"Should be on the shelf of every edu_____
ent interested in our culture's fascination with fantasy. It is an
honest, straightforward, and vitally important tool for friends and
foes of fantasy alike."

—**Bill Myers,** bestselling youth and
children's fiction author

"An extraordinary resource containing a clear presentation of the
issues as well as practical tools of discernment....This book
should be in every home."

—**Michael O'Brien,** bestselling author of
the Father Elijah series

"Towers above other discussions of the Harry Potter books in
relation to the fantasy stories of J.R.R. Tolkien and C.S. Lewis....
Built on four virtues: in-depth and comprehensive research of the
title's subjects, fair-mindedness regarding rival viewpoints, schol-
arly rigor, and careful analysis of the material."

—**Leland Ryken,** author of *The Christian Imagination*
professor, Wheaton College

"Abanes has carefully documented not only the state of present-
day children's fantasy, but also its influence and effects."

—**Marcia Montenegro,** founder of "Christian
Answers for the New Age" Web site
and former astrologer

Harry Potter, Narnia, and The Lord of the Rings

Richard Abanes

HARVEST HOUSE PUBLISHERS

EUGENE, OREGON

Cover by Terry Dugan Design, Minneapolis, Minnesota

HARRY POTTER, NARNIA, AND THE LORD OF THE RINGS
Copyright © 2005 by Richard Abanes
Published by Harvest House Publishers
Eugene, Oregon 97402
www.harvesthousepublishers.com

Library of Congress Cataloging-in-Publication Data
Abanes, Richard.
   Harry Potter, Narnia, and The lord of the rings / Richard Abanes.
      p. cm.
   Includes bibliographical references and index.
   ISBN-13: 978-0-7369-1700-1   ISBN-10: 0-7369-1700-4 (pbk.)
   1. Fantasy fiction, English—History and criticism. 2. Children's stories, English—History and criticism. 3. Tolkien, J. R. R. (John Ronald Reuel), 1892-1973. Lord of the rings. 4. Lewis, C. S. (Clive Staples), 1898-1963. Chronicles of Narnia. 5. Rowling, J. K.—Characters—Harry Potter. 6. Potter, Harry (Fictitious character). 7. Middle Earth (Imaginary place). 8. Children—Books and reading. 9. Christianity and literature. 10. Narnia (Imaginary place). 11. Magic in literature. I. Title.
   PR888.F3A234 2005
   809.3'8766—dc22   2005004199

Printed in the United States of America

05   06   07   08   09   10   11   12   13   / DP-KB /   10   9   8   7   6   5   4   3   2   1

To my friend Othmar, a brilliant scientist and progressive thinker—an individual about whom I still understand far too little, but whose wisdom and insights I look forward to someday exploring more completely. I am indebted to your important work, which has enabled me to think more clearly and finish this project.

Thanks to—

Bob Hawkins Jr.
Terry Glaspey
Paul Gossard
Carolyn McCready
Mr. S.Q., Esq.
L. Philip
Mr. Tursle
T. Angus
R.F. Andreas
Patterson
Mrs. Acoon
Juan Prospero
Ray Malloy
Evangeline, my loving wife

For more information about Richard Abanes
and his endeavors, visit:
www.abanes.com/abanesbio.html

Contents

Family Fun

Foreword by Gene Edward Veith

Reading any story "clicks in" the imagination—that faculty of the mind that conjures up mental pictures—allowing readers to experience events, characters, challenging situations, and ideas impossible in real life.

For generations the marvelous pastime of reading endured as the most common form of entertainment enjoyed by adults and children alike. Today, however, reading is no longer the popular pursuit it used to be. Thanks to high-tech digital imaging, we now have movies that can depict not just realistic scenes, but *ultra*realistic scenes. We also have "reality" TV shows, alternative programming (for example, MTV and pay-per-view), and television dramas that are hypersexualized, violent, or both (not to mention some fairly racy sitcoms).

And, just as real-life experiences create learning and growth, so also do entertainment experiences—those realized through imaginative participation in the experiences of others. They can shape a person's values, sensibilities, beliefs, and even personality. Unfortunately, in today's culture, respectful attention to what any given form of entertainment teaches has largely been supplanted by an uncritical acceptance of whatever kind of experience a "fun" activity puts us through.

This is true especially when it comes to children's books. Parents today are so glad if their child picks up a book instead of

turning on the TV (or playing a computer/video game) that they pay little attention to what the book is about or what it does to their child. But a fair question is, "What is being taught by the books my child is reading?" There are other equally important questions to be asked: "What is a particular movie showing my child?" "What values might a certain TV show be promoting?"

Richard Abanes's understanding of these issues is strikingly evident in *Harry Potter, Narnia, and The Lord of the Rings*—a book that is pro-literature, pro-fantasy, and pro-fun. He makes a strong case for the value of imaginative literature, movies, and TV. But while arguing for the positive effects of these entertainment forms, Abanes also raises vital distinctions between healthy entertainment and unhealthy entertainment.

How do books, movies, and television affect children? Do certain forms of entertainment make evil repellent or attractive? Does a particular book, movie, or TV program motivate a child to emulate what is good or what is bad? If there is violence, does it move a child to sympathize with those being hurt, or does it give the impression that hurting others is pleasurable?

These are just some of the questions this book deals with. And Abanes is no outside observer. He is a self-professed *Star Trek* fan who has been nourished by fairy tales, science fiction, and fantasy. He also is a professional actor (and singer and dancer) who has a deep appreciation for the movie industry and TV, including their power to influence. He understands that determining whether or not a certain form of fantasy (or entertainment) is appropriate for children is not just a matter of isolated imagery—that is to say, whether a story has a "witch," "magic," or "violence."

Abanes knows that to judge any form of entertainment requires attention not simply to its details, but also to the specific nature of the vicarious experience it creates using those details.

To understand the meaning of a book, movie, or TV program calls for interpretation as well as information and context.

Interpretation and Information

This is what *Harry Potter, Narnia, and The Lord of the Rings* provides. For example, it covers the impact of commercialism on children's literature and its resulting downward drift into a world of decidedly dark subjects. Consider the kiddy-horror novels of R.L. Stine, which serve up senseless, albeit titillating, accounts of murdered schoolmates and cannibal parents. How different these tales are from classic horror stories such as *Frankenstein*, which is not simply scary, but is filled with important messages about human limits and the boundaries of science.

The Harry Potter books by J.K. Rowling, of course, are better written than Stine's novels, but they have the same publisher—Scholastic Press—and offer similar points of appeal. The main controversy over Harry Potter, however, relates to the question of whether these absorbing novels about a school for witches might cause young readers to pursue an unhealthy interest in *real-world* occultism.

Rowling's defenders say, "Of course not. Kids won't turn into witches by reading about Harry, anymore than reading Tolkien will make them hobbits." But Abanes, it seems, has found evidence to the contrary. Judging from what children are posting on thousands of Harry Potter fan Web sites, many of them *are* becoming interested in learning how to do *real* witchcraft. Abanes also has gathered quotes from Wicca devotees and other occultists who are hailing the Potter series as a prime recruitment tool.

More pertinent is how the children's book industry, in an attempt to cash in on the craze, is publishing guidebooks on occultism that directly target young Harry Potter fans. Titles like

So You Want to Be a Wizard, Teen Witch, and *Spells for Teenage Witches* sell themselves with blurbs similar to that of *The Witch and Wizard Guide,* which claims to be "a complete guide to doing the magic in Harry Potter using modern Wiccan techniques."

Unfortunately, anyone today presuming to criticize such things is instantly branded with the charge of censorship. Abanes, however, is not advocating censorship, nor the banning or the burning of anything—especially books. He does not even say that a certain book or movie will definitely be harmful to every child. He is concerned, though, about the possible effects of some entertainment forms on some children—and he demonstrates the validity of his concerns using child-development research.

Supervising how children entertain themselves (the TV shows they watch, the movies they see, the computer or video games they play, the Web sites they visit, and the books they read) is not the job of the government but, as nearly everyone agrees, is the responsibility of the parents. Fortunately, *Harry Potter, Narnia, and The Lord of the Rings* gives the information all of us need to know in making good decisions.

Abanes contrasts the works of J.K. Rowling, J.R.R. Tolkien, and C.S. Lewis, successfully illuminating each of their fantasy worlds. This, I believe, will help everyone move much closer toward rescuing the great tradition of children's literature from the wasteland of modern commercialism, adult manipulation, and a spiritually impoverished culture.

—Gene Edward Veith, PhD
Culture Editor, *World* magazine
Professor, Concordia University

To Be a Child Again

Books fall open, you fall in,
Delighted where you've never been;
Hear voices not once heard before,
Reach world on world through door on door;
Find unexpected keys to things,
Locked up beyond imagining...[1]

—DAVID MCCORD

By the first grade, my love for fantasy had already manifested itself. *Winnie the Pooh, Charlotte's Web, Peter Pan, The Wizard of Oz*—I loved them all. And I still do. Then I discovered The Chronicles of Narnia and The Lord of the Rings. These works, too, found their way into my heart.

After my father surprised the family with a color TV, I came to appreciate cartoons. My favorite was *The Bullwinkle Show*. This series, of course, featured that lovable moose, Bullwinkle, and his sharp-minded friend, Rocky, the flying squirrel. I could not get enough of their antics and adventures.

Most delightful to me was one specific segment of their show, "Fractured Fairy Tales," narrated by Edward Everett Horton. To this day, I can't help but chuckle to myself when I recall those hysterical twists on classic fairy tales and the humorous lines they contained. They brought many smiles into my childhood.

13

I also now see that the stories taught me a great deal about right and wrong, good and evil, cleverness and stupidity, and—to some extent—how life works. I remember, for instance, as a third grader, choosing to not taunt another student being picked on by others—a poor student. I made my choice thanks to a fractured fairy tale I had seen wherein paupers were contrasted with rich nobility.

A few years later I found another television series that would exert even more influence over me: *Star Trek*. Its September 8, 1966, television debut changed the world—*my* world, anyway. Although my dad would always be my number-one role model, the 1960s sci-fi series presented me with a second male figure to emulate: James T. Kirk, captain of the starship *Enterprise*.

I didn't want to just be *like* Kirk—I actually, desperately, wanted to *be* him—a gallant, handsome, strong, brave, tough guy who always seemed to make the right decisions and ended up the hero. And, of course, he always had a beautiful woman falling in love with him. (At seven years old, my odd gladness over this aspect of Kirk's life was still a bit baffling to me. But I would understand it more within a few years.)

I can still remember myself, in about the fourth grade, turning my miniature rocking chair upside down and sitting at an angle. I'd nestle myself into its underside between the two curved rockers (it was the closest thing I could find to a captain's seat). Nearly every afternoon, from 4 PM until my mother called me for dinner, I commanded my own starship.

"Mr. Sulu, warp factor two," I'd shout to my stuffed rabbit. "Deflector shields up! Bring us around, Mr. Sulu. Let's give those Romulans something to think about."

An imaginary Spock, stationed in front of my dresser, would invariably turn from his sensors and give a predictable word of

warning: "Captain, I must caution you. We are now in the Neutral Zone."

"I'm well aware of that, Mr. Spock," was my usual response. "Lock phasers on target, Mr. Chekhov!"

"Phasers locked on target, sir." (Chekhov never gave me any back talk.)

"Hold your course, Mr. Sulu...easy...FIRE!"

Of course, I would score a direct hit every time, and the explosion's concussion would invariably knock me out of my captain's chair (a perfect excuse to roll around on the floor). Then, after a few congratulatory remarks to my invisible crew, the next mission would begin.

"Mr. Spock, didn't Starfleet Command report Klingons in the Gamma Quadrant?"

"Yes, Captain. At least four Klingon warbirds have been reported, but they may have cloaking devices."

I was thrilled.

"Mr. Sulu—set a course for the Gamma Quadrant, warp factor three!"

"Aye, aye, Captain."

Thanks to Kirk, I spent most of my childhood longing to be an astronaut. I couldn't get his words out of my mind: "Space, the final frontier." I just knew that an exciting life among the stars awaited me. But imagination gradually gave way to reality, and I eventually became a writer. (I still, however, watch *Star Trek* as often as possible.)

Joy, Wonder—and Controversy

Today, countless children continue to experience the joy and wonder of fantasy and science fiction as they become preadolescents, teens, and then young adults. And in this era of technology

nearly every kid owns what I never had—computer and video games. They offer a whole new range of interactive possibilities that in many ways mirror reality quite effectively (so much for my upside-down chair and stuffed rabbit).

And Hollywood, now more adept than ever at special effects, has added a previously unknown dimension to films—superrealism and wildly exhilarating images. There seems to be no limit to what can be put on the silver screen, as evidenced by the films based on J.K. Rowling's Harry Potter series and J.R.R. Tolkien's classic trilogy, The Lord of the Rings.

Both works have made quite an impact not only on many youths, but also on our entire culture. The books, along with their spin-off movies, computer/video games, and merchandise, have been raking in hundreds of millions of dollars.[2] And as of December 2005, when the movie version of C.S. Lewis's *The Lion, the Witch, and the Wardrobe* is released by Walt Disney Pictures, the world will have yet another fantastic source of fantasy-related entertainment.

The influence of such books, movies, and games, however, has not been without controversy. Many parents are concerned about their depiction of occult themes, violence, good, evil, and morality. This has been especially true of Harry Potter. Consider these recent headlines: "Locals Protest at 'Occult' Potter"; "Australian College Bans Potter"; "Harry Potter and the Clergy's Ire."[3]

Adding fuel to the fire is evidence suggesting that *some* Potter fans may indeed be developing an interest in occultism. The results of a 2002 Barna Research Group poll of U.S. teens between 13 and 19, for instance, found that, of the 9 million who had been exposed to Harry Potter books or films, 12 percent said they had become more interested in witchcraft as a result of their exposure: "4% said they were a lot more interested [in occultism], and 8% were a little more interested [in occultism] as a result of the book or movie."[4]

In other words, of the teenagers polled, about one out of every twenty said that Harry Potter had made them more interested in witchcraft. These statistics certainly represent a minority of teens, but "it still accounts for about 5% of all U.S. teenagers and projects to more than a million students nationwide who claim that the Potter stories have made them more interested in witchcraft."[5]

In light of such findings, I offer *Harry Potter, Narnia, and The Lord of the Rings.* My hope is to provide a balanced look at the controversies surrounding the fantasy works of J.K. Rowling, J.R.R. Tolkien, and C.S. Lewis. The following pages discuss both the pros and cons of fantasy, how various forms of entertainment affect kids (with an emphasis on specific developmental stages), and the place of occultism in our society. All of these subjects are interwoven and must be examined if parents are going to make wise decisions regarding the entertainment they allow their children to enjoy.

Before moving on, I must stress a key and crucial point. To be perfectly clear, *I do not endorse book burning, book banning, or rigid censorship.* But I do believe that care must be taken when we're faced with today's entertainment choices, especially in light of the misinformation and disinformation that has been circulating about fantasy.

Confusion has resulted in the minds of many people—the religious, the nonreligious, the half-religious, and even the irreligious. Only by carefully looking at well-documented information can anyone understand the facts surrounding the many concerns being expressed about various forms of entertainment for kids.

Some concerns are justified—others, in my opinion, are not. All final judgments, of course, are up to you, the reader, as you sift through the material that awaits you.

So I invite Rowling fans and foes, Tolkien supporters and detractors, Lewis lovers and critics, to journey with me into the wonderful (but often controversial) world of fantasy. I hope all of us will learn a few lessons along the way.

"Mr. Sulu—warp factor nine! Mr. Chekhov—deflector shields up!"

Part One
Focusing on Fiction

The character of fantasy...is that of a fiction evoking wonder and containing a substantial and irreducible element of supernatural or impossible worlds, beings or objects.

—C.N. MANLOVE
Lecturer in English Literature,
University of Edinburgh

1

Fantasy's Fall

Children's book publishing was rescued by the fast-growing chain bookstores to be found in malls....To attract children and adults as consumers of literature, the very nature of the book—its design and contents—began to change.[1]

—JACK ZIPES
folklore expert, University of Minnesota

Once upon a time, children's literature was carefully chosen and published by editors whose main goal was to inspire and elevate young minds. But today, according to many publishing insiders, consumerism is driving the children's book industry. Tom Engelhardt, a longtime editor at Pantheon Books, alleges that the main goal of too many publishers today is the facilitation of sales relating to expensive book spin-offs such as DVDs, clothing, movies, and computer or video games.[2]

In the words of one expert, publishing is now "in the hands of the financiers."[3] Hence, many children's book producers (most of which are tied in to food or toy companies) now do little more than create in kids an appetite for specific kinds of literature. Then, to satisfy that appetite, they mass-market only those types of books—right alongside their costly side-products.

As folklore expert Jack Zipes observes, "Rather than opening new worlds to children," book publishers are now inviting them "to repeat certain predictable and comforting experiences that they can easily and affordably buy into."[4] Fantasy author Donna Jo Napoli agrees: "The market right now is for a particular kind of book, constructed by the publishers because they happen to be making money on it."[5]

But there is more to this disturbing story. Once children's books became big business, publishers saw that the actual money-holders (that is, parents) had to be motivated to lay down cash for whatever was being offered. So book producers, with the help of well-meaning librarians and teachers, began painting a frightful portrait of millions of illiterate youths glued to the TV or video games—all because they had not developed good reading habits. Fear soon replaced critical thinking about children's literature, which in turn caused many adults to no longer care about *what* kids were reading. The new goal was just to get them reading again—reading anything!

In a hard-hitting 1991 article, "Reading May Be Harmful to Your Kids," Tom Engelhardt complained that the habit of reading "was invoked with reverential seriousness by the people producing the flood of new books....The issue was increasingly not so much what you read but that you read at all."[6]

This modern approach to children's reading, however, is little more than a panic response to false notions about the academic performance of students. "The best evidence we have on the reading crisis indicates that no crisis exists on average in United States reading," says Jeff McQuillan, author of *The Literacy Crisis*. "Despite a few minor shifts, reading achievement has either stayed even or increased over the past thirty years." American nine-year-olds, for example, "ranked second in the world" in a 1992 study, and "fourteen-year-olds ranked a very respectable

ninth out of 31."[7] Even the assumption that kids are reading less today than they did a generation ago is "difficult to prove," says a 2002 article in *Book Magazine*.[8]

There are indeed hurdles to be overcome with regard to helping youth develop better reading habits.[9] But the problems are not new. In "Youth and Reading: A Survey of Leisure Reading Pursuits of Female and Male Adolescents," two researchers showed that adolescent reading habits have changed little since 1927, when reading ranked third among children's leisure activities (following sports and spending time with friends).[10]

To Read, or Not to Read?

The real issue today, then, is not that kids are *not* reading. Rather, it's the substance of what they *are* reading:

> People are reading more and more trash and less and less serious literature. One of the odd situations facing the country is that we have too...many writers and not enough readers. I don't know what the answer to this dilemma is.[11]

In other words, some children's books might get kids to read, but not necessarily in a good way. Consider Harry Potter. In "Literacy in America," Patrick Clinton cautions that the series represents the very kind of literature that could "push back the day when kids turn to the kind of serious, adult reading that has always played an important role in teaching kids about complex language, shifting points of view and the like."[12]

Who is primarily responsible for the presence of such material? The likely culprit is corporate America. Its campaign to warn the public about the dangers of juvenile illiteracy has resulted in a global acceptance of the highly flawed and perilous

idea that *any* reading is better than *no* reading. Most adults, in fact, seem entrenched in the false notion that reading is intrinsically good regardless of the quality of material being read.

This misconception has allowed for a steady stream of less-than-admirable but highly profitable "children's" books. Moreover, although some of these works contain fairly mature themes, anyone daring to call for even *moderate* care in offering them to young children is vehemently shouted down by terror-stricken adults worried about only one thing: getting kids to read again.

Some commentators see this widespread fear as a major driving force behind J.K. Rowling's meteoric rise to literary stardom—the Harry Potter books "are pitched to kids, and today's parents are so terrified the little ones won't read anything, won't even learn to read, that sensible mothers and fathers will line up at the Potter altar with good money, just to see their offspring turning pages."[13]

Rowan University writing professor Diana Penrod agrees: "Someone saying negative things about the Harry Potter series practically elicits the same reaction as cursing motherhood, apple pie, and baseball—how dare anyone question something, anything, that motivates children to read?"[14]

The plain truth is that far too many adults are not only overlooking the content of children's books, but they are not recognizing that the current glut of mass-marketed volumes reflect "a calculated way of looking at children as consumers with a common denominator, and many of the products represent a dumbing down of children rather than a challenge to their creativity."[15]

In reference not only to this ongoing problem, but also to the media's inundation of kids with gratuitous violence and overt sexuality, respected film critic David Denby wrote a scathing

1996 essay for *The New Yorker* titled "Buried Alive: Our Children and the Avalanche of Crud":

> The danger is not mere exposure to occasional violent or prurient images but the acceptance of a degraded environment that devalues everything—a shadow world in which our kids are breathing an awful lot of poison without knowing that there's clean air and sunshine elsewhere. They are shaped by the media as consumers before they've had a chance to develop their souls.[16]

Denby also lambasted pop culture in general, noting that it "consumes our children." He then criticized parents for allowing their kids to be turned into cookie-cutter victims of mass-market interests and materialism.[17]

If Denby is correct, then the foe we find ourselves facing is not really illiteracy, but rather, a money-making industry that has co-opted the formerly honorable label "Children's Literature." It is a corporate industry force-feeding today's youth anything and everything—as long as it sells. And fantasy, thanks to media marketing strategies, has been at the center of this whole controversy.

The Billion-Dollar Book

The most obvious example of consumerism's link to kids' books is the hysteria over Harry Potter. Even J.K. Rowling's supporters have noticed the merchandising push of her fantasy, as one Internet fan site complained in 2004: "Why must everyone's vision of the HP series become corrected and unified by movies, posters, and memorabilia?"[18] Jack Zipes observes,

Phenomena such as the Harry Potter books are driven by commodity consumption that at the same time sets the parameters of reading and aesthetic taste....What readers passionately devour and enjoy may be, like many a Disney film or Barbie doll, a phenomenal experience and have personal significance, but it is also an *induced* experience calculated to conform to a cultural convention of amusement and distraction.[19]

Zipes, a well-respected and knowledgeable children's literature specialist, additionally feels that the Harry Potter novels are not only formulaic, but also sexist. Interestingly, for expressing such views during radio shows, he has been "aggressively attacked" by callers accusing him of demeaning Rowling.[20]

And Zipes is not alone. A number of others who find Harry Potter to be fairly ordinary (or even substandard) when compared to similar literature have been castigated by Rowling's fans. The critics have been labeled either arrogant snobs or jealous know-nothings too rigid to see the excellence of Harry Potter.[21]

Literary critic Harold Bloom, for instance, took off the proverbial gloves in his *Wall Street Journal* article titled "Can 35 Million Book Buyers Be Wrong? Yes." Then, during a PBS interview, Bloom candidly remarked, "They're just an endless string of clichés. I cannot think that does anyone any good. That's not *Wind in the Willows*. That's not *Through the Looking Glass*....It's really just slop."[22]

Needless to say, Harry Potter fans were not happy. But even greater disdain has been directed at anyone daring to raise the slightest hint of concern about the "child-appropriateness" of Harry Potter. Such critics have been called stupid, narrow-minded, and ignorant.

The most vilified critics, however, continue to be persons concerned about occultism in Rowling's fantasy (see chapter 7).

They have been called everything from hate-mongers to extremists comparable to the Taliban and terrorist Osama bin Laden.[23] Oddly, such reactions rarely address the actual objections that have been made but instead concentrate on blasting religion, with an emphasis on deriding Christianity.[24]

This overdefensive attitude might be related to "Pottermania" itself. Once any phenomenon begins, especially one that is media-driven, people habitually lose the ability to reason or think objectively. Zipes explains:

> The ordinary becomes extraordinary, and we are so taken by the phenomenon that we admire, worship, and idolize it without grasping fully why we regard it with so much reverence and awe except to say that so many others regard it as a phenomenon and, therefore, it must be a phenomenon.[25]

It is undeniable that blind allegiance to anything (whether a piece of literature, a religion, a politician, or an entertainment personality) opens a Pandora's box of detrimental and destructive consequences. Yet this is precisely what is taking place within our society as certain kinds of fantasy and fiction are being marketed to children. Such books are known as "shock fiction" for kids and are nothing short of reprehensible—morally, intellectually, and spiritually.

Goosebumps on Fear Street

In 1970, child-education expert James Higgins noted, "No one has to remind parents that a bad book can seduce."[26] But that was 1970. Today, many adults have indeed forgotten that some books, though entertaining, might not be so good for kids. All manner of reading material is now being introduced to

impressionable minds. The Fear Street books and Goosebumps series by R.L. Stine typify—indeed, have served as a prototype for—such books.

Stine (born 1943) gained notoriety in 1986 with *Blind Date*, his first horror story for teenagers.[27] Three years later he started releasing his Fear Street series for pre-teens and teens. It now numbers more than 100 titles and has sold more than 80 million copies.[28] It is often read by nine- to ten-year-olds.

Fear Street depicts nonstop gruesome events that befall people living on or near "Fear Street" in the fictional town of Shadyside. The teen characters in the books encounter all kinds of mayhem, violence, brutality, murder, and oftentimes, occult phenomena. A publicity blurb for *Halloween Party* (1993), for instance, reads, "An invitation to a Halloween party hosted by the beautiful but mysterious Justine Cameron spells danger, terror, and murder for the guests."

Other titles are equally revealing: *Spring Break: Sun, Fun... Murder!* (1999); *Graduation Day: Will Anyone Get Out Alive?* (1999); *Dance of Death* (1997); *Killer's Kiss* (1997); and *Who Killed the Homecoming Queen?* (1997).

Moreover, Stine's books often feature the nonstop terrorization of women. This subject matter is all the more disturbing given his book-cover illustrations—they often depict attractive teenage girls being stalked, or kidnapped, or lying dead. The plots are almost misogynistic in their incessant portrayal of women being verbally and physically victimized.

Fiction writer Diana West argued, "In this literary landscape, narrative exists solely to support a series of shocks occurring at absurdly frequent intervals. Push-button characters serve as disposable inserts to advance the narrative shock after shock."[29]

How have parents responded? In an interview with *New York Newsday*, a mother of an 11-year-old exclaimed, "I'm thrilled."

She added, "He's literally reading a book a day. He always says, 'Just a few more pages.'...He devours [them]." The mother of a 9-year-old explained, "They just weren't my choice of subject matter. But I'm happy he's reading. If he wasn't reading this, he wouldn't be reading anything at all. Now he's at the point where he's constantly reading. He's fixated on horror."[30]

For even younger readers (aged eight to nine), Stine has written his Goosebumps series. It has sold 300 million copies in 28 languages since 1992.[31] These books are packed with ghastly plots involving murder, revenge, violence, occultism, and pure gore.[32] The titles are telling: *Return to Horrorland: No Time to Scream*; *Welcome to Dead House: It Will Just Kill You*; and *Piano Lessons Can Be Murder*. Michael O'Brien, author of the bestselling *Father Elijah*, makes these observations:

> For sheer perversity these tales rival anything that has been published to date....Shock after shock pummels the reader's mind, and the child experiences them as both psychological and physical stimuli. These shocks are presented as ends in themselves, raw violence as entertainment.[33]

It is no surprise that Stine's books have caused immense controversy in public schools. Some parents have even demanded that libraries ban the volumes. (In 1997 they topped the American Library Association's list of Most Challenged Books.) But such protests have been drowned out by the same argument: "At least the kids are reading." (Interestingly, the producer of these grisly volumes is none other than Scholastic, the U.S. publisher of Harry Potter.)[34]

Predictably, Stine feels that kids should have virtually no restrictions placed on their reading material: "Kids are the best

judge of what they should read and not read....I think kids are really smart, and I don't think they will read anything that is inappropriate for them....I think everyone is glad that kids are reading."[35]

This is virtually the same mind-set held by J.K. Rowling, who enjoyed complete freedom as a child. She revealed in 1999, "I was really very lucky growing up—my parents let me read anything and everything. Adult books. The works." Elsewhere she has explained, "I don't believe in censorship for any age group." And in reference to some of the darker, more adult scenes in her own books, she declares, "My parents never censored what I read, so I wouldn't say don't read them to a six-year-old."[36]

Librarian Shirley Emmert of a Minneapolis suburb school district used a similar line of reasoning in 1997 during a debate over Goosebumps. When interviewed by KTCA-TV, she was asked, "Your approach would be to get the kids to read?"

Emmert replied, "Yes."

"No matter what they're reading, to begin with?" asked the KTCA newsman.

"Yes," she responded.

"And then worry about exactly what they read later on?"

"Yes, yes."[37]

Emmert's attitude continues to be advanced by many parents, teachers, and librarians.[38] But others disagree. Fourth-grade teacher David Edholm, who was part of the 1997 St. Paul–Minneapolis area controversy, stated, "For them to say at least the kids are reading, if they're reading a wrong message, their reading skill does not mean that much." He added, "The same argument could be used if middle school boys aren't reading, you know, do we put erotic novels in the middle school library so that they would read?"[39]

Unfortunately, the now popular "let's just get kids reading" perspective, coupled with Stine's success, has only encouraged other writers to produce similar volumes (for example, Christopher Pike's Spooksville books, targeting children aged 9 to 12).

Author Diana West has pinpointed perhaps the most damaging aspect of these books. She argues they show a lack of respect for the journey from childhood to adulthood:

> Stine's audience is being encouraged at a critical age to engage in literary pursuits devoid of content, crammed with shock....[We should object to] shock fiction, for its role in desensitizing the very young, stunting the life of the mind before it has even begun.[40]

Steve Russo, author of *The Devil's Playground* and coauthor of *The Seduction of Our Children* and an expert in the occult, also has expressed concerns. He admits it would be too extreme to say that all children reading Goosebumps will end up Satanists or perpetrators of a heinous crime. He does, however, offer a word of caution: "They will become desensitized to evil and violence. This type of desensitization is subtle and can affect the child long term."[41]

Russo further believes that Goosebumps and similar works also might serve as a gateway into the world of the occult. "Evil is enticing," he says. "And for some kids a hunger for more can easily develop, causing them to search down the wrong path to satisfy their appetite by dabbling in the darkness."[42]

"His Dark Materials"

Another popular fantasy series for young readers is Philip Pullman's His Dark Materials, which has sold several million copies worldwide. Although these books may not be as horrifying

as those written by Stine, or as laced with real-world occultism as Harry Potter (see chapters 7 and 8), they are blatantly antireligious—more specifically, anti-Christian. Nevertheless, his trilogy—*The Golden Compass* (1995), *The Subtle Knife* (1997), and *The Amber Spyglass* (2000)—has garnered many honors, including the prestigious Whitbread Award (2001).

But amid the rave reviews and accolades, the anti-Christian venom that permeates His Dark Materials has caused great controversy. Even *The Times* of London agreed that "religion is spared no indignity" in the series.[43] Another British publication, *The Mail on Sunday*, criticized Pullman even more pointedly:

> In his worlds, the Church is wicked, cruel and child-hating; priests are sinister, murderous or drunk....The one religious character who turns out to be benevolent is that liberal favourite, an ex-nun who has renounced her vows and lost her faith.[44]

Lyra and Will

The complex plot of His Dark Materials involves two children from two separate worlds. Twelve-year-old Lyra Belacqua possesses the Golden Compass, which can be used to discern the truth of any situation. Will Parry, a boy who is Lyra's age, has the Subtle Knife, which can slice open windows to other worlds.

The series begins in a time and place similar to ours, but with a few changes. The Roman Catholic papacy no longer exists, having been dissolved after the death of the final pope, John Calvin. There are no Protestants. The Eastern Orthodox Church is not to be found. And heaven is "a lie."[45]

The sole "Church" is a nightmarish caricature of Roman Catholicism—an evil, greedy, and tyrannical institution that

rules Lyra's world with an iron fist. It is led by an utterly corrupt hierarchy known as the "Magisterium," which controls the masses via propaganda about a false "God" called the "Authority."[46]

The Church was founded by "God," who in arrogance and selfish ambition, instituted church-enforced rules to destroy human freedom, stifle creativity, advance ignorance, and foster a slave mentality. Both Lyra and Will are swept up in the politics of it all, traveling between worlds and having adventures until they discover the purpose of their lives and relationship: They are destined to be the new Adam and Eve.

It is basically a reworking of the Genesis story. But in this version, the innocent couple does not *damage* humanity, but instead, *delivers* it. Through their love for each other, they rescue everyone else from a spiritually darkened state (what Pullman disparagingly labels the "Kingdom of Heaven"). How is such a feat accomplished? By killing the Authority—or rather, by killing the angel who falsely set himself up as "God."

According to His Dark Materials, this nasty creature is the same being we find exalted throughout the Old Testament:

> The Authority, god, the Creator, the Lord, Yahweh, El, Adonai, the King, the Father the Almighty—those were all names he gave himself. He was never the creator. He was an angel like ourselves—the first angel, true, the most powerful, but he was formed of Dust as we are....The Authority was the first of all. He told those who came after him that he had created them, but it was a lie.[47]

Perhaps the best summation of this trilogy's theme can be found in the statement made by one of its characters—the ex-Christian, former-nun character mentioned earlier. She says, "I

thought physics could be done to the glory of God, till I saw there wasn't any God at all and that physics was more interesting anyway. The Christian religion is a very powerful and convincing mistake, that's all." The series also tells us, "Every church is the same: control, destroy, obliterate every good feeling."[48]

Fortunately for Lyra and Will, the Authority is annihilated by the conclusion of The Amber Spyglass. His death scene paints the Judeo–Christian God thus: "Demented and powerless, the aged being could only weep and mumble in fear and pain and misery." He mumbles, whimpers, grinds his teeth, picks at himself, and in the end, after being led into the sunlight, dissolves into nothingness.[49]

Religion Is Evil

Pullman, a self-professed atheist–agnostic,[50] sees religion and the religious as little more than dispensers of "lists of rights and wrongs, tables of do's and don'ts."[51] And he holds a special contempt for Christians.

Even some fans of His Dark Materials have expressed concern over the transparent way that Pullman presents his antireligious views. But he has responded, "Every time I thought I was overdoing it, up came another scandal about brutal monks mistreating children in Irish schools, or sadistic nuns tormenting children in Scottish orphanages, to name but two."[52]

Pullman's rancorous stand against religion is reflected at various points throughout his fantasy, especially where one character condemns the Church: "It's tried to suppress and control every natural impulse. And when it can't control them [natural impulses], it cuts them out."[53] In 2002 he detailed why he specifically targeted Christianity:

> When you look at organized religion of whatever
> sort—whether it's Christianity in all its variants, or

whether it's Islam or some forms of extreme
Hinduism—wherever you see organized religion and
priesthoods and power, you see cruelty and tyranny
and repression. It's almost a universal law. It's not just
Christianity I'm getting at. The reason that the forms
of religion in the books seem to be Christian is
because that's the world I'm familiar with. That's the
world I grew up in and I knew.[54]

A distinction must be made at this point. His Dark Materials
is not against the idea of a God *per se* (even though Pullman has
publicly stated not only "I am all for the death of God," but also,
"If there is a God and he is as the Christians describe him, then
he deserves to be put down and rebelled against."[55]) Technically,
the trilogy condemns only the evils that have come from religions built around faith in God. This is a fine distinction, to be
sure, *and one that is not made at all in the series.*

But in fairness, one must recognize Pullman's intentions.
When one fan asked Pullman point-blank, "Why do you hate
God so much as it appears in your books?" the fantasy writer
answered:

> Well, it is not that I hate God, it is just because I don't
> believe in God, it is just that I think the people who
> do believe in God and persecute the people who don't
> believe in God are thoroughly dangerous, that is the
> way I would put it.[56]

Pullman is even more explicit on his Web site, where he
explains that his trilogy "is against those who pervert and misuse
religion, or any other kind of doctrine with a holy book and a
priesthood and an apparatus of power that wields unchallengeable
authority, in order to dominate and suppress human freedoms."[57]

Confused About Religion

The tragic irony here is that Pullman's stand against religious abuse actually echoes Christianity—which is based on love, forgiveness, gentleness, kindness, patience, and humility. Jesus nowhere teaches his followers to kill, persecute, dominate, or suppress others. Although Pullman recognizes this inescapable fact, he still fixates on the bad that has been done in the name of religion:

> The greatest moral advances have been made by religious leaders such as Jesus and the Buddha. And the greatest moral wickedness has been perpetrated by their followers. How many millions of people have been killed in the name of this religion or that one? Burnt, hanged, tortured. It's just extraordinary.[58]

But apparently, for some reason, Pullman does not find as equally extraordinary the many *positive* contributions that Christianity has made to society: art, music, hospitals, orphanages, and the elevation of women from near-slavery to a status on par with men (see John 20:17-18; Romans 8:17; Galatians 3:26-28).

And what about the many Christian physicians, scientists, and educators throughout history? Why does Pullman also not mention the long list of Christian activists throughout the world who have stood against social injustice and oppression? How can he overlook the multitude of humanitarian relief efforts spearheaded by Christians (most recently, for example, the assistance and donations provided by churches to Asian tsunami victims in 2004 and 2005)?

Instead of giving any honor or credit to Christianity, Pullman incessantly harps on gross abuses committed by so-called Christians. His final conclusion, which is based on the worst assumptions about religion, basically condemns everything and everyone connected to faith:

Churches are malevolent forces in our world. If we look at the history of the Christian church alone we see persecution, hanging, burning and torture carried out the name of the God of Love. It's a history of infamy almost without parallel, and we don't have to look very far in the world today for examples of zealotry entirely fuelled and sustained by religious hatreds of one sort or another.[59]

One can only wonder why Pullman has targeted religion, rather than atheism, since so many brutal totalitarian regimes in history have been atheistic.[60] He has admitted that repressive power has been "wielded at various times in the name of religion as well as in the name of 'scientific' atheism."[61] He concedes that "the most dogmatic materialist is functionally equivalent to the most fanatical believer, Stalin's Russia [is] exactly the same as Khomeini's Iran. It isn't belief in God that causes the problem."[62]

His "main quarrel," he clarifies, is really "with the literalist, fundamentalist nature of absolute power, whether it's manifested in the religious police state of Saudi Arabia or the atheist police state of Soviet Russia." Elsewhere he has said he is *not* opposed to "Christianity, but every religion and fundamental organization where there is one truth and they will kill you if you don't believe it."[63]

Yet none of these points appear in His Dark Materials. Instead, children and teens—the ones to whom his books are marketed—receive blanket denunciations of religion, Christianity, the church, and faith.[64] It is slipped into their minds under the guise of "fantasy." Pullman himself agrees, "All stories teach, whether the storyteller intends them to or not. They teach the world we create. They teach the morality we live by. They teach it much more effectively than moral precepts and instructions."[65]

Guarding Your Family

Despite the drawbacks of some fantasy, the genre can provide a wonderful way for children (and adults) to live vicariously through the adventures of fictitious characters. Fantasy also can help us learn how others might handle certain problems, which in turn can alter how we look at our own situations. Fantasy, then, is not intrinsically evil. But because it sends powerful messages, care ought to be taken when choosing material to read. So exactly how does one evaluate a children's fantasy book?[66]

First, consider the text itself, including its plot, language, and underlying message. Check for what you may consider disturbing or child-inappropriate images. Read the description of the book on either the inside cover flap or the back cover. Take a moment to read about the author and see what other kinds of books he or she has written.

Second, know why you are buying the book for your child. Is it for private reading? Classroom reading? Will you be reading it to your child, or will your child be reading it unsupervised? What message, values, or lessons will the book impart?

Third, read a few chapters. Many bookstores now have a café where you can relax and peruse a volume before purchasing it. You also might want to use the Internet to look up some reviews of the book from sources you trust, making sure to read the comments of at least two or three different reviewers.[67]

In light of the current esteem for horror/fantasy novels, it should be remembered that some children can be negatively affected by scary images (visual and textual). According to Nicholas Tucker, an educational psychologist at the University of Sussex, even a child able to distinguish fantasy from reality may have difficulties with some literature. "There are still some books that by the very force and vividness of their detail can overcome

his defenses and make him dread the light going out and the bad dream."[68]

Tucker also has raised a cautionary flag over stories that "dwell on certain details with such lingering and even gloating effect that this too can become difficult for a child who is not yet ready for them."[69] Gratuitous, says Tucker, are scenes of "unnecessary nastiness.... Although young children can take some horror, there is a difference between a story containing a ghost and a *ghost story*. One mentions fears, the other aggrandizes them."[70]

In the book *A Landscape with Dragons*, author Michael O'Brien addresses this same issue by comparing the horror of Goosebumps with classic scary tales:

> The momentary horrors that occur in classical tales always have a higher purpose; they are intended to underline the necessity of courage, ingenuity, and character; the tales are about brave young people struggling through adversity to moments of illumination, truth, and maturity; they emphatically demonstrate that good is far more powerful than evil. Not so with the new wave of shock-fiction.[71]

Lastly, the morality in some fantasy also may pose a problem. Celebrated novelist Jan Mark (*The Ennead* and *Nothing to Be Afraid Of*) has found that "in contemporary popular fiction, it's sometimes very difficult, if you are not told, to decide which of the main characters is the hero and which is the villain, because their behavior and attitudes are so morally dubious."[72] Throughout Harry Potter, for instance, "good" characters often indulge the kind of "bad" behavior usually linked to evil characters (see chapter 8).

✧ ✧ ✧

Fantasy should not be forgotten by anyone seeking good children's literature. As Lillian Smith (1887–1983), the first children's librarian in Great Britain, said, "We should put into their hands only books worthy of them, the books of honesty, integrity, and vision—the books on which they can grow."[73]

Of course, giving children "appropriate" literature does not mean giving them sanitized, lifeless volumes that shy away from difficult issues, intense emotion, or frightening scenes. Mild violence may be an appropriate and necessary part of the story (for example, the battles in The Lord of the Rings). Furthermore, such encounters can help children deal with real-world dangers and evils. How so? By providing "mock battles" that can "better prepare a child to live a pure life in a fallen world."[74]

But there is a proper way to deal with such issues. Parents, of course, should be the final arbiter of what is and what is not proper reading for their children, especially when it comes to the horror-style of books so popular today. Only a parent knows their child well enough to make determinations concerning appropriate reading material.

In conclusion, then, fantasy can be used either for good or for evil; to extol morality or glorify immorality; to terrify or to teach. There is no reason to reject outright the whole genre just because negative examples within that category exist. A little discernment and care can go a long way.

Such an approach is especially true when it comes to those works of modern fantasy wherein real-world occultism is a featured element. This is something relatively new to fantasy, and as such, must be considered. What is occultism? How has it crept into children's books? Why is occultism so popular? Why is it so potentially dangerous? These questions will be answered in our next chapter.

2

Abracadabra Adventures

> The phenomenal interest aroused by the Harry Potter books, written by J.K. Rowling, indicates a burning desire on the part of young and old to enter the enticing world of magic.[1]
>
> —THE GNOSTIC SOCIETY
> "True Magical Practices and Harry Potter"

The overall spiritual picture in America suggests there has been a mass exodus away from the Christian church and its teachings.[2] If people are no longer seeking solace in the arms of Christianity (allegedly "America's religion"), then where is the public looking for spiritual fulfillment? According to a 2001 issue of the Gallup Organization's newsletter, *Emerging Trends*, there has been a substantial increase in acceptance of "psychic, paranormal and occult phenomena over the past decade."[3] The accuracy of these findings can be seen in how American views have changed since the 1970s with regard to several occult subjects:

Which, if any, of the following do you believe at least to some degree?[4]		
Belief	*1976*	*1997*
Spiritualism (communication with the dead)	12%	52%
Astrology	17%	37%
Reincarnation	9%	25%
Fortune-telling	4%	14%

These findings suggest that today's most popular forms of spirituality are associated in some way with the occult, neopaganism, witchcraft, or a combination of them. (More discussion to come on all of these.) Religion scholar Mircea Eliade foresaw this trend with great clarity as far back as 1976:

> I cannot fail but be impressed by the amazing popularity of witchcraft in modern Western culture and its subcultures....The contemporary interest in witchcraft is only part and parcel of a larger trend, namely, the vogue of the occult and the esoteric.[5]

Since Eliade's prophetic pronouncement, the number of individuals embracing occult practices, neopagan beliefs, and principles of modern Witchcraft (also known as Wicca) have grown dramatically. And their ranks continue to swell.[6] But what is neopaganism? What do Wiccans/Witches believe? How do Wiccans differ from neopagans? What practices fall under occultism? And how are these spiritual phenomena being reflected in the fantasy literature being offered to children and teens today?

The Occult–Neopagan Connection

The word *occult*, taken from a Latin word meaning "to hide," was originally used of the hidden knowledge of various "mystery religions" and secret societies. Occultism dates back thousands of years to when people thought "deviations from natural law involved mysterious and miraculous 'supernatural' or occult laws, deriving from gods, invisible entities or the souls of the dead."[7]

Individuals and cultures subsequently developed "magick" rituals in hopes of tapping into these laws of power. Such practices in turn gave rise to witch doctors and shamans, who claimed special ability to perform magick. Thus began humanity's quest to control an uncontrollable world through the alteration, refocusing, or suspension of natural laws.

Modern occultists still seek to gain "secret powers" of the body, mind, and spirit and by so doing, alter reality. The occult, then, is a vast system of spiritual study, theory, practice, and beliefs that allegedly enable participants to obtain knowledge by which they can control, or at least influence, the world—for example, change the future, attract a mate, heal the sick, secure sudden wealth, evolve to a higher spiritual level.

Occultism encompasses countless activities, including alchemy, astrology, channeling, crystal-gazing, dowsing, extrasensory perception (ESP), fortune-telling, numerology, Ouija, out-of-body travel (astral projection), palm-reading, psychic healing, pyramidology, tarot cards, necromancy (or talking with the dead), and voodoo. Paranormal things that seem to contradict natural explanation (such as ghosts) also fall within occultism. This makes discussing the occult a daunting task:

> Occult belief comprises traditions both of immense antiquity and great complexity in which it is nearly

impossible to find any degree of uniformity and consistency, and the followers of occultism are themselves notoriously given to mystification so that their
own accounts of a subject are full of strange pseudo-
scientific jargon and merely add to the confusion.[8]

It also is difficult to categorize occultists since a majority of
them tend to be eclectic in their views.[9] But of those who do fall
into some sort of classification, the largest cross-section is *neopagan*
(or "new pagan")—in other words, people who practice and
preach modern forms of paganism.

The word *paganism* is from another Latin word, meaning
"country dweller." It refers to primitive folk of the pre-Christian
era who developed religion as a means of explaining the world.
Such forms of spirituality thrived in the West for untold millen-
nia until they were suppressed by the rise of Christianity.

No one really knows exactly which beliefs held sway over all,
or even most, ancient pagans. Contrary to what is popularly
believed, there was no single paganism. There were countless
forms of ancient paganism   numerous diverse *paganisms*   that
revered "dozens or hundreds of gods, goddesses, spirits, and less
easily defined supernatural entities." Although some paganisms
had only male gods, most had at least one male and one female
deity.[10]

Today's paganism—*neopaganism*—is a bit more streamlined. It
is based mostly on acceptance of 1) a mother goddess, who represents creation, birth, food-gathering, agricultural plenty, and the
summer; and 2) the horned god, male consort of the mother goddess, who represents the hunt, death, and winter.

To personalize their faith, modern neopagans will usually
assign to these god figures any one of a variety of names gleaned
from ancient mythology and paganism: Isis, Pan, Osiris, Odin,

Diana, Astaroth, Brighid, Aphrodite, Athena, Ceres, Hecate, Kali, and Cybele. The mother goddess is especially popular, often being referred to as Gaia or Sophia.

But beyond acceptance of multiple deities, it is impossible to affix any *rigid* set of beliefs to all neopagans. Each neopagan shapes his or her faith according to what "feels" right. As one neopagan Web site puts it, "Pagans pursue their own vision of the Divine as a direct and personal experience."[11] However, of the many traditions of paganism that exist, none is more popular or influential today (including in fiction/fantasy literature) than Wicca, also known as either Witchcraft or simply the Craft.

Something Wiccan This Way Comes

Wicca is one of the most misunderstood religions of our day (see this chapter's note 39 for more discussion).[12] Just the word "Witch" is enough to conjure up images of old hags, who at Satan's beck and call boil brews in cauldrons and fly on broomsticks. In reality, modern Witches tend to be peace-loving, nature-honoring individuals who take somewhat of a "you-leave-me-alone-and-I'll-leave-you-alone" approach to life.[13]

As with paganism, Witchcraft has many strains. The most common elements[14] binding them are:

❖ exaltation of experience over any dogmatic beliefs or creeds

❖ acceptance of "diversity of beliefs" as healthy and essential to "the survival and harmony of humanity...as well as to spiritual growth and maturation"

❖ denial of absolute truth, meaning that no single "religion or morality" is objectively right. ("Truth is what is true for you; right is what is right for you; but neither is necessarily right

for me....Your path may not be my own, but both are equally viable trails of truth and spirituality.")

❖ adherence to the Wiccan ethical code (the Wiccan Rede): "If you harm none, do what ye will"

❖ the working of magick and various divination techniques

❖ development of personal psychic abilities

Most alluring is Wiccan morality, or rather, the lack of it. Wiccans adhere to their "own path" of right and wrong, which ultimately amounts to a denial of any standard definition for good or evil. As Wiccan priestess Vivianne Crowley admitted: "In the circle there are no absolutes—no rights and wrongs."[15]

Wiccans, simply put, follow their own self-interests. They judge what is "moral" by their subjective determination of what may be harmful to someone else (see the Wiccan Rede). But such a broad code of conduct leaves room for a plethora of activities that range from sexual promiscuity, to illegal drug use, to stealing, to lying—as long as a Witch feels he or she is not hurting anyone else. It is all based on subjective feelings.

The Wiccan Rede, therefore, will *always* result in moral relativism and ethical inexactness. Therefore, a potential hazard to children is posed because Wicca basically advocates little more than the pursuit of one's selfish desires. No self-interest is out of bounds, as long as a Wiccan can convince himself or herself that what they are doing is not harmful. As Starhawk, founder of Covenant of the Goddess (the leading neopagan association), plainly states: "In witchcraft, we do not fight self-interest, we follow it."[16] Even the most sympathetic researchers of Wicca agree that the morality inherent in Witchcraft is confusing at best.[17] Religion professor Phillip Davis, author of *The Goddess Unmasked*, warns that encouraging people to think they are

divine is very dangerous. It takes the limits off and doesn't leave any moral restraints."[18]

Magick Is As Magick Does

Although not every pagan is a Witch, all Witches are pagan.[19] So while retaining their distinctiveness, these two systems do share some beliefs. Persons in both camps are antidogmatic, anti-authoritarian, polytheistic, and nature-exalting; they are concerned with psychic abilities and extol humanity's inherent divinity.[20] Another critical component of both Witchcraft and neopaganism is occult *magick* (as opposed to fantasy "magic"):

> the attempt to control, manipulate, bend, shape, twist, turn, or direct reality for one's own ends or goals. This is supposedly accomplished by invoking or employing spirits or extra-dimensional entities or beings, or mysteries, unknown or relatively unknown, or seldom used powers, forces, rules, guidelines, and/or laws [of nature].[21]

Magick normally is accomplished through spells or incantations. These usually consist of physical rituals and highly evocative imagery expressed through repetitive phrases, power words, or both, which are designed to summon either 1) external forces—including spirit beings of some kind—or 2) inner powers of the self.[22]

The theory behind spell-casting is based on the notion that there exists an intimate connection between words spoken and whatever objects or persons they signify. Witches and other neopagans believe that under the right conditions they can use this connection to create change in accord with their wishes. This is accomplished by chanting about or describing the desired result

while mentally relating those words to the objects/people/spirits involved.[23] This is one aspect of magick that is often misunderstood. Most people mistakenly think that magick always involves either the summoning of spirit beings (considered by Christians to be demons) or the use of forbidden *supernatural* powers.[24]

On the contrary, many occultists see magick and spell-casting as something quite natural, rather than supernatural. In *Witchcraft: The Old Religion*, Leo Martello says, "I make no claims as a Witch to 'supernatural powers,' but I totally believe in the *super* powers that reside in the *natural*."[25]

Wiccan author Scott Cunningham agrees:

> Folk magic cannot and could not be construed as a supernatural, otherworldly process....It's a perfectly natural process that most of us simply haven't used...Folk magicians don't use supernatural powers....They simply sense and utilize natural energies which have not yet been quantified, codified and accepted...[by] science.[26]

What actually unifies occultists is not demons, spirit beings, or supernatural forces of any kind, but their shared concept of the purpose of magick—which was concisely articulated by the infamous Aleister Crowley (1875–1947) who popularized the spelling of *magick* with a "k." He said, "Magick is the science and art of causing change to occur in conformity with will." The promise of being able to cause change in conformity with one's own will has undoubtedly helped bolster the image of Witchcraft, which some researchers see as "the fastest-growing religion in America."[27]

This new level of acceptability is more than apparent. "Proud to Be a Witch" bumper stickers now adorn cars. Web sites

extolling the virtues of Wicca, magick, and paganism abound. And bookstore shelves dedicated to paganism, Wicca, and occultism are jam-packed with volumes covering the subjects. Wicca is gaining ground in America, Canada, Australia, New Zealand, Germany, the Netherlands, and Scandinavia.[28]

Marketing Magick to Minors

According to book-buying patterns, various surveys, and a number of research reports, a large percentage of persons today buying occult-related volumes are children and teens. Wicca in particular seems to be generating the most interest. For example, one source lists these indicators:[29]

✣ the percentage of small bookstores carrying Wiccan and other Neopagan books

✣ the percentage of Wiccan books in bookstores' New Age section

✣ the numbers of Emails received by this website from teenagers with questions about Wicca

✣ media reports of the number of conflicts between Wiccan students in public high schools and their school boards over the wearing of pentacles

Book publishers many years ago began capitalizing on the occult-obsessed youth market. Various scholars have noted as much. For example, Dr. Frances Chan said, "To measure the commercial power and influence of witchcraft books in today's market, simply consider the Harry Potter phenomenon."[30]

But it did not start with Harry Potter. Today's occult harvest grew from seeds sown decades ago, particularly those planted back in 1983 by Diane Duane's Young Wizards series, which is

about a teenage witch and her wizard boyfriend. The eight-book set initiated what has become an obsession among teenage girls—the female teen-witch character. Duane also helped open the publishing door for other occult-based novels targeting children and teens.[31]

Recent additions to this growing body of literature include the Sweep series (14 titles) by Cate Tiernan, the T*Witches set of books (10 titles) by H.B. Gilmour and Randi Reisfeld, and the Circle of Three novels (15 titles) by Isobel Bird. All three offerings paint a tremendously attractive portrait of occultism, magick, and Wicca.

According to Jean Feiwel, editor-in-chief at Scholastic (publisher of T*Witches and Harry Potter), this brand of fiction is just tapping into an increased teen fascination with witchcraft. "It's almost gotten—dare I say—acceptable," Feiwel said in a 2001 news article.[32] This same story reported that "practicing witches are amused by this trend in teen books" and that "the books are selling so well that the writers have been given contracts to write more volumes."[33]

Swept Away by Sweep

The Sweep series, which features such titles as *The Coven*, *Blood Witch*, and *Dark Magick*, follows the adventures of 16-year-old Morgan Rowlands. When we meet her in Book I, she is a drab and shy teenager who has fallen for a handsome high school heartthrob: Cal. He is a Wiccan, as is his mother.

Morgan would love to attract him, but she is only a plain-looking Catholic girl embarrassed to still be a virgin. Then, she discovers she is exceptionally sensitive to natural energies and is unusually adept at magick, especially when it comes to channeling occult power. The story continues with Morgan joining Cal's

coven and learning how to perform Wiccan rituals, complete with praises to "the Goddess."[34]

Week after week Cal teaches Morgan and her friends more about Wiccan history, rituals, spells, and powers. An occult bookstore becomes Morgan's favorite hangout and her main supplier of occult paraphernalia.[35] The saga goes on to exalt Wicca as the most exciting, fulfilling, and rewarding of all religious belief systems. And with the help of magick, Morgan blossoms into a strong, confident, and powerful young woman.

Tiernan's series effectively doubles as a thinly veiled evangelism tool for Wiccans.[36] The joys of Wicca and the magnificence of "magick" shine through brilliantly to readers of Sweep. Teens and younger children have no problem understanding the author's message about Wicca (see note 37 for fan reviews).[37]

Not only does Sweep exalt Wicca and denigrate Christianity (the religion in which Morgan was raised by her adoptive parents), but it puts forth several highly dubious yet oft-repeated claims, including the assertion that Wicca is based directly on verified prehistoric beliefs and ancient Celtic traditions.[38]

In reality, *modern* Wicca has only loose connections, at best, to a few ancient pagan traditions that have now been significantly altered. Charlotte Allen, in an enlightening article on Wicca that appeared in *The Atlantic Monthly*, writes,

> Historically speaking, the "ancient" rituals of the Goddess movement are almost certainly bunk....In all probability, not a single element of the Wiccan story is true. The evidence is overwhelming that Wicca is a distinctly new religion, a 1950s concoction influenced by such things as Masonic ritual and a late-nineteenth-century fascination with the esoteric and the occult, and that various assumptions informing the Wiccan view of history are deeply flawed....Scholars generally

agree that there is no indication, either archaeological or in the written record, that any ancient people ever worshipped a single, archetypal goddess—a conclusion that strikes at the heart of Wiccan belief....

In the 1950s [Gerald] Gardner introduced a religion he called (and spelled) Wica. Although Gardner claimed to have learned Wiccan lore from a centuries-old coven of witches who also belonged to the Fellowship of Crotona...no one had been able to locate the coven....[It appears] that Gardner had invented the rites he trumpeted, borrowing from rituals created early in the twentieth century by the notorious British occultist Aleister Crowley, among others.[39]

Despite the availability of such information, the Sweep series has lulled untold numbers of teens into thinking Wicca is something it is not.

Twin Witches and the Circle of Three

Similarly crafted to make Wicca look attractive are the T*Witches books by Scholastic (publisher of Harry Potter). They tell the tale of identical teen twins, Camryn and Alexandra, who were separated at birth. Camryn can foresee the future, and Alexandra can read people's minds. When both are reunited, they begin sharing adventures as Wiccans. The novels are so popular that "the Disney Channel is turning T*Witches into a made-for-TV movie!"[40]

Scholastic has devoted an entire "Kids-Fun-Online" Web site to T*Witches. Children not only can find out which T*Witch they most resemble, but also locate their horoscope. The site even includes a "Magick Tips Archive" to assist children with their "own private spell-binding."[41] (In this archive the word

magick is spelled in its occult form, using a "k." See note 41 for samples.)

Finally, Scholastic provides the "Spellbook," which lists spells submitted by *children* who practice magick.[42] There are incantations posted by children wanting to help their peers learn and use a wide range of spells. Although juvenile in content, they accurately reflect Wiccan and neopagan procedures for properly casting spells.

Scholastic's Web site shows just how effectively books can promote religious ideas to kids. (Coincidentally, Scholastic also is the British publisher of His Dark Materials series—see chapter 1.) Most disconcerting about Scholastic, however, is its unparalleled influence over children as "the largest publisher and distributor of children's books and...the largest operator of school-based book clubs and school-based book fairs in the United States."[43] T*Witches, for example, regularly appears at public school book fairs.

However, the Circle of Three series by Isobel Bird is the most overt attempt made by any fiction author to woo teenagers into the world of Wicca. Bird, a long-time Wiccan, blatantly seeks to make Witchcraft "a viable religion." A 2001 *School Library Journal* review observed that Bird's representation of Wicca would certainly "wet the appetites of teens interested in the subject."[44]

Circle of Three presents Wicca so positively that Wiccan Ellen Dugan recommended it (and Tiernan's Sweep series) in her nonfiction book *Elements of Witchraft: Natural Magick for Teens*.[45] Teens are finding the series both exhilarating and mind-expanding. Teenreads.com exclaims, "Want to learn more about witchcraft but don't want to slog through some boring—and frankly weird—New Age book about Wicca? Teenreads has the answer for you: the Circle of Three series."[46] Children, too, have been enjoying the books; children as young as nine years old.[47]

In 2002 the success of Circle of Three increased even more after the American Library Association (ALA) listed the series among its "Quick Picks for Reluctant Young Adult Readers." According to the ALA, this list "is geared to the teenager who, for whatever reason, does not like to read....Teen input is a vital aspect in the final decision of the committee."[48]

Calling All Kids

Meanwhile, seemingly unfazed by the possible dangers posed to children by occultism, publishers continue churning out books that pique youth interest in the subject. Wiccans and neopagans also have responded to the occult publishing boom by producing not only fiction works lauding their religion, but also *nonfiction* volumes on Witchcraft. These books, which boldly teach Wicca to children and teens, include many popular titles such as: *Spells for Teenage Witches*; *The Real Witches' Handbook*; and *To Ride a Silver Broomstick: New Generation Witchcraft*.

Both fiction and non-fiction books related to Wicca and neopaganism are indoctrinating an incalculable number of children and teens. But what is the attraction? There are at least eight types of individuals who usually end up in the world of the occult:[49]

✤ "The curious," who have no fully formed system of religious beliefs—those who are merely dabbling with occult forces out of nothing but sheer curiosity (for example, teenagers).

✤ "The conformist, who looks around at this peer group and says, 'Everyone does it,' and decides to be another who 'does it.'"

✤ "The dissatisfied, whose religious experience has left him unfulfilled and skeptical."

❖ "The sad, whose bereavement inclines him towards any-thing that offers knowledge of the dead."

❖ "The rebellious, who recoils from the status quo in the church and in society, and seeks a viable alternative else-where."

❖ "The psychically inclined, who wants to develop suspected latent powers."

❖ "The offspring of practicing occultists, who are condi-tioned from childhood."

❖ "The credulous," who are ready to believe just about any-thing and everything.

Occultism in general can help people, through rites and rituals, stamp out feelings of powerlessness—something that most children and teens struggle with daily. Such feelings, of course, are a normal burden that all young people must bear until they mature into adults, at which time they gain autonomy. Here is the danger and the draw of occultism: the so-called "power" it pledges. For would-be Witches the promise of a changed life is as close as a spell, rite, or ritual that can be performed by simply knowing how to execute a magickal formula.

Whether or not the expected results actually materialize is inconsequential. The sheer promise of a result, coupled with the personal feeling of power received from occult involvement, is enough to form a bond between a youth and occult activity. Wielding power, even the mere *hope* of wielding it, can be tan-talizing.

And any fantasy about children who seem to already possess some degree of autonomy via magick is going to have great kid-appeal. Such stories offer youths an entertaining outlet for their

unmet desires to experience freedom from parents, teachers, and other authority figures. J.K. Rowling worked this into Harry Potter, saying, "I was thinking of a place of great order but immense danger, with children who had skills with which they could overwhelm their teachers."[50]

These types of stories, however, pose a risk if by their content they suggest that children in the real world can, and should, truly seek to exercise personal power or autonomy over their own lives and the lives of others.

Magick vs. "Magic"

In light of the very legitimate concern over occult magick in children's literature, one question consistently raised by parents, especially those from within the religious community, has to do with the positive portrayal of *magic* in fantasy and fiction: Is it a danger? Magic, of course, is a common element not only in fantasy, but also in fairy tales, folktales, myths, fables, and legends. It serves as an essential tool to propel the plot and characters forward.

In fact, magic is as central to fantasy as advanced technology is to science fiction. Both magic and advanced technology allow for things to happen in their respective genres that otherwise could not happen. While few parents would harbor concern over the "phasers" or "dilithium crystals" in *Star Trek*, many parents do feel uncomfortable with the "magic" in some stories for children.

But the "magic" in most works of fantasy should not be equated with real-world magick. They are two altogether different things. As J.R.R. Tolkien said, true fantasy is filled with images and imagery that "are not only 'not actually present,' but which are indeed not to be found in our primary world at all, or are generally believed not to be found there."[51]

Magic without a "k"—the kind found in most fantasy—is imaginary. It bears little resemblance to the occult beliefs and practices of our real world. Fantasy magic will only have a *transient* similarity to anything in the actual sphere of reality. Objects associated with "magic" in fantasy tend to be wholly invented for the sake of the story, and if not wholly invented, then at least significantly altered (either in their use or appearance) in order to distance them from vaguely similar real-world objects.

In The Chronicles of Narnia, for example, devout Christian C.S. Lewis positively speaks of a "stargazer," which in our world normally would refer to an astrologer. Such a reference would completely contradict Lewis's faith. However, the fact is that his "stargazer" is a centaur (a mythological beast) living in Narnia. Furthermore, the entire cosmological system is different in Narnia—"the planets and stars are living beings."[52] Hence, this would be much better interpreted as an allusion to some sort of astronomer, or a person whose function is to discern divine messages that Aslan (Lewis's Christ figure) has allowed to appear in the stars of Narnia.

What we see in Lewis is how certain objects or practices in fantasy, even if they are not changed enough to make them *totally* unrecognizable, can still be arranged within an entirely different system, thereby taking them far away from any real-world context. Consequently, such objects and practices need not pose a problem for religious parents worried about any direct links to the occult. In other words, because fantasy often takes place in an alternate reality, different definitions, meanings, and laws of existence apply.

Parents must not automatically reject a fantasy book just because it may mention witches, spells, or magic. Such elements are not necessarily reflecting real occultism. Many fantasy books, for instance, feature magicians (or wizards). But these characters

often serve as symbols of benevolence and help, which is why they are often seen fighting evil. Evil wizards are depicted, to be sure, but these characters usually have gone bad and are warring with good wizards. In either case, their "magic" diverges from anything in our reality.

To J.R.R. Tolkien, fantasy "magic" is so different from anything in our real world that he thought perhaps the very word *magic* should not be used. He said that occult magick "produces, or pretends to produce, an alteration in the Primary World [our world, as opposed to a fantasy world]....It is not an art but a technique; its desire is *power* in this world"[53] (an issue we touched on a few pages earlier).

Fact or Fiction?

It cannot be legitimately argued that fiction does not affect how readers think, feel, and respond to the world. The extent to which this happens might vary from person to person, but the most susceptible fiction fans will always be children, who are in their formative years. According to children's education specialist James Higgins, a young reader of fantasy and realistic fiction might actually confuse "the terrain of the author's world with that of his own."[54]

When fiction/fantasy contains magick, this confuses the worlds of fiction and reality, especially for younger children. Unfortunately, in addition to the Wiccan fiction we've already considered, this is also happening today in certain forms of "parallel world" fantasy, where authors heavily draw upon real-world occultism in an effort to create works reflecting society's current fascination with the occult.

Of course, the more realistic a book is, the higher the probability that a child will mistake it for reality. One key issue, then,

is whether or not a work of fantasy could be detrimental if taken more realistically than intended. Equally important is whether or not a particular fantasy could guide children in a potentially harmful direction.

This concern has caused all three of the most popular fantasy works of our era—Harry Potter, The Lord of the Rings, and The Chronicles of Narnia—to be eyed with great suspicion by adults. But is this fair? Is it accurate to view them all as similar? If they are different, how are they different? What about those readers who say the fantasy novels present identical structures, religious allusions, and underlying messages?

To answer these questions, Part Two will take an in-depth look at the works of J.R.R. Tolkien, C.S. Lewis, and J.K. Rowling. Feel free to jump ahead to this section! However, for those readers who may want slightly more information on literature and how kids learn by reading, chapters 3 and 4 should be your next stop.

3

Long Ago and
Far Away

Wonder—...emotion excited by the perception of
something novel and unexpected, or inexplicable;
astonishment mingled with perplexity or bewil-
dered curiosity.

—THE OXFORD UNIVERSAL DICTIONARY

Many persons today, both young and old, fail to see how a fictional tale could relate to their life. Others assume that reading
will not be as entertaining as a "great movie" or an "awesome
video game." Some nonreaders also harbor the illusion that most
literature is either boring or just too difficult to comprehend.
However, as literary critic Northrop Frye (1912–1991) noted,

> Literature gives us an experience that stretches us ver-
> tically to the heights and depths of what the human
> mind can conceive, to what corresponds to the con-
> ceptions of heaven and hell....No matter how much
> experience we may gather in life, we can never in life
> get the dimension of experience that the imagination
> gives us.[1]

"A good story lets you know people as individuals in all their particularities and conflict; and once you see someone as a person—flawed, complex, striving—then you've reached beyond stereotype,"[2] says one author. The written word (like music, art, drama, and dance) can express some of the deepest parts of our humanity: joy, grief, love, anger, and desire.

But unlike other forms of creative expression, literature also merges the art form being enjoyed with the one who is enjoying it. There is a marriage of sorts that takes place so the story and the reader become one, thereby creating a "virtual" experience of the mind and heart. This event then adds to who we are as individuals.[3]

Once upon a Time

One of the most popular types of literature of our era is fantasy. (Its close relative, science fiction, which might best be thought of as high-tech fantasy, also has seen a recent increase in popularity.) Fantasy developed from an immense body of work known as *folklore*, a genre that is difficult to define. It is nearly as broad a category as fiction itself since it includes poems, nursery rhymes, proverbs, fables, and even folk songs.[4]

Folklore is perhaps best viewed as simply "the great stream of anonymous creation that is the accumulated wisdom and art of everyday people," and it has always emerged from a community as an expression of their beliefs, customs, memories, and fears. It is no surprise that folklore has often been referred to as the "cement of society."[5]

Folktales and fairy tales are the most obvious examples of folklore. They "come out of the most distant deeps of human experience and human fancy."[6] Both kinds of tales address universal

themes such as fear, anger, jealousy, grief, revenge, and love. And they often contain spiritual overtones:

> They tell of immortality, of the souls of beasts and birds and other living things. They tell of perpetual spiritual combat. However, they never leave out the stubborn facts concerning greed and hate; sometimes even daring to tell how these may ride roughshod over virtue and goodness.[7]

In general, fairy tales and folktales tend to have the same overall themes. They usually focus on some hero or heroine who demonstrates courage, loyalty, bravery, cleverness, perseverance, or other admirable virtues.[8] (It is easy to see why fairy tales like "Sleeping Beauty," "Cinderella," and "Puss in Boots" have been so enjoyed and told for generations.) The importance of exposing young readers to this kind of fantasy cannot be overstated. Nicholas Tucker, children's book author and senior lecturer in cultural studies at the University of Sussex, remarks,

> Fairy stories provide the child with the "knowledge that he is born into a world of death, violence, wounds, adventure, heroism and cowardice, good and evil." Children will probably not yet know this to be true from their own experience, but this knowledge may still strike a chord within them, possibly even from memories of their own more violent fantasies and nightmares. It may also start providing them with some sort of mental preparation for those more violent aspects of adult society which they will soon also notice, for example by watching television news bulletins.[9]

The poet Richard Le Gallienne (1866–1947) probably articulated the deep significance of fairy tales best when he wrote,

> The wonder of the world! Perhaps that is the chief business of the fairy tale—to remind us that the world is no mere dustheap, pullulating with worms, as some of the old-fashioned scientists tried to make us believe; but that, on the contrary, it is a rendezvous of radiant forces forever engaged in turning its dust into dreams, ever busy with the transmutation of matter into mind, and mind into spirit—a world, too, so mysterious that anything can happen, or any dream come true.[10]

The beauty of folk and fairy tales lie in their ability to communicate truths and virtues to children in an uncomplicated way. Kids are able to see in them the reality of good and bad, the consequences of wrongdoing, and the rewards of doing right without having to "dig" for the message. And although there exists little ambiguity in such tales, they still leave room for reflection and discussion.

Surprising Depth

Far from being naive or innocent works, folk and fairy tales "have been to the end of experience and back."[11] Their depth can be traced to the fact that they were not originally written for young readers:

> Originally conceived of as adult entertainment, fairy tales were told at social gatherings, in spinning rooms, in the fields, and in other settings where adults congregated—not in the nursery.[12]

Some fairy tales were thematically so mature that they never made it into modern-day children's books. Consider the earliest version of "Sleeping Beauty," titled "Talia, Sun, and Moon." In addition to the recognized aspects of "Sleeping Beauty," the original tale also includes the rape of the sleeping Talia by a king, her resulting pregnancy, and the king's abandonment of her. The king eventually returns, but only after he has already married another woman—a murderous one with cannibalistic tendencies. The story ends with the evil wife being burned alive on the bonfire she intended for Talia![13]

Photos from early fairy tale stories show their original adult nature. In "Jack the Giant Killer" (recorded about 1820), we have a gruesome execution: "Then Jack with his pickaxe commenced; the giant most loudly did roar." And the cover illustration from the original *Little Red Riding-Hood* (1823) features the little girl's tombstone. This reflects the story's ending, where Red Riding-Hood is eaten by the wolf—no lumberjack saves the day. (Photos courtesy of the University of Southern Mississippi, McCain Library and Archives, de Grummond Children's Literature Collection.)

Modernized fairy tales are much less adult in nature, so they can be used as powerful tools for helping kids grasp morality and ethics. As folklore expert Jack Zipes has observed, "Knowledge of a story's featured 'sin' can, in the context of children's natural curiosity, help make the answers to their questions more meaningful." He also believes that as children listen to fairy tales and project themselves into characters, they receive "a stage upon

which they can play out inner conflicts."[14] This can be especially beneficial for children needing to resolve tension relating to how they feel about themselves and others around them.

Myth and Legend

Myths and legends date back to the origins of recorded history. These wondrous sagas developed as people gathered together, often around an open fire, and infused their own personal struggles and experiences with supernatural elements.[15] Additionally, the tellers of myths and legends made their stories far more epic in scope than the folktales or fairy tale, usually by setting them in far-off lands or mystical regions.

Myths normally revolved around invented characters whose existence explained the mysteries of the world—natural phenomena such as lightning, thunder, rain, wind; the origins of humanity; and the history of religious beliefs and customs. Moreover, myths often explained difficult aspects of life, such as suffering, danger, disease, misfortune, and death.[16]

Legends, on the other hand, were often based on the life of an ancient ancestor, a regional hero, or some other real-life person or persons. Unlike myths, legends served to highlight concepts relating more to personal human drama and tragedy than to natural phenomena or universal issues.

Anything mysterious, frightening, or harmful could be explained by myth and legend. They might symbolically depict hostile warriors or peoples. Sickness or death might be represented as a curse of either gods or demons. Misfortune might be blamed on the antics of diverse creatures, seen and unseen: fairies, gnomes, or elves, to name but a few.

But unlike fairy tales or folktales, myths and legends are so all-encompassing that with few exceptions they take place within

worlds separate from the one in which we live. They also include moral lessons relating to life and sometimes even the afterlife. They are prime examples of the kind of stories that have the potential to convey weighty truths about humanity, our world, and the metaphysical realm.

Clearly, a story is not necessarily bad just because it contains supernatural beings, bizarre creatures, or scary situations. More important is how those characters are portrayed. What are they doing? What are they saying? What is the tale's overall message? This brings us to that form of fiction directly descended from myths and legends—epic fantasy. For many readers, it is the best of all genres rolled into one.

From Faerie to Fantasy

Fantasy on a grand scale is probably best typified by *The Hobbit* and The Lord of the Rings trilogy by J.R.R. Tolkien (see chapter 5). These works offer, in a most striking way, what Tolkien said was the basis of all good fantasy: the "aventures of men in the Perilous Realm" ("Perilous Realm" usually meaning some kind of alternate reality; a locale removed from the real world).[17]

There is no end to the places fantasy can take us. In *Realms of Fantasy*, science-fiction writers Malcolm Edwards and Robert Holdstock identify at least five fantasy environments: the ancient past, the distant future, present-day lost worlds, other planets, and fantasy Earths similar to, but different from our own. Tolkien fondly referred to these secondary worlds as "sub-creations."[18]

But why is fantasy so popular? Escapism, at least to some extent, drives the joy of retreating into a fantasy book's alternate reality. Probably more significant, however, is the intense satisfaction we derive from safely immersing ourselves into a place

that in many ways is better than ours. Through imaginative literature we are able to manufacture an internal vision of the society
in which we want to live, as opposed to the one in which we
already do live—our *ideal* world versus our *real* world.

Even if a fantasy world starts off in poor shape (as in C.S.
Lewis's witch-ruled Narnia of *The Lion, the Witch, and the
Wardrobe*), there exists the thrill of ultimately achieving a better
world via adventure. Whatever sorrows may be experienced
along the way, the story and the storyteller lead us onward. We
ourselves meet every dread and face every danger along with the
fantasy hero or heroes. In the end, all of us are victorious.

Children's book author Natalie Babbitt agrees: "Fantasy literature lets us share the hero's hopes and eventual triumph."[19] In
other words, fantasy can be highly therapeutic, both emotionally
and psychologically. We can obtain comfort by seeing evil
unmasked, condemned, and destroyed. We gain hope by seeing
that at least somewhere, even if it is in another world, good has
triumphed.

Fantasy, of course, need not always be epic in scale. It can be
light and whimsical, like *Winnie the Pooh* or Beatrix Potter's *The
Tale of Squirrel Nutkin*. Fantasy also can be sensitive and sentimen-
tal—for example, *Charlotte's Web*. Adventure, too, might drive the
story, as in *Journey to the Center of the Earth* by Jules Verne.

Award-winning sci-fi writer Everett Bleiler has commented:
"Fantasy may be almost all things to all men."[20] Every kind of
fantasy, however, somehow deals with life as it might be in an
alternate reality where natural laws are suspended. In fantasy,
science does not exist as we know it, and magic is everywhere in
some form. Children respond to it because it activates their
imagination—a key to psychological maturation. Kids never
encouraged to enter the fantasy world are "quite literally,
deprived children."[21]

Fantasy can even help children see with spiritual eyes by training them to look beyond what's visible toward other possible worlds. In *The Ordinary and the Fabulous*, British writer Elizabeth Cook says that legends, fairy tales, and fantasy possess "a sense of the strange, the numinous, the totally Other, of what lies quite beyond human personality and cannot be found in any human relationships."[22]

In other words, fantasy can be extremely beneficial. But there remains a problem with fantasy, as with all forms of fiction for young readers. According to recent studies into child development, which confirm the commonsense observations of parents, literature that is good for some kids might not be good for others.

4

Trusting Souls

Literature helps children realize their potential during a particular stage of development and fosters progress toward the next stage....The books children read are formative in their lives; it is our responsibility to know their books....We need to develop guidelines for choosing the best....The books we select influence children in lasting ways....We cannot just say, "This is a good book," but must ask ourselves, "Good for whom?"[1]

—BERNICE CULLINAN
former president of the International
Reading Association

People bring their own background, experiences, and biases to any book they read. Consequently, different children often understand, interpret, and respond differently to the same piece of literature.

This is also the case with adults. But subjectivity is especially pronounced in kids not only because they are less developed emotionally, psychologically, intellectually, and spiritually, but also because they have fewer life experiences from which to draw

71

when they read. In other words, it is not necessarily the content of a given piece of literature that will most influence a child's response, but the child's personal background, life experiences, maturity, and overall developmental level.[2]

The trick is to provide children with enough enjoyable literary experiences that reading becomes a habit—one that will broaden their intellectual and emotional horizons for the rest of their lives. A good book for a child, teen, young adult, or even a mature reader must be worth the effort. As C.S. Lewis said, "No book is really worth reading at the age of ten which is not equally (and often far more) worth reading at the age of fifty."[3]

Making Good Choices

But there is more to reading than just an intellectual recognition of text. A literary work takes on life as it is "realized" by the reader, "who is in turn acted upon" by the text.[4] Stated another way, the book comes alive.

The coming to life of a book should be "fun." But what is "fun" for many children (or adults) is not necessarily healthful, as children's book author Elizabeth Fitzgerald Howard comments:

> We read for delight. But at the same time we must read with a discerning eye and mind, with the intention of defining that delight. So on one hand or with one eye, we are reading with a receptive spirit, eagerly and non-judiciously, unconsciously becoming the child that is still with us. But with the other eye, we must go beyond our own delight to the nuts and bolts, the very basic hardware, of how and why this book delights us and what could make it a source of delight for child readers.[5]

Children are not little adults—they need guidance. But in this day and age, many children are the ones making the critical choices with regard to the books they read and the movies they watch, not to mention the computer/video games they play. This has led to a troubling reversal in the traditional family structure that has children making choices previously left up to parents.

Of course, children should have a great deal of input when it comes to reading material and other forms of entertainment in which they desire to participate. But the final decision *must* remain in parental hands. The all-too-frequent lament of today's moms and dads is, "Well, I really don't want them reading that book, but what can I do? They're just going to do what they're going to do."

Simply put, parents ought not be afraid to use that necessary, but certainly most difficult of words (the one all kids dread): "no." As the preamble to the United Nations' Declaration of the Rights of the Child (1959) reads, "The child, by reason of his physical and mental immaturity, needs special safeguards and care." Choosing literature for children undoubtedly falls under this guiding principle, and parents must not shy away from acting upon it. To do otherwise could easily prove harmful—not only to the literary development of a child, but also to their spiritual and emotional well-being.

Language—The Key Component

Material that is too simple for a child's language skills will probably inspire little more than boredom, which in turn might cause them to reject reading for entertainment and learning. On the other hand, material that is too advanced could devastate a child's self-confidence, especially if reading difficulties provoke

ridicule from peers. At the very least, such results may lead to frustration stemming from an inability to follow the story line.[6]

A good way to test a child's development in this area is to read aloud to them, letting them take turns reading as you go along. Then pause periodically to discuss the themes and events of the book, checking their comprehension. (This is critical because some children might be able to "read" the words on the page but not be proficient enough with language to comprehend what they are reading.)

Books take children outside their world. Therefore, it is important that the new situations, events, and conflicts presented to them are understandable. The material can then contribute to the store of information the child uses to interpret life. Fortunately, good stories place new words and concepts in contexts that explain their meaning. A parent, however, must always be on hand to clarify to the child any concepts still vague.

Knowing Right from Wrong

Everyone has a sense of right and wrong, of morality and ethics, of good and evil. But from where do we get these concepts? That aspect of our development begins early in life and progresses through several stages. Literature helps children and teenagers work through these stages of development and can be very influential in determining their moral direction.

According to researchers who study such issues, the earliest stage (the *morality of constraint* stage) involves obedience to adult rules ("good" behavior) primarily through fear of punishment. This emerging grasp of right and wrong is what makes the morality in typical fairy tales easy for children to accept. The stories meet them at their level of moral development.[7]

Eventually, this stage is replaced by a *morality of cooperation* phase, which is entered gradually as children begin noticing that their actions affect themselves and others. This new understanding engenders some level of respect for their fellow human beings.

Further, the "morality of cooperation" stage usually includes the discovery of something called *motive*. Children come to see that motive exists not just in their own decisions, but also in those of others. Suddenly, with an understanding of motivation, a child can appreciate not only *what* a character does, but also *why* a character does it.

Herein lies a great benefit of literature—it facilitates discussions with children that delve into the actions of fictional characters and legitimacy of those actions. Such talks can help children in developing their problem-solving skills, enable them to build a sense of security with their own moral convictions, and force them to examine why they believe what they believe. Each of these reading benefits can only help a child in future years.

Of course, there are some dangers here. What if a parent's ethical–moral conscience is undeveloped? What if a teacher discussing morals and ethics with a child seeks to impose his or her own standards on that child, rather than allowing them to reach their own conclusions? What if the morals or ethics put forth and glamorized by a story are incompatible with a parent's convictions? Children's literature experts Zena Sutherland and May Hill Arbuthnot offer several observations and suggestions:

> Children's literature often reflects the values that adults think are important to encourage, and those who select books for children should be aware of the author's values and assumptions as well as of their own. If an author's attitude toward parent-child relationships, sex

mores, civil rights, or any other issue is in agreement
with our own, we may tend to approve of the book as a
whole, but if the values and assumptions are at variance
with our own, we may tend to dismiss it, regardless of its
other qualities. For these reasons, it is particularly
important for us to analyze books carefully and objectively....It is often illuminating to compare a book
with the author's other books and with other authors'
books on the same topic or in the same literary genre.[8]

There is just no way to avoid some risks. But if parents can be
careful about choosing books for their children, the risks will be
well worth taking.

I Think, Therefore I Read

Literature also is inextricably linked to how children acquire
knowledge and make choices in life. Good books help young readers mature intellectually, especially with regard to how they process
information. Closely tied to how literature helps in this area is the
universal practice of personal storytelling—a basic human activity
enjoyed by both adults and children. Engaging in it enables us to
process, reflect upon, and put to use all we perceive.

Respected language and literature authority James Britton
described storytelling as "an assimilative function through which
we balance out inner needs with external realities."[9] Literature
merges with this natural form of expression when kids take symbols and characters from stories (for example, witches, fairy god-
mothers, giants, trolls, wizards) and adapt them for use in their
own personal tales.[10]

Young children also borrow phraseology from stories to make
their own tales. "Once upon a time" is commonly taken as a
beginning, and "they lived happily ever after" is a typical ending.

According to Bernice Cullinan, this borrowing shows the extent to which children "have assimilated literature and dramatically illustrates the potential power of literature to affect language as well as cognitive and affective development."[11]

Gradually, as children move through the stages of maturity, they progressively interact more on an analytical basis with literature until finally reaching the *formal operational mode* of thinking (late adolescence).[12] This is marked by an ability to reason with abstractions and symbols. Signs of this stage can be seen in most kids by around 9 to 11 years old—the age when they can both identify with and emulate the traits of characters in books.

Me, Myself, and Others

Literature can significantly affect a child's ability to interact socially. Bernice Cullinan remarks,

> One world is around us, the other is a vision inside our minds, born and fostered by the imagination, yet real enough for us to try to make the world we see conform to its shape....Literature plays a strong role in helping children envision a world they do not see....[It] feeds the imagination; it helps us create a vision of society to work toward.[13]

Since the future of our society is in the hands of our children, it seems reasonable they should have their imaginations educated and exercised. But when it comes to the literature we allow them to read, there is a crucial question parents must ask: What kind of "vision of society" is a particular book presenting?

Answering this question alone may be enough for a parent to know whether or a not a book is appropriate for their child. We must never underestimate the power that a certain piece of

literature, or body of literature, can have over a generation. It can ultimately affect society in general on a very large scale in years to come.

Magical Appeal

Literature can affect children so deeply that their reading experience becomes a kind of spiritual event. Children instinctively meet the world as a place where "the material and the spiritual are so intricately entwined that they are one and the same." Fantasy in particular, like the mind and heart of a child, "integrates the spiritual and the material into a unified whole."[14] Professor James Higgins commented,

> Story offers the child another key to the understanding of the universe—a universe which stretches multi-light-years in time and distance beyond the reader's own experience. Literature accepts the imagination of the child as a legitimate vehicle for passing beyond the differences of appearance and into the unity of truth....[T]here is something spiritual and mystifying about almost any good story written about children, and many good books written for children.[15]

As we have seen, C.S. Lewis, George MacDonald (1824–1905), and J.R.R. Tolkien were all very adept at capturing the spiritual/mystical within the pages of their fantasy works. The same could be said about several contemporary authors such as Stephen Lawhead (born 1950) and Lloyd Alexander (born 1924). The spiritual undertones of their fantasy works are undeniably apparent.

The eminent poet Richard Le Gallienne saw the presence of such spirituality as an indispensable facet of good fantasy (or fairy

tale), saying: "The earth cannot get along all by itself. It is always in need of help from the stars. This is one of the many morals of the fairy tale, which thus gives expression to the holy hunger of the human heart."[16]

Lloyd Alexander also saw the immense benefits of fantasy, at least four of which he discussed in "Wishful Thinking—or Hopeful Dreaming":[17]

❖ Fantasy makes possible the "sheer delight" of "let's pretend" and the "eager suspension of disbelief." He observes "an exuberance in good fantasy quite unlike the most exalted moments of realistic literature."

❖ Fantasy elicits our emotions as vividly as a dream does. The fantasy adventure "seems always on a larger scale, the deeds bolder, the people brighter." He adds, "In fantasy, we have more plausible scope for strong feelings....We can laugh harder, weep longer—and be a little corny."

❖ Fantasy can be wonderfully influential in the area of morality. The genre offers clear values, true heroes, ultimate justice, endless mercy, and fierce courage. "Fantasy, by its power to move us so deeply, to dramatize, even melodramatize, morality, can be one of the most effective means of establishing a capacity [in children] for adult values."

❖ Fantasy, including science fiction (and to a degree even some types of horror), can offer hope, which he describes as "one of the most precious human values."

Given Alexander's last point, a word must be said here about the issue of horror, which according to many respected authors is an essential thread of all fantasy genres. Award-winning fantasy/sci-fi writer Terry Pratchett comments:

The morality of fantasy and horror is, by and large, the strict morality of the fairy tale. The vampire is slain, the alien is blown out of the airlock, the evil Dark Lord is vanquished and, perhaps at some loss, the Good triumph—not because they are better armed, but because Providence is on their side. Let there be goblin hordes, let there be terrible environmental threats, let there be giant mutated slugs if you really must, but let there also be Hope.[18]

G.K. Chesterton expressed a sentiment many years ago in reference to fairy tales. His comment is just as applicable to fantasy, and it's one that should be a watchword for parents who want their children to develop a moral outlook on life: "The objection to fairy stories is that they tell children there are dragons. But children have always known there are dragons. Fairy stories tell children that dragons can be killed."[19]

Part Two

Realms of Imagination

Christian fans of Tolkien also tend to be fans of C.S. Lewis, whose seven-volume series The Chronicles of Narnia is also a work of Christian imagination that involves magic and wizardry. The Harry Potter books, on the other hand, have met with decidedly mixed reactions among Christian readers. In both Catholic and Protestant circles, some have enthusiastically embraced Rowling's popular series, at times even explicitly making comparisons to Tolkien and Lewis....Others, however, have attacked the young hero of Rowling's series as a veritable poster child for the occult.

—STEVEN D. GREYDANUS
"Harry Potter vs. Gandalf," decentfilms.com

5

Life in Middle-Earth

Tolkien changed fantasy; he elevated it and rede-
fined it, to such an extent that it will never be the
same again.

—GEORGE R.R. MARTIN
award-winning author, screenwriter

We are all deeply in J.R.R. Tolkien's debt, writers perhaps even more than readers. He gave us the greatest fantasy of our time.

—Poul Anderson
award-winning fantasy author

The fantasy world of Middle-earth created by John Ronald
Reuel Tolkien (1892–1973) began taking shape in 1914 in the
form of a short poem titled "The Voyage of Earendel the Evening
Star." It included a passing reference to Westerland, which
Tolkien would later define as the land of the immortals.[1]

He then wrote a collection of related poems, but unexpectedly had his writing interrupted by World War I, which took him
to France. It was there that Tolkien's 11th Battalion saw some of
the heaviest action witnessed by troops, including that at the

Battle of Somme in 1916. At last, in November, Tolkien con-
tracted trench fever. It so ravaged his body that he was evacuated
to a nearby hospital. But when the illness did not abate, he was
sent home to England.[2]

Tolkien was safe, but the bloody confrontations he had witnessed fundamentally changed his demeanor. The scenes were
not easily forgotten and often plagued his mind. Horrific images
took on even greater life each time word reached him about various Oxford companions who had died in what he called "the
'animal horror' of trench warfare." Many years later he remembered, "By 1918 all but one of my close friends were dead."[3]

Tolkien eventually returned to Oxford, where he received
both an education and a teaching position. There he continued
writing various mythic poems and interesting tales, all of which
took place in Middle-earth, his own sub-creation. These stories
eventually become *The Silmarillion*, a historic narrative tracing
the events of Middle-earth.

The expansive saga, however, was never published during
Tolkien's lifetime; in fact, he would never even finish it. That
task, which fell to his son Christopher, would not be completed
until just prior to its release to the public in 1977—four years
after Tolkien's death.

These earliest writings contributed in many ways to his most
famous tale, The Lord of the Rings. That story however, would
not see the light of day until well after the 1937 publication of yet
another Tolkien volume, which began unexpectedly around 1930,
while Tolkien was correcting exams on a warm summer day.

While alone at his desk, he turned over one of the exam papers
and found that the student had for some unknown reason left the
page blank. Bored, he casually scrawled on it a single sentence that
had mysteriously popped into his mind. It would forever change

the fantasy genre. That sentence read, "In a hole in the ground there lived a hobbit."[4]

There and Back Again

Tolkien had no idea what his sentence about a "hobbit" meant. It seemed to have come from nowhere in particular. In looking back at the incident, he admitted, "Eventually I thought I'd better find out what hobbits were like."[5] After much thought he concluded that hobbits were small people having little or no magic about them at all, and they were very much like him.[6]

As Tolkien further explored the nature, character, and habits of hobbits, he wove a tale that would become his first published book about Middle-earth: *The Hobbit, or There and Back Again*. It follows the adventures of Bilbo Baggins, a respectable hobbit whose story begins with a visit from a powerful wizard named Gandalf. The wizard reveals that Bilbo's destiny is to travel with a group of 13 dwarves to a mountain where an evil dragon dwells.

The group's goal is nothing less than death-defying—slay the dragon and steal his treasure, which rightfully belongs to the dwarves. Despite his fears, Bilbo ultimately ends up traveling far from home with the dwarves to the Lonely Mountain, where the dragon Smaug sits in his lair on mounds of the stolen wealth. During the quest Bilbo and his companions face numerous hardships and dangers. Additionally, when the hobbit becomes separated from the group, he confronts a particularly vile creature named Gollum.

Eventually, Bilbo escapes Gollum and is reunited with the dwarves, and Smaug is slain. The hobbit returns home not only wealthy, but in possession of money and a few extraordinary treasures, including a magic ring with which anyone can become invisible:

His gold and silver was largely spent in presents, both useful and extravagant—which to a certain extent accounts for the affection of his nephews and his nieces. His magic ring he kept a great secret, for he chiefly used it when unpleasant callers came.[7]

C.S. Lewis, after reading *The Hobbit*, wrote, "[It] will be funniest to its youngest readers, and only years later, at a tenth or a twentieth reading, will they begin to realize what deft scholarship and profound reflection have gone to make everything in it so ripe, so friendly, and in its own way so true....*The Hobbit* may well prove a classic."[8]

The Lore of the Rings

The Hobbit, published in 1937, was seen as a story of quest—one of the oldest of universal themes. Moreover, it took place in another land, far away from the real world, in a realm where moral abstractions were made concrete. Heroes fought bravely. Good was rewarded. Evil was defeated. And noble virtues such as mercy, kindness, courage, love, and gentleness were esteemed.

Such a work seemed tailor-made for a world watching Hitler reverse the Treaty of Versailles by rebuilding his army and moving troops into the Rhineland. War was imminent. People could feel it and longed to escape reality. Tolkien opened for them a doorway to Middle-earth. His book's success was almost assured.

It quickly became apparent that there would need to be a sequel to *The Hobbit*. But thanks to World War II, Tolkien's ongoing work as an Oxford professor, serious editorial problems, and publishing delays, that sequel—The Lord of the Rings—would not be published until 1954 and 1955!

But the wait was worthwhile. The masterpiece trilogy consisting of *The Fellowship of the Ring*, *The Two Towers*, and *The Return*

of the King forever changed the standard by which all good fantasy is measured. C.S. Lewis wrote one of the first public reviews of *The Fellowship of the Ring:* "This book is like lightning from a clear sky....To say that in it heroic romance, gorgeous, eloquent, and unashamed, has suddenly returned...is inadequate."[9]

The trilogy merges with *The Hobbit* by beginning 60 years after the end of that tale. Bilbo Baggins is making preparations for his one-hundred-eleventh birthday party. He plans on using the occasion to leave his home in the Shire. All of his possessions, including his house, will go to his nephew, Frodo—including his magic ring, which he leaves behind only at the insistence of his friend, Gandalf the wizard, who is visiting.

Gandalf now suspects the ring to be a very dangerous item, and he soon discovers that it is an inestimably powerful object created in the distant past. It is *the* Ring originally owned by the Dark Lord, Sauron, who tried to conquer all of Middle-earth.

Sauron vanished for a time after being defeated by armies of Men and Elves, but in *The Fellowship of the Ring* he has risen again and is seeking the Ring in order to restore his powers. If he succeeds, he will be invincible. The only way dwellers of Middle-earth will ever defeat Sauron is if someone (that is to say, Frodo) destroys the Ring in the volcanic fires where it was forged.

Frodo, however, meets enemies. There are the nine Black Riders, terrifying specters who were once human kings but succumbed to the power of the magic rings they wore in life and were corrupted and transformed by Sauron into "undead" servants. Their invisible forms, clothed in dark robes and armor, ride black horses throughout the countryside, hunting for the one Ring. Nothing can stand in their way.

Another foe of Frodo is Gollum, the creature in *The Hobbit* from whom Bilbo originally acquired the Ring. Most interesting is the fact that at one point in *The Hobbit*, Bilbo had an opportunity

to kill Gollum, but out of mercy he let him live. Early in The Lord of the Rings, Frodo laments, "What a pity Bilbo did not stab the vile creature, when he had a chance!" Gandalf corrects Frodo: "Pity? It was Pity that stayed his hand. Pity and Mercy: not to strike without need." Gandalf adds a profound thought: "Many that live deserve death. And some that die deserve life. Can you give it to them?...Do not be too eager to deal out death in judgment. For even the very wise cannot see all ends."[10]

Frodo and his hobbit companions—Sam, Merry, and Pippin —continue their mission to destroy the Ring. Along the way, however, they are separated and must face unending perils while at the same time avoiding enemies seeking to capture them. Meanwhile, it is discovered that Saruman, once a good wizard, has turned toward evil and is himself seeking the Ring of power.

Frodo, too, must fight the psychological and emotional strains of the Ring itself. It seeks to overtake Frodo's will and consume him just as it had consumed Gollum. The struggle against the Ring's power is so overwhelming that by the time Frodo reaches the Crack of Doom, he cannot bring himself to destroy the object and decides to keep it. Providentially, Gollum is nearby and attacks, biting off Frodo's finger to reclaim the Ring. But the creature loses his balance and falls, along with the Ring, into the Crack of Doom.

Simultaneously, Sauron's evil hordes are converging on the last stronghold of Middle-earth's defenders. The Armageddon-like battle seems destined to be won by Sauron's armies. But just as the last shreds of hope evaporate, the Ring's annihilation breaks Sauron's power. Good triumphs. And Middle-earth is saved from the Dark Lord's tyranny.

Yet it is a bittersweet victory. Although Sauron has been defeated, the Ring's destruction marks the beginning of the end of Middle-earth, for its allotted time has passed. The world of

hobbits, dwarves, and elves is giving way to the time of men. Middle-earth must be replaced by another kind of Earth—one where magic will be all but nonexistent. And so the trilogy ends with the Ring-bearers (Bilbo and Frodo) sailing west across the sea, out of Middle-earth.

Middle-Earth Spirituality

Jeffrey Richards of Lancaster University expresses exactly what fans of Tolkien's trilogy have been feeling for decades:

> The Lord of the Rings is a work of unique power, scope and imagination. Tolkien's language is rich and allusive, his vocabulary extensive and varied. His descriptive writing is wonderful. His evocation of such invaluable virtues as loyalty, service, comradeship and idealism is inspiring. Above all, he creates a universe of myth, magic, and archetype that resonates in the deepest recesses of the memory and the imagination....The more children, indeed the more people of all ages, who read The Lord of the Rings, the better it will be not only for the literary level of this country but for its spiritual health.[11]

One can easily see from such comments why Tolkien's masterpieces have remained in print for more than 50 years and have sold upward of 100 million copies in some 40 languages. It is much more than a children's story. As one 2000 article observed, "The Lord of the Rings is a completely adult tragedy with profound moral and religious implications."[12]

These themes sprang from Tolkien's devout faith in not only a personal God, but in the death, burial, and resurrection of Jesus Christ, whom Tolkien unabashedly proclaimed as his Lord and

Savior. This is not to say that The Lord of the Rings contains any explicit references to "God," Jesus, churches, prayers, or other elements of Christianity. Such references are nowhere in the text.

Nevertheless, the saga of Bilbo and Frodo is a thoroughly Christian work with Roman Catholic underpinnings. Tolkien himself noted as much in 1953, explaining that The Lord of the Rings "is of course a fundamentally religious and Catholic work; unconsciously so at first, but consciously in the revision."[13]

This aspect of Middle-earth (that is to say, its spirituality) is easily adduced from The Silmarillion and numerous letters Tolkien wrote to his fans. From his correspondence, for example, we learn that Middle-earth's "wizards," contrary to popular belief, are not human. Each one, including the well-known Gandalf, is a Maia—an angel-like being that has taken on human form.[14]

These Maiar (plural of Maia) were sent into Middle-earth to render assistance to Elves and Men. Gandalf, Sauron, and every other wizard illustrate good angels and evil angels (demons). Their powers are not supernatural or occult-based, but are natural aspects of their race.[15] In a 1951 letter, Tolkien said he never intended to link them to occultism (see note 16).[16]

He also did not necessarily even want to utilize the word wizard, but was forced to do so by the limitations of English, calling the word "perhaps not suitable," but necessary.[17] He ran into the same problem with his concept of "dwarves," as opposed to the standard Germanic dwarf of mythology.[18]

He spoke not only of wizards and dwarves, but also of another race—the Valar:

> [Wizards] are actually emissaries from the True West, and so mediately from God, sent [by the Valar] precisely to strengthen the resistance of the "good," when

the Valar became aware that the shadow of Sauron is taking shape.[19]

The Valar, according to *The Silmarillion*, are an even higher order of spiritual being than Maiar. One example of a *Vala* (singular of Valar) is the Dark Lord Morgoth—perhaps the most powerful of the Valar—a satanic character who tried to subjugate Middle-earth.[20] His wickedness resulted from direct rebellion against the divine authority presiding over everything: the Creator of all, *Eru*, also known as *Ilúvatar*. This entity is the supreme deity—the One God of Middle-earth.

Tolkien did not hesitate to say that "religion" in any pagan (or polytheistic) sense was false worship in Middle-earth. The *Númenóreans*, for example—the most honorable men throughout Tolkien's grand fantasy—originally were monotheists before their loss of integrity as a nation. He declared that "[Middle-earth] is a 'monotheistic but sub-creational mythology.' " Using even starker terms, he later wrote, "There are no 'Gods,' properly so-called, in the mythological background of my stories." (Then again, some years previous, he noted, "There is only one 'god,' *Eru Ilúvatar*." [21]

Frodo's God

The influence of Ilúvatar over the affairs of Middle-earth is plainly seen in one segment of the trilogy where Gandalf is speaking to Frodo about the Ring. From their interaction we learn that the seemingly random series of events that led to the hobbit's dire situation are far from random.

Frodo acknowledges that he was, in some cosmic way, "chosen" for his mission. But he is not pleased. Gandalf, however, offers a word of hope that reveals his faith in the sovereignty of Ilúvatar, who is watching Middle-earth's events unfold according

to his plan. Sauron's schemes are but a small part of a much larger, unknown plan, one held in place by Ilúvatar.

> "I wish it need not have happened in my time," said Frodo.
>
> "So do I," said Gandalf, "and so do all who live to see such times. But that is not for them to decide. All we have to decide is what to do with the time that is given us....It was not Gollum, Frodo, but the Ring itself that decided things. The Ring left *him*."
>
> "What, just in time to meet Bilbo?" said Frodo.
>
> "...It was the strangest event in the whole history of the Ring so far: Bilbo's arrival just at that time, and putting his hand on it, blindly, in the dark. There was more than one power at work, Frodo...there was something else at work, beyond the design of the Ring-maker [Sauron]. I can put it no plainer than by saying that Bilbo was meant to find the Ring, and not by its maker. In which case you also were meant to have it. And that may be an encouraging thought."[22]

This passage and others from The Lord of the Rings brought Willis Glover—emeritus professor of history at Mercer University—to a significant conclusion. In "The Christian Character of Tolkien's Invented World," Glover stated that the sense of history in Tolkien's fantasy is far more biblical than that of other modern novels because it suggests the existence of an "unnamed authority" to whom the "actors are responsible and who works in history in ways inscrutable to finite creatures."[23]

When Sin Entered the World

In addition to a sovereign God presiding over Middle-earth, Tolkien also wove into his mythology a heaven of sorts, called

Valinor, home of the Valar and Ilúvatar. One story relating to Valinor that is most interesting involves the shape of Middle-earth, which according to *The Silmarillion*, originally was flat. Valinor, or heaven, was connected to Middle-earth and could be reached via sailing ships.

But like Adam and Eve, the Númenóreans were not content with their original state. Despite having been granted longer life than other humans (a triple span), they envied the immortality of the Elves. It became an obsession, which in turn caused their spans of life to wane. Finally, near the end of Middle-earth's Second Age, the Númenóreans attacked Valinor, thinking they would achieve immortality by controlling the heavenly realm. They failed.

Sauron had deceived them into doing it. Nevertheless, by disobeying they brought death into the world and lost intimate contact with Ilúvatar when a great chasm opened in the sea and swallowed the land of Númenór (a reflection of the Atlantis legend). Tolkien said their delusion was initiated by a "Satanic lie." This tragic event changed all of Middle-earth. It not only became a round world, but its physical connection with heaven was severed forever.[24]

Many similarities between Middle-earth and Christianity exist, according to Professor Tom Shippey, Tolkien's successor at Oxford. Shippey notes that

> *The Silmarillion* bears a kind of relationship to Christian myth [by "myth" Shippey simply means a traditional tale, not one that is untrue]. The rebellion of Melkor [who became Morgoth], and his subordinate spirits, is analogous to the Fall of Lucifer and the rebel angels....The origin of the fall is also the same in both cases, for the sin of Lucifer was (according to C.S. Lewis) the urge to put his own purposes before those

of God, and that of Melkor was "to interweave matters of his own imagining" with the "theme of Ilúvatar [the Creator]." This "fall of the angels" also leads in both mythologies to a second fall: the Fall of Man and the exile from the Garden of Eden in the Book of Genesis, the loss of elvish innocence and the emigration from Aman (which becomes an exile) in The Silmarillion....

He also built in, or rather left a space for, the traditional story of the Fall of Man....When the humans do enter Middle-earth from the east all that is known about them to the elves...is that something dreadful had happened to them already, a "darkness" which "lay upon the hearts of Men."[25]

The Lord of the Rings also contains Christian symbolism, albeit obscured. For instance, we see Sauron and Morgoth as demonic figures. Gandalf fulfills a prophetlike role. The Elven "way-bread," lembas, might even represent holy communion.[26] And certain traits of the Elf queen Galadriel mirror aspects of the Roman Catholic concept of the Virgin Mary.[27] Even more fascinating are two time reckonings that certainly must have been deliberate:

In Appendix B of The Lord of the Rings we are told that the fellowship leaves Rivendell to begin its mission on December 25 [Christmas]. Frodo and Sam destroy the ring by throwing it into the Crack of Doom. This heralds the new era on, according to the Gondorian reckoning, March 25....In the old English tradition (a subject about which Tolkien was quite familiar), March 25 was the date of the first Good Friday, the date of Christ's crucifixion. This means

that the main events in the story of how the ring is destroyed and Sauron is defeated are played out during the mythic period between Christ's birth on December 25 and his death on March 25.[28]

The narrative further contains numerous events that serve to advance Christian values and virtues, including self-sacrifice, steadfast devotion, and faith. Also featured in the tale are distinctly religious topics such as temptation, sin, betrayal, mercy, repentance, and forgiveness. Finally, we see Tolkien dealing with a host of other issues that relate directly to a Christian's life with God: simplicity, generosity, friendship, hospitality, suffering, resurrection, humility, trustworthiness, wisdom, hope, submission, stewardship, courage, mirth, foolishness, perseverance, celebration, justice, and love.[29]

A Man of Faith

Although The Lord of the Rings is undoubtedly a "Christian" fantasy of sorts, the *underlying* Christianity of the story likely ended up in the text simply because "what Tolkien believed was part of him, and that belief became part of what he created."[30]

Tolkien was a devout Christian, as we have noted. He "habitually referred to Jesus as 'our Lord' and possessed an unshakeable conviction in the power of prayer." His son John, who became a Roman Catholic priest, maintained that faith "pervaded all [his father's] thinking, beliefs and everything else."[31]

Understandable, then, is Tolkien's admission that he intended The Lord of the Rings "to be consonant with Christian thought and belief."[32] Indeed, he unreservedly declared his love for God, and he emphasized the centrality of the Creator to not only the very meaning of life but to his work:

> The chief purpose of life, for any one of us, is to increase according to our capacity our knowledge of God by all the means we have, and to be moved by it to praise and thanks. To do as we say in the Gloria in Excelsis…"We praise you, we call you holy, we worship you, we proclaim your glory, we thank you for the greatness of your splendour."[33]

Tolkien's faith shaped his understanding of human beings also, which was inextricably linked to his fiction. Creating fantasy worlds (or "sub-creations"), he believed, demonstrates an inescapable primal urge in all of us because such activity is part of our nature. It is a reflection of our having been made in the image of God (Genesis 2): "We make in our measure and in our derivative mode, because we are made: and not only made, but made in the image and likeness of a Maker."[34]

He further believed that each individual is implanted with not only the desire to be a sub-creator, but also with some sort of natural attraction toward fairy tales, fiction, mythology, and fantasy.[35] All humans are endowed with this predilection, albeit some to a greater extent than others. Moreover, he viewed all mythology as to some degree pointing to Christianity:

> I believe that legends and myths are largely made of "truth," and indeed present aspects of it that can only be received in this mode; and long ago certain truths and modes of this kind were discovered and must always reappear.[36]

The late Humphrey Carpenter, who wrote the authorized biography of Tolkien, summarized his views as follows:

We have come from God, and inevitably the myths woven by us, though they contain error, will also reflect a splintered fragment of the true light, the eternal truth that is with God. Indeed, only by myth-making, only by becoming a "sub-creator" and inventing stories, can Man aspire to the state of perfection that he knew before the Fall. Our myths may be misguided, but they steer however shakily towards the true harbor.[37]

Both Tolkien and C.S. Lewis, in fact, maintained that the Gospel stories of the Bible present the greatest of all myths—the one that became fact. Lewis said that the story of Christ was a "true myth, a myth that works on us in the same way as the others, but a myth that *really happened*."[38] About the Gospels, Tolkien commented,

[They contain] many marvels—peculiarly artistic, beautiful, and moving: "mythical" in their perfect, self-contained significance....There is no tale ever told that men would rather find was true, and none which so many skeptical men have accepted as true on its own merits. For the Art of it has the supremely convincing tone of Primary Art, that is, of Creation.[39]

For Tolkien then, "the Gospel story constitutes the perfect fairy-tale by the most potent of all authors—God himself."[40]

True Good Meets True Evil

One of the most interesting aspects of The Lord of the Rings is its philosophy of good and evil: "Nothing is evil in the beginning." This perspective, expressed by the elf leader Elrond, again echoes Christian thought. Tolkien believed that God created

everything good (see the book of Genesis). Put another way, evil has no independent existence. It came into our world, just as it came into Middle-earth: by the perversion, twisting, or corruption of a good thing.[41]

In Christianity, Lucifer began life as a mighty angel, but he became Satan, the devil, only after rebelling in pride and selfish ambition against God. So too, we hear from Elrond that Sauron (like Lucifer) was not initially evil, but became so via self-seeking. This leads to yet another facet of Tolkien's concept of good and evil: the corrupting effects of power. Elrond declares,

> We cannot use the Ruling Ring....[It] is too great for anyone to wield at will, save only those who have already a great power of their own. But for them it holds an even deadlier peril. The very desire of it corrupts the heart....If any of the Wise should with this Ring overthrow the Lord of Mordor, using his own arts, he would then set himself on Sauron's throne, and yet another Dark Lord would appear. And that is another reason why the Ring should be destroyed: as long as it is in the world it will be a danger even to the Wise.[42]

The Ring will always destroy the one who bears it. Tolkien's story perfectly illustrates the observation made by historian Lord Acton (1834–1902): "Power tends to corrupt and absolute power corrupts absolutely."[43]

At the same time, however, Tolkien is careful to demonstrate that evil also is always self-destructive. The end of evil will be judgment—a theme intrinsic to the Bible (see Psalm 1:4-6; 9:5-6; 11:6; Proverbs 10:24-25; Galatians 6:7-8). "Evil is self-blinded, too. That which it does in malice, that which seems to be its

greatest victory, proves to be its own undoing." This concept is revealed as Tolkien gradually exposes Sauron's shortcomings, which include overconfidence, desperation, and delusions of superiority. His own fears, coupled with the blind assumption that everyone, like him, will seek the power of the Ring, is what leads to his downfall.[44]

Despite the many examples of Christian symbolism in Tolkien's works, many have taken a decidedly negative view of The Lord of the Rings. Their concerns are primarily based on the belief that the trilogy contains occult imagery and practices, particularly "magic" and "wizards."

Tolkien on Trial

The concerns expressed by Christians regarding The Lord of the Rings commonly rest on several misunderstandings of the text. For example, as previously stated, Tolkien's wizards are not the kind of wizards condemned in the Bible. They are, for all intents and purposes, angels. No reference to "wizards" suggests a link to occult "wizards."

And as for the "magic" that the wizards (angels) use, there is a difference between it and the occult "magick" found in our Primary World (see chapter 2). Tolkien thoroughly disliked having to use the word *magic*, but was forced to do so because he could find no other word closer to the meaning he intended.[45]

He attempted to alleviate the problems associated with the word by placing *very strict* limitations on it, including who possessed it, how it was used, and why it was used. In various letters, he made it clear that "magic" in the context of Middle-earth is in no way connected to supernatural power. It is a natural attribute, one that is given *only* to Elves—not humans.

Even though he took great pains to make such distinctions, he often lamented his use of the word "magic." It failed miserably in his estimation to adequately or accurately say what he wanted to say in his story:

> [Magic] is for them [Elves] a form of Art, and distinct from Wizardry or Magic, properly so called....We need a word for this Elvish craft, but all the words that have been applied to it have been blurred and confused with other things. Magic is ready to hand, and I have used it above, but I should not have done so: Magic should be reserved for the operations of the Magician [a practitioner of magick]....
>
> Magic [that is to say, magick in the Primary World] produces, or pretends to produce, an alteration in the Primary World. It does not matter by whom it is said to be practiced...it is not an art but a technique; its desire is power in this world, domination of things and wills.[46]

Like Tolkien's Elves, the Maiar and Valar are just exercising their God-given (*Eru*-given) abilities when they practice "magic," either for good or evil.[47] Magical power belongs to no other race depicted in the trilogy, including men, orcs, trolls, dwarves, and hobbits. As Tolkien said, "It is in an inherent power not possessed or attainable by Men as such."[48]

Interestingly, in Middle-earth there are always drastic and negative consequences when its nonmagical residents (non-Elves) get too close to magic. The Nine Riders, for instance, became servants of the evil Sauron through exposure to their magical rings. Gollum likewise was corrupted by a magic Ring. Bilbo, too, began to be changed for the worse by his Ring. And

Frodo, after his long journey with the Ring, is never physically or psychologically the same. He tells Gandalf that he has been forever "wounded" by the ordeal.[49]

The "magic" in Middle-earth is clearly different from magick in our real world though it is similar in this: In Middle-earth all who dabble in powers not meant for them are ensnared by those powers. The character Elrond emphasizes this message, saying, "It is perilous to study too deeply the arts of the Enemy, for good or for ill."[50]

It is best argued, therefore, that The Lord of the Rings is a Christian classic, rather than anything derived from paganism. Summing up this point, Joseph Pearce, author of *Tolkien: Man and Myth*, asserts,

> *The Lord of the Rings* is a profoundly Christian myth....The values that emerge in *The Lord of the Rings* are the values that emerge in the Gospels. In the characterization of the Hobbits, the most reluctant and the most unlikely of heroes, we see the exaltation of the humble. In the figure of Gandalf we see the archetype of an Old Testament patriarch, his staff apparently having the same power as that possessed by Moses. In his apparent "death" and "resurrection" we see him emerge as a Christ-like figure. His "resurrection" results in his transfiguration....The character of Gollum is debased by his attachment to the Ring, the symbol of the sin of pride....

Ultimately, the bearing of the Ring by Frodo, and his heroic struggle to resist the temptation to succumb to its evil powers, is akin to the Carrying of the Cross, the supreme act of selflessness. Throughout the whole of *The Lord of the Rings* the forces of evil are seen as powerful but not all-powerful. There is always the sense that divine providence is on the side of the Fellowship and that, ultimately, it will prevail against all the odds. As Tolkien put it succinctly, "Above all shadows rides the Sun."[51]

Why does The Lord of the Rings continue to be interpreted by some as a kind of promotion of occultism? Though it may be due in part to unfamiliarity with the work, a more notable cause may be society's obsession with occultism in general and the explosive growth of occult-based belief systems such as Wicca and neopaganism (see chapter 2).

Another fantasy saga that is similarly misunderstood and misjudged sometimes is The Chronicles of Narnia by C.S. Lewis, a close friend of Tolkien. Lewis, in fact, became a Christian through his contact with Tolkien at Oxford. This fortuitous meeting, the ensuing friendship, and the resulting work of fantasy from the pen of Lewis will be the subject of chapter 6.

6

A Land Called Narnia

As to Aslan's other name....Has there never been
anyone in *this* world who (1) Arrived at the same
time as Father Christmas (2) Said he was the Son of
the Great Emperor (3) Gave himself up for someone
else's fault to be jeered at and killed by wicked
people (4) Came to life again (5) Is sometimes
spoken of as a Lamb?...Don't you really know His
name in this world?[1]

—C.S. LEWIS
letter to an American girl

Around 1925 to 1926, Tolkien and several of his peers at Oxford
began meeting to discuss what they were reading, writing, and
thinking. They called their little club the Coalbiters, after the
Icelandic *kolbíter*, a lighthearted term for people huddled "so
close to a fire in winter that they could almost bite the coals." It
was a "Who's Who" list of Oxford's best minds.[2] Others wanted
to join, but that honor came by invitation only. One person they
invited was Clive Staples Lewis (1898–1963), better known as
C.S. Lewis.

Lewis met Tolkien in 1926, then recorded in his diary, "[Tolkien] is a smooth, pale, fluent little chap…thinks all literature is written for the amusement of *men* between thirty and forty….No harm in him: only needs a good smack or two." They became best friends. Tolkien in turn wrote in his diary, "Besides giving constant pleasure and comfort, [it] has done me much good from the contact with a man at once honest, brave, intellectual—a scholar, a poet, and a philosopher."[3]

But it was an unlikely camaraderie: Tolkien, a dyed-in-the-wool Roman Catholic and Lewis, a non-Christian. Lewis, in fact, did not even believe in a God! He became a theist in 1929, only after having many conversations with Tolkien and others.[4] Not until 1931 did he become a Christian. Around this same time the Coalbiters drifted apart, prompting Tolkien and Lewis to form another group: the Inklings.

They met from the 1930s into the 1940s on Thursday nights. Anywhere from 10 to 15 men would sit long into the evening, listening to each other's literary works in progress. Everyone "would then give their comments, often not sparing the feelings of the poor soul who had just read out something he had been working on for months."[5]

Lewis's presentations to this circle eventually included a delightful tale he called *The Lion, the Witch, and the Wardrobe.*[6] It would turn into the first volume in a series of seven books collectively titled The Chronicles of Narnia, published from 1950 to 1956, and is now a classic.

Aslan's World

The other-dimensional land of Narnia, we learn in *The Magician's Nephew* (Book VI),[7] came into existence during the late Victorian Era in our world, around 1900. Its first contact

with our realm took place because of a boy named Digory Kirke, whose mother was dying. The series opens with them staying in London with Digory's Uncle Andrew.

Andrew is an eccentric magician, who convinces Digory and a neighbor girl, Polly Plummer, to participate in an experiment with magic rings. The result is not good. Both Digory and Polly are transported to Charn, a dying world that has been devastated by Jadis, an evil witch. She is under a spell, however, and can cause no more damage to anyone; that is, until she is awakened by Digory.

Even worse, Jadis follows the children back into our world, where she unleashes havoc. Digory and Polly, however, are able to transport the witch and themselves out of our world. But they find themselves in another dimension that is totally empty; a place of Nothing. Then, from out of the darkness, they hear a creation song being sung by King Aslan, who turns out to be a magnificent lion that can talk. He also is the Son of the Emperor Beyond the Sea.

They have witnessed the birth of Narnia. But now Jadis is there! Aslan, however, reveals that her powers can be bound if Digory can retrieve an apple from a magic apple tree in a distant valley. Its seed will produce a tree that will protect Narnia. Digory not only accomplishes his task, but also is able to bring back another magic apple to London. His mother eats it and is healed. He then plants the apple's core, and from it springs a marvelous apple tree, the wood of which is eventually used by Digory to build a wardrobe.

Forty or so years later this very same wardrobe serves as a portal into Narnia for the Pevensie children: Peter, Edmund, Susan, and Lucy. When they arrive, however, Jadis (now the White Witch) has risen and by her magical power holds the whole land

in a state of unending winter where there is never any Christmas (see *The Lion, the Witch, and the Wardrobe*).

All of the children except Edmund, who falls under the spell of the Witch, side with Aslan in the battle for Narnia. Edmund is doomed. But Aslan offers himself to the White Witch in exchange for her release of Edmund. She agrees. So Edmund is freed, and Aslan willingly dies on his behalf at the witch's hands.

But unbeknownst to Jadis, there existed an altogether different kind of magic that only Aslan knew about; a deep magic based on love and self-sacrifice. This "magic" actually resurrects Aslan and brings life to all of Narnia. Winter fades away, and its passing brings the witch's destruction. All four children subsequently grow up in Narnia to reign as kings and queens over the land's Golden Age. But when they eventually return to our world through the wardrobe, they find that no time has passed at all. They are still children.

The sequel to this story, *Prince Caspian* (Book II), continues the saga a thousand years in Narnia's future. The Golden Age has passed, the Old Narnians who battled with the White Witch are gone, and the throne is occupied by the tyrant Miraz. But he has usurped his position. Prince Caspian is the rightful heir.

The prince needs help, and so he summons the children back to Narnia by blowing the magic horn of Queen Susan, which she had left behind. But time is so different in Narnia that when Peter, Edmund, Susan, and Lucy are swept back into the land, even though it has been a thousand years, they are still children. They join Prince Caspian, and with Aslan's assistance, destroy Miraz.

The next book, *The Voyage of the Dawn Treader* (Book III), reads much like Homer's *Odyssey*. It follows a myriad of characters in adventures that range from searching for lost kings to seeking the land of Aslan himself at the world's end—past the Eastern Ocean. It is literally a volume of quests.

The Silver Chair (Book IV) again takes place in Narnia, after many years have passed. Young Prince Caspian is now an old king whose son is missing. Though one of the most memorable books in the series, it is also scary. Caspian's wife has been murdered by the Green Witch. There are Giants who eat humans. And Aslan gives commands that seem to make no sense. It is a mature tale, but one that is packed with lessons about faith, trust, hope, and perseverance.

Next is *The Horse and His Boy* (Book V). It takes readers backward in time to Narnia's Golden Age and revolves around Shasta, a boy who grew up in a fishing village. His real name is Prince Cor, and he is the lost son of a king. It also features a young girl, Aravis, who meets Shasta. Together they discover a plot to overthrow Narnia, and it is up to them to warn everyone.

Finally, in *The Last Battle* (Book VII), we have the initiation of a New Narnia (reminiscent of a New Heaven and a New Earth) after all of the land's inhabitants are judged by Aslan—in much the same way that Jesus, according to Christian belief, will judge humanity. It is an extraordinary work of fantasy that captured the prestigious Carnegie Award for the best children's book of 1956.

Christ in the Chronicles

The Chronicles present Christian ideas and beliefs in a far more obvious way than Tolkien's fantasy. Although not a true allegory of the Gospel story, it comes about as close to being one as is possible without crossing over the line. Parts of it *could* be read allegorically (for example, when Aslan dies for Edmund and then is resurrected). But a true allegory would *have to be* read as a symbolic representation of a deeper message.

Such is not the case with the Chronicles. Its Christian parallels were not deliberately inserted. "[Christianity] pushed itself in of its own accord," Lewis explained.[8]

> I did not say to myself "Let us represent Jesus as He really is in our world by a Lion in Narnia"; I said, "Let us suppose that there were a land like Narnia and that the Son of God, as he became a Man in our world, became a Lion there, and then imagine what would happen."[9]

Lewis's "Let us suppose" ultimately inspired "an imaginative expression of Christian truths, which could bring insights to readers....But, in the freedom of interpretation of myth, they need not necessarily be apprehended as such."[10] According to Lewis, his series works itself out as follows:[11]

- ✧ *The Magician's Nephew*—creation and how evil entered Narnia

- ✧ *The Lion, the Witch and the Wardrobe*—the crucifixion and resurrection

- ✧ *Prince Caspian*—restoration of the true religion after a corruption

- ✧ *The Horse and His Boy*—the calling and conversion of the heathen

- ✧ *The Voyage of the Dawn Treader*—the spiritual life

- ✧ *The Silver Chair*—the continuing war against the powers of darkness

- ✧ *The Last Battle*—the coming of Antichrist (the ape); the end of the world and the last judgment

Clearest of all are the allusions to Christ, who is represented by Lewis as Aslan—a regal lion reflecting the Bible's figurative depiction of Jesus (Revelation 5:5). Christ's dual nature (human and divine) is represented in Aslan by the Lion's presence that is at once both terrifying and inviting.[12] And just being near Aslan refreshes both body and soul, sometimes by way of life-giving water[13]—a hint at Christ, who is the source of living water (see John 4:10; 7:37).

Then, in *The Magician's Nephew* we see Aslan, again like Christ, as Creator (Colossians 1:16). And in *The Horse and His Boy*, Aslan reveals his identity in a way that is reminiscent of the name by which God revealed himself to Moses, "I AM THAT I AM" (Exodus 3:14 KJV; compare Christ's use of "I am" in John 8:58). Aslan, like God in the Old Testament, is asked, "Who *are* you?" Aslan answers three times, "'Myself,...and again, 'Myself,'...and then a third time 'Myself,' the triple response being a Trinitarian allusion."[14]

Aslan also is the only one who offers wrongdoers an opportunity to repent. They can then correct their mistakes, or if needed, be healed or changed by Aslan: Uncle Andrew and Digory (*The Magician's Nephew*), Edmund (*The Lion, the Witch, and the Wardrobe*), the Dwarfs (*The Last Battle*), Eustace (*The Voyage of the Dawn Treader*), and Aravis (*The Horse and His Boy*).

In *The Voyage of the Dawn Treader* we even have Aslan appearing as a Lamb—the quintessential symbol of Christ, "the Lamb of God who takes away the sin of the world" (John 1:29 NKJV). Here also Lucy asks Aslan if there is any way into his country from her world. He answers yes and adds,

> But there I have another name. You must learn to
> know me by that name. This was the very reason why

you were brought to Narnia, that by knowing me here
for a little, you may know me better there.[15]

And Lucy does indeed learn her lesson, for she says at the end
of The Last Battle, "In our world too, a Stable once had something
inside it that was bigger than our whole world."[16]

Biblical Narnia

In addition to the inclusion of a Christ figure in Lewis's fantasy, there can be found numerous aspects of Christian theology,
including the characteristics of God, doctrines surrounding salvation, and beliefs about the end times.

For example, the Christian assertion that Jesus is the only way
to God and that all religions are not equal can be seen in The Last
Battle. In this book, some characters claim that Aslan and the
pagan god Tash are one and the same. They go so far as to begin
using the term "Tashlan" for the supposed Tash/Aslan ruler of
Narnia. But in the end, Aslan proves them wrong by revealing
himself, and then allowing Tash—a terrifying monster—to
destroy all those who worshiped him.

Concepts linked to Christian salvation through faith in Jesus
are displayed in Narnia each time an individual submits to Aslan
and is subsequently obedient to his commands. According to
Paul F. Ford, a renowned expert on C.S. Lewis, obedience is "a
major theme in all of Lewis."[17] As Jesus said, "If you love me,
keep my commandments" (John 14:15).

Even more interesting is John 14:21, in which Jesus, in a very
Aslan-like way, promises, "Whoever has my commands and obeys
them, he is the one who loves me. He who loves me will be loved
by my Father, and I too will love him and show myself to him."
Aslan basically echoes this promise when, during his creation of
Narnia in The Magician's Nephew, the animals he has brought to

life "pledge their obedience." Their Creator responds: "I give you myself."[18]

The revealing, or revelation, of Aslan–Christ is a recurring theme in the Narnian Chronicles. Again and again Aslan shows himself to those willing to obey him. Lewis, however, is not interested in advocating submission that is given begrudgingly. Instead, he depicts what Paul Ford's *Companion to Narnia* describes as followers who are "freely attentive" rather than "slavishly devoted."[19]

As Lewis said during a 1945 lecture, "Authority exercised with humility, and obedience accepted with delight are the very lines along which our spirits live."[20] Closely linked to this concept are faith and trust in Aslan–Christ. Consider the scene in *The Silver Chair* in which Rilian tells the children he must be bound at night or else he will kill them.[21] They have no idea that these words actually are a result of his bewitchment.

So at night he is bound. But that is precisely when the enchantment leaves and he is restored to a sound mind! He pleads in the name of Aslan to be released. A dilemma is presented because Aslan had previously said that the children's success would depend on "the first person" who asks them to do something "in the name of Aslan."[22]

They must make a decision in the midst of Rilian's entreaties. One character asks, "Do you mean you think everything will come right if we do untie him?"

Another replies, "I don't know about that." He adds, "You see, Aslan didn't tell Pole [one of the characters] what would happen. He only told her what to do. That fellow will be the death of us once he's up, I shouldn't wonder. But that doesn't let us off following the sign."[23]

They decide to be obedient and release Rilian, which turns out to be the best thing they could have done.

This does not mean that those who swear allegiance to Aslan are perfect.[24] They are flawed followers, but Aslan is always there to guide them back on course, often using their missteps to reveal to them a hidden weakness. And after they learn their lesson, they are better for it—more courageous, honest, faithful, trusting, hopeful, kind, and sensitive. Aslan's loving corrections present a most poignant and accurate reflection of how Jesus deals with his followers.

The reader, in fact, is inundated with Christianity. Lewis pulls so much inspiration from his faith that the Narnian Chronicles contain subtle rephrasings of, and allusions to, many Bible passages (see note 25).[25] Yet all of these hints of Christianity are overshadowed by grandeur and import of the fantasy's climax. It is a majestic portrait of Christ's final judgment upon humanity—Narnian style.

The Last Battle offers the most explicit depiction of how our choices here affect our destiny there—that is, in the eternal realm. Our destination depends on whether or not we have chosen to follow Aslan–Christ. Lewis paints a profound, as well as a disturbing, portrait. Lewis expert Kathryn Lindskoog described the scene in *The Lion of Judah in Never-Never Land*:

> At the end of Narnia millions of creatures, all of the living men and beasts of that world, came streaming toward the doorway where Aslan waited. As they approached him, some of their faces filled with fear and hate. And these swerved to his left, disappearing into his huge black shadow. Those who loved him came in at the Door at his right.[26]

The parallel to Jesus' eschatological imagery about one day separating the sheep from the goats is undeniable (see Matthew

25:31-46). The reference to Aslan's followers entering his eternal country (or "True Narnia") through a "Door" likewise draws our minds to Christ, who called himself the door of life (John 10:9).

Like today's Christians who joyfully await the second coming of Christ, the Narnians longed for Aslan's return. An old rhyme recited by the goodly Mr. Beaver in *The Lion, the Witch, and the Wardrobe* sums it up nicely:

> *Wrong will be right, when Aslan comes in sight,*
> *At the sound of his roar, sorrows will be no more,*
> *When he bares his teeth, winter meets its death,*
> *And when he shakes his mane, we shall have spring again.*[27]

The Anti-Lewis

Despite his popularity among adults and children alike, Lewis is not without critics. As of 2005, the most visible and vitriolic detractor continued to be bestselling author Philip Pullman, author of the series His Dark Materials (see chapter 1). Thanks to Pullman's widely publicized condemnations of Lewis, he has earned himself a title with which he seems completely at ease: "The Anti-Lewis." And his trilogy has correspondingly been labeled "C.S. Lewis for Atheists."[28]

However, against the dark background of Pullman's secular writing and criticisms, the generous and Christian nature of the Chronicles of Narnia is illuminated even more brightly than we have already seen.

Pullman has explained that when he first read the Chronicles as an adult he "realized that what he [Lewis] was up to was propaganda in the cause of the religion he believed in." Elsewhere he has described the fantasy series as "loathsome, full of bullying and sneering, propaganda, basically, on behalf of a religion whose

main creed seemed to be to despise and hate people unlike your-self."[29]

Pullman has also castigated Lewis personally, falsely accusing the beloved Christian author of holding the vilest of views:

> When he was writing fiction…he went mad.…What I really cannot understand is why C.S. Lewis's books are…hailed as great Christian books. They're not! In many ways they contradict what you read in the Gospels.…They're profoundly racist. They're misogy-nistic. He hates girls and women. He thinks they're no good at all—they're weak; they're useless; they're stu-pid. In fact, he hates life, basically. 'Cause at the end of them the greatest reward these children have is to be taken away from it, and be killed in a railway acci-dent.[30]

Pullman expresses his overall view in a word: "I hate the Narnia books, and I hate them with a deep and bitter passion."[31] He, of course, is entitled to his opinions. However, the serious accusations he makes are problematic. First, and foremost, Pullman is being terrifically hypocritical in lodging any com-plaint against Lewis for writing "propaganda." Does he really think that the His Dark Materials books, which preach atheism, are not propaganda for certain beliefs (or nonbeliefs) about "God" and related issues?

This is not hard to see. Britain's The Guardian reviewed His Dark Materials, saying, "At their core, Pullman's books are pro-foundly humanistic." And the Church of England Newspaper noted, "By setting out to do the opposite of Lewis, Pullman's own work is propaganda."[32]

The two main differences on this issue between Pullman and Lewis are 1) Lewis's fiction advances theism, while Pullman's fiction advances atheism; and 2) Lewis's talent enabled him to avoid *explicit* pro-Christian declarations, while Pullman was forced to use blatant "in your face" anti-Christian remarks and references. (Regarding the latter issue, religion journalist Amy Welborn has commented, "[Pullman] fails as a writer in His Dark Materials, not because of his views on religion, but because he simply cannot resist the temptation to preach about them, putting art to the service of manipulating his young readers' opinions."[33])

A Microcosm of Misogyny?

According to Pullman, The Chronicles of Narnia are "disparaging of girls and women" to the point of being "misogynistic" (woman-hating). This is not only inaccurate, but also odd, given the way Lewis exalts the girls that appear in his stories.

We have Lucy, for example. She is the initial Pevensie to see Aslan and throughout the series continues to see him most often. She is one of his "closest friends."[34] Although the youngest of the children, Lucy is in many ways central to the entire series.[35] She comes to be known during Narnia's Golden Age as Lucy the Valiant. Interestingly, it is through Lucy, rather than one of the boys, that "Lewis expresses his own religious and personal sensibilities."[36]

The Chronicles also feature Polly Plummer, who like Lucy, paves the way for others. She is a born leader: independent, brave, trustworthy, rational, sensible, cautious, perceptive, and insightful.[37] Susan and Aravis have dispositions that are more complex. They each display admirable traits as well as serious weaknesses, but overall are obviously "good." The difference between them is the path they eventually choose. Aravis pursues a relationship with Aslan that not only brings out her best qualities, but also

imparts to her qualities that make her fit to be a queen: humility, gratitude, and a forgiving heart. Susan, however, allows the cares of the world to overshadow what should be uppermost in her mind: serving Aslan. We never know how her story ends.

Finally, the White Witch and the Green Witch are set at the opposite extreme of Lucy and Polly. They typify the worst traits of *all* humanity—not just women. Nothing is said that suggests their femaleness means anything. They are simply vehicles that help round out the complete spectrum of good and evil.

Lewis the Racist?

Equally overstated is Pullman's claim that the Narnian Chronicles promote racism. He is no doubt referring to parts of the series that refer to Narnia's enemies: the Calormenes, who live to the south, across the desert. They and their society are definitely modeled after Middle Eastern cultures.

In truth, some of his comments do irritate modern sensitivities—and rightly so. For instance, at one point in *The Last Battle*, wicked Dwarfs refer to the Calormenes as "darkies."[38] The Calormenes also are artistically inept, barbarous, and enemies of Aslan. Is this "racist"? Or was Lewis simply voicing the expressions and perceptions of his day?

According to Gregg Easterbrook's article "In Defense of C.S. Lewis," the British author was "employing language then in common parlance." Easterbrook also notes that "many older books contain race or gender references discordant to modern ears....We don't stop reading Twain or Darwin because they used racial terms no author uses today."[39]

But it must be admitted that Lewis's portrayal of Middle Eastern–like individuals is unflattering. They are dirty, cruel, and inhospitable. Lewis showed insensitivity toward, and ignorance of, Middle Easterners. And these blind spots invaded his

otherwise stellar tale. Such insensitivity and ignorance, however, is *not* racism. It is, at most, mild prejudice born of ignorance.[40]

The truth is that the "profoundly racist" charge has become a very convenient way to quickly stigmatize someone. As one article astutely noted,

> Pullman is using crass propaganda here. Racism and sexism have become such large problems in contemporary culture that the words have almost stopped having any objective meaning. They are just dirt-words, to throw at anyone whose opinions you do not like, in the hope that some mud will stick.[41]

So although Lewis may have harbored false stereotypes about Middle Easterners, he was not a racist. He was uneducated about a certain people. This is not Lewis's fault. Only recently, with the advent of better communications, a more global society, and greater cultural exchange have Europeans and Americans started to understand the Middle East and its people (although a great deal remains to be learned).

Death Is Delightful?

Perhaps the most outlandish accusation Pullman has made against Lewis is that "he hates life" because at the end of the Narnian series the children and several others are "taken" from life (that is to say, they are killed) "in a railway accident." Pullman is appalled, declaring that the Narnian books "celebrate death." "For the sake of taking them off to a perpetual school holiday or something, he kills them all in a train crash. I think that's ghastly. It's a horrible message…It's a filthy thing to do," he rants further concluding that the God Lewis depicts in his fantasy "is a god who hates life."[42]

But Lewis's message is only "horrible" and "filthy" to Pullman because he is an atheist—and for him, this life is all there is. It is no surprise that as an atheist he would find multiple deaths highly offensive (if not very disconcerting). Pullman's atheism, however, utterly blinds him to what Lewis is conveying: the *celebration* of life—real life in the truest and most perfect sense of the word.

Death happens. And kids can either be taught that it is the *end* of all they know, or an *extension* of all they know—plus more. Lewis is celebrating the latter, what we call the afterlife. Pullman's fantasy, on the other hand, celebrates life *only as it exists here*, as he clearly declares: "I believe in the absolute preciousness of the here and now. Here is where we are and now is where we live."[43]

The railway accident is a tragedy, to be sure, but it also is an occasion for joy. The most faithful characters in Narnia get what they have always wanted: life with Aslan in his country forever. They will not only enjoy new adventures and unimaginable peace and bliss, but also be reunited with the old Narnians who lived during the Golden Age and the courageous Reepicheep, who is featured in *The Voyage of the Dawn Treader*.[44] Lewis explained it most beautifully himself:

> We can most truly say that they all lived happily ever after. But for them it was only the beginning of the real story. All their life in this world and all their adventures in Narnia had only been the cover and the title page: now at last they were beginning Chapter One of the Great Story which no one on earth has read: which goes on for ever: in which every chapter is better than the one before.[45]

In the words of Aslan, "The term is over: the holidays have begun. The dream is ended: this is the morning."[46]

Weird Sexuality or Wise Commentary?

Finally, a word must be said in response to Pullman's rather off-the-wall notion that in *The Last Battle*, "one girl was sent to hell because she was getting interested in clothes and boys."[47] What he is referring to here is the passage in Lewis's concluding volume where we learn that Susan (formerly Queen Susan the Gentle during Narnia's Golden Age) has lost her love for Narnia and Aslan.

She has convinced herself that it was all just make-believe, a childish delusion. The character Jill tells us that the adolescent Susan is "interested in nothing now-a-days except nylons and lipstick and invitations."[48] As a result she is not with her siblings at the railway station when the fatal train accident whisks them all away to "Aslan's country"—heaven.

Pullman explained his interpretation thus, claiming that "for Lewis, a girl's achieving sexual maturity was 'so dreadful and so redolent of sin that he had to send her to Hell.' "[49] But why, according to Pullman, would Lewis write something so atrocious and cruel?

> This seems to me on the part of Lewis to reveal very weird unconscious feelings about sexuality. Here's a child whose body is changing and who's naturally responding as everyone has ever done since the history of the world to the changes that are taking place in one's body and one's feelings. She's doing what everyone has to do in order to grow up.[50]

But if any "weird unconscious feelings about sexuality" are to be found, they will not be located inside Lewis's mind. As a recent article rightly observed, "Lewis's grand theme is about individuals' transformation of character through knowing and being known by Aslan." On the other hand, "Pullman's grand theme is about individuals' transformation through puberty and by throwing off any beliefs or rules imposed by the church."[51]

Sexuality is pivotal to Pullman, who presents it in His Dark Materials books as a kind of litmus test of maturity, independence, self-expression, and ultimate love—everything that the "evil Christian church" has tried to suppress. Pullman seems to view sexuality (especially a child's increasing curiosity about it) as one of the truest marks of adulthood, or at the very least, of one's progress toward it.

In truth, it is Pullman's own apparent preoccupation with sexuality that he imposes on Jill's comment about lipstick, nylons, and invitations. The remark indicates to *his* mind that Lewis was depicting "childhood as a golden age from which sexuality and adulthood are a falling away." He alleges, "Susan is shut out from salvation because she is doing what every other child who has ever been born has done—she is beginning to sense the developing changes in her body and its effect on the opposite sex."[52]

However, although Susan did not go to heaven (Aslan's country) with those who died in the railway accident, *nothing* says she did not go later on, presumably when she died. Then, sexuality has nothing to do with the line about lipstick, nylons, and invitations. These things are merely symbols of Susan's long-standing fixation on being "adult."

The problem is, "Nylons and lipstick and invitations have not been *added* to her other interests and tastes, but have replaced them."[53] As the character Jill tells us, Susan is interested in "nothing" but them. Susan is so overwhelmed by them that she

has lost sight of what is really important. Lucy agrees: "Nowadays all she cares about are parties." So rather than being a sign of her "growing up," these interests show her ongoing immaturity!

Susan is stuck at *wanting* to be an adult, without moving on to *becoming* an adult by cultivating deep insight, thoughtful reflection, and spiritual maturity. The sad result is childishness.

Worse, Susan has relegated Aslan and Narnia to the illusory world of childhood make-believe, even when the other children try to talk to her about it. As religious-studies professor Robert Houston has noted, "For Susan, being grown-up means regarding God, beauty, and imagination as worthless fantasies."[54]

This runs contrary to true maturation, according to Lewis, and contravenes the very reason the children were brought into Narnia. Aslan wanted them to recall their experiences there, and by doing so, discern his identity here: that is, his identity as Jesus Christ.[55] Things like sexuality, curiosity about sexuality, and sexual experiences have nothing to with being grown-up, mature, and more adultlike—not to Lewis. That is all in Pullman's mind. Lewis, instead, sees maturity as something irrespective of both age and sexuality. Growing up means growing closer to God.

A Shining Beacon

C.S. Lewis's legacy is one of incalculable worth. Beyond his fiction, he produced some of the finest available works on philosophy and Christian apologetics. Even Philip Pullman has had to acknowledge that "when he was writing the books of Christian apologetics such as *The Screwtape Letters,* for example, he is perceptive, and very psychologically shrewd."[56]

But Lewis also was a man "in love with imagination," and as such, he wrote fiction that imparted a "real though unfocused gleam of divine truth fallen on human imagination." He used

fantasy as a means of converting the reader "in the same manner in which Lewis himself was first drawn to Christianity: by baptizing the imagination in the hope that the reason will follow."[57]

To accomplish his goal, Lewis (like Tolkien) firmly rooted his fantasy in Christian doctrines, morality, ethics, and biblical ideals relating to life, love, eternity, and spiritual growth. He could not have done otherwise, for as he once explained, an author's views will spontaneously arise "from whatever spiritual roots" that author has "succeeded in striking during the whole course" of life.[58]

In a very natural way, then, Lewis's Christian faith wove its way into his fantasy. Authors still infuse their works with whatever spirituality or morality they have embraced. Unlike in Lewis's day, however, many of our most popular authors are creating a whole new kind of fiction culled from decidedly non-Christian spiritualities, moral perspectives, and ethical ideals.

This new kind of fantasy makes explicit use of real-world occultism, magick, or both (see chapter 2). The most prominent example, and a typical one, is J.K. Rowling's mega-bestselling Harry Potter series—the subject of chapter 7.

7

Welcome to Hogwarts

It is good to see that the best-selling series of books in the Western world is such a positive tale about witches and wizards.

—THE CHILDREN OF ARTEMIS
Wicca/neopagan Web site

One of today's most popular works of fantasy is the multivolume Harry Potter saga by Scottish author J.K. Rowling. It is about an orphaned boy-wizard, Harry Potter, and his struggles against the evil sorcerer, Lord Voldemort. Fans say it is a classic good-versus-evil saga, complete with lessons that exalt courage, loyalty, and selflessness. Rowling herself declares, "The theme running through all of these books is the fight between good and evil."[1]

The story begins with the infant Harry being delivered to his relatives, the Dursley family: Aunt Petunia, Uncle Vernon, and their son, Dudley, who is the epitome of a spoiled brat. Harry must live with them because his parents, James and Lily, have been murdered by Voldemort.

But Vernon and Petunia are hardly fitting stand-ins for James and Lily, both of whom were greatly beloved by their fellow

witches and wizards. The Dursleys, in fact, are thoroughly detestable *Muggles* (nonmagical people). They abhor and fear magic so much that they conceal from Harry his true identity and actually tell him his parents died in an automobile accident.

Harry lives a miserable and lonely life, oblivious to the magical world—that is, until he begins receiving mysterious letters just prior to his eleventh birthday. These turn out to be from Hogwarts School of Witchcraft and Wizardry, the same school his parents attended. He is to be a wizard-in-training at Hogwarts, which, as one character says, is "the finest school of witchcraft and wizardry in the world."[2]

The remainder of Book I (*Harry Potter and the Sorcerer's Stone*) follows Harry as he goes off to Hogwarts to hone his magical skills. This book also brings into focus the series' villain, Lord Voldemort, explaining that his diabolical goal is threefold: 1) recover the power he lost by attacking the Potters; 2) kill Harry; and 3) draw to himself a band of followers through whom he can rule the world.

Subsequent volumes released thus far—*Harry Potter and the Chamber of Secrets*, *Harry Potter and the Prisoner of Azkaban*, *Harry Potter and the Goblet of Fire*, *Harry Potter and the Order of the Phoenix*, and *Harry Potter and the Half-Blood Prince*—detail Harry's yearly activities. Each one covers another school term wherein Harry must face an array of predicaments that demand he solve mysteries and dodge dangers (often due to Voldemort's nefarious schemes). Meanwhile, he and his friends continue learning how to be more powerful and competent witches and wizards.

Practical Magick

Unlike The Lord of the Rings and The Chronicles of Narnia, Harry Potter is set against the backdrop of *real-world*

occult traditions, beliefs, practices, and historical figures. (I am not referring to any of those things in Harry Potter that are plainly unrealistic: dragons, flying broomsticks, enchanted candies, magic mirrors, talking hats, invisibility cloaks, or other fantastic elements.)

The problem is the astrology, numerology, divination, potions, magick, clairvoyance, herbology, alchemy, spell-casting, necromancy (communication with spirits), and occult lore in the series[3]—all of which are listed in the *Encyclopedia of Wicca & Witchcraft*.[4] Consider, too, this post from a Wiccan on a neopagan Web site:

> There are things in Harry's world that are "accurate" representations of what we believe....Animals are seen as valuable magical beings and partners. Study is encouraged; magic does not come easy and the principles must be learned. And...one should call all things by their real name, for fear of a name increases fear of the thing named. So, yes, there are some good parallels.[5]

According to Duke University's Thomas Robisheaux, history professor and teacher of magick/witchcraft courses, "Rowling discusses alchemy and the whole range of occult arts—including natural, or 'good' magic, and divination—so well known in the Renaissance."[6] Her use of occult concepts and symbolism makes for some striking parallels to real-world magick.

For instance, the school supplies for Hogwarts students match what most neopagans use: cauldrons and magick wands, among others. The pets owned by Rowling's characters hearken back to medieval associations between witches and animals and reflect the value of animals to Wiccans.[7] Additionally, Hogwarts classes

mirror courses offered by some occult groups, like London's Ordo Anno Mundi (see note 8).[8] Even the names of books read by Rowling's characters closely match books that have been circulating in the neopagan/Wiccan community for many years (see note 9).[9]

Compliments of the Dark Side

The realism permeating Harry Potter comes from the wellspring of occult knowledge its author possesses. She has admitted quite openly to having "done research on witchcraft and wizardry" in order to find material consistent with her plot. Rowling also has said that "some of the magic in the books is based on what people used to believe really worked"—about "one third" of it.[10]

Harry Potter also contains the basic occult definition of magick ("Magic is magic—it is neither good nor bad, it just is!").[11] This belief, which has been advanced by innumerable persons from the occult tradition, is voiced by one of Voldemort's followers: "There is no good and evil; there is only power and those too weak to seek it."[12]

Although the words come from an evil character, they convey the similarity in how magick is 1) depicted in Harry Potter and 2) viewed by real-world neopagans, witches, and occultists. Consider the comment made by one practicing neopagan:

> "There is no good and evil, there is only power, and those too weak to seek it."...This might actually offend some, but it hides one of the great truths of Witchcraft, that there is no White or Black Magick, there is only Magick, and it is the use we make of it that defines its purpose, although, we usually see a dark use of Magick as weakness, rather than strength.[13]

Given such parallels, it is no surprise that *The Sorcerer's Companion* (a fan-written reference guide to Harry Potter) lists dozens of occult entries relating to the series: amulets, arithmancy (divination with numbers), astrology, charms, crystal balls, divination, magick (ritual, natural, high, low), mandrakes, palmistry, poltergeist, talismans, and female sexual demons (called *veela*).[14] And the delineation between our world and Rowling's "fantasy" fades yet further thanks to the occult figures referenced:

❖ Vablatsky, an anagram for *Helena Petrovna Blavatsky* (1831–1891), founder of Theosophy, an occult blend of Eastern philosophy, metaphysical thought, mental healing, spiritualism, and pseudo-science[15]

❖ *Paracelsus* (1493–1541), a Swiss alchemist who stands as "one of the most striking and picturesque figures" in occultism[16]

❖ *Cornelius Agrippa* (1486–1535), an occultist whose writings "influenced generations of thinkers that followed and became part of the heritage of folk magic practiced by witches" and who "embraced astrology, divination, numerology and the power of gems and stones" and of whom "it was said that he practiced necromancy [or communing with the dead] for divination"[17]

The agreement between Harry Potter and occultism was highlighted in a 2001 article wherein neopagans Lisa Braun and Michael Sichmeller said the first Harry Potter movie, although a bit exaggerated, embodied their beliefs respectfully and accurately. The interviewer reported that the occultists were "particularly impressed with the characters' use of wands, which wiccans believe 'can direct energy.' "[18]

A similar comment appeared on the "Pagan Perspectives" message board at witchvox.com. Although spells are not cast simply by the flick of a wand, noted the writer "the overall depiction of magick and witchcraft, though, is as accurate a reflection of our knowledge of them as could be asked for." She added, "The lessons about proper use of magick, etc., are realistic and perfectly placed in the story."[19] Another enthused that the Potter

> books and in the movie form, are a wonderful metaphor of how we, as Witches/Wiccans/Pagans/Magickal people, perceive our own spirituality/work/studies, and our vision of the world. The symbolism is strong, and I have found myself reacting so many times, by reading between the lines and looking beyond the exaggerated way their magical acts and spells is depicted, and reacting positively, mostly thinking "This is SO right!"[20]

Particularly noteworthy is yet another Web site, "The Harry Potter Witchcraft Spellbook," designed by a Harry Potter fan whose screen name is "IO." The site is subtitled "Wherein is Explained Old Magical Secrets the Likes of Which J.K. Rowling's Book Series Was Based Upon." IO declares,

> Rowling has done her homework. Her hidden references are so numerous, and her knowledge so deep, that I'm certain she has done much research on the subject of real sorcery. Many of her characters are named after famous occultists of the past, many of her fantastic spells actually exist, and her magical creatures are straight out of ancient mythology. She is writing about the same witchcraft that I study at home, far away from Hogwarts!...I recognise much of

J.K. Rowling's work from Middle Age grimoires [spell-books] I've read. These charms and spells are more than just mere fantasy! They have a historical basis. And I will be more than happy to share it with you, here, on my website.[21]

Such close associations between Harry Potter and witchcraft may be why celebrated witch Phyllis Curott, in referring to her own Wiccan volume, *Book of Shadows*, said, "I wouldn't mind subtitling my book Harry Potter for Adults."[22]

The "W" Dilemma

An important word of clarification is needed here—Rowling's novels do not teach "Witchcraft" *per se*. Nowhere do they present or promote Wiccan doctrines or "deal with the philosophical precepts of Wicca."[23] This must be emphasized. Harry Potter does not outline the *technical* teachings of Wicca or instruct children to study Wicca.

But the series does contain witchcraft. How is such an apparent inconsistency possible? It all involves terminology. Although Harry Potter makes no reference to the technical doctrines *specific* to Wicca, it does include *generalized* practices and concepts inherent to Wicca.

These two categories of "witchcraft" are differentiated by Wiccans and neopagans through use of either a capital or lowercase "w." One Witch gives these explanations:

> *Witchcraft*, spelled with a capital "W"—A religion recognizing the divine in nature and following the seasonal changes and moons.

witchcraft, spelled with a small "w"—A magickal system which may or may not be used within a religious framework.[24]

Most neopagans practice witchcraft, but not necessarily Witchcraft (or Wicca). Wren Walker, a practicing Wiccan and cofounder of The Witches Voice (an organization for Wiccans worldwide), sought to dispel the confusion, noting that Rowling's books

> really don't have anything to do with a "capital w" witchcraft as practiced by a large number of people. It's something more to do with a "small w" witchcraft, which can be done by any other religion.[25]

Simply put, Harry Potter presents **w**itchcraft while simultaneously avoiding **W**itchcraft. By doing so it gives a sketch of real magick and occultism, but does not necessarily provide a narrowly-defined religious belief system (namely, Wicca).

Way of the Witch

Failure to make this crucial distinction has led many persons, including J.K. Rowling herself, to misunderstand the heart of concerns being expressed over Harry Potter. "I absolutely did not start writing these books to encourage any child into witchcraft," she has said. "I'm laughing slightly because to me, the idea is absurd."[26]

The famous author, however, is missing the obvious—just because she did not intentionally write the books to "encourage" children "into witchcraft" does not mean that her fantasy will not motivate kids to dabble in it. The fear that Harry Potter *might* inspire *some* children (even *some* adults) to experiment with witchcraft is far from "absurd."

Experimentation and investigation of anything usually springs out of a curiosity or interest that has been aroused. In this case, the stimulus is Harry Potter, as a 2002 article, "Potter Prompts Course in Witchcraft," revealed:

> A growing interest in sorcery and witchcraft generated by Harry Potter stories has prompted an Australian university [Adelaide University] to launch a special course....[It] will explore the witchdoctors of Africa, shamans...witches...and others who practice magic.[27]

If Harry Potter is getting college students and other adults interested enough in occultism to begin studying it, then common sense tells us that at least some children reading Harry Potter might also become curious about occult-related issues. However, Rowling's fantasy exerts a particular influence over children because the series so perfectly mirrors several aspects of childhood: school, friendships, a longing for autonomy, and peer rivalry.[28]

Even older children, who know it is just pretend, may become so enthralled with magic and wizardry that they will seek out neopaganism, witchcraft, or magick in the real world. Kids are already dressing up like Rowling's characters at bookstore-hosted parties. Many stores hold "wizard breakfasts." And some children are actually trying out Harry Potter spells. "I have met people who assure me, very seriously, that they are trying to do them," says Rowling. "I can assure them, just as seriously, that they don't work."[29]

But adults must ask, Will the ineffectiveness of Rowling's silly spells put an end to every child's desire for magick, or will it only be the start of a child's drift in that direction? Where will the fascination and emulation end? With playing dress-up? With

dabbling in "fun" occult practices like divination and spell-casting? With signing up for college courses on magickal phenomena? As Harry Potter fans mature, will they desire to delve deeper into occultism?

Multiple studies have proven that media images of violence and sexuality affect the behaviors, attitudes, and beliefs of kids (see chapters 10 and 11).[30] Is it really so absurd to theorize that exciting images and depictions of occult spirituality might also have an affect of some children? Many Christians think it is possible that Harry Potter and similar works could influence a whole generation. And they are not alone in holding this opinion.

What Do Witches Think?

Ultimately, Rowling's books could desensitize tens of millions of children to the dangers of occultism (see appendix A), which in turn could create in them a general curiosity about witchcraft. This concern is being voiced by many respected and nonextreme observers of the Harry Potter phenomenon.[31]

Interestingly, neopagans and Wiccans too have theorized that untold numbers of children, teens, and adults will probably be influenced by the Potter books to investigate occultism and magick—perhaps to join the Wiccan fold:

❖ "Harry Potter happens to be one of the best things for witchcraft, and the understanding of it."[32]

❖ "Will it draw people to the craft[?] It will probably make some people very curious and therefore more open."[33]

❖ "I think that more people will start exploring witchcraft because of the movie [Harry Potter]."[34]

❖ "As to whether Harry Potter generates interest in Paganism, of course it does! Many people will explore Paganism because of Harry Potter."[35]

❖ "[Harry Potter] will bring more attention to Paganism and the study of Magick....The open-minded people will go out and buy a few 'Wicca 101' books to learn more about witchcraft in the real world."[36]

At witchvox.com, a self-described "urban witch" named Henbane explained how Harry Potter mirrors in some ways her own concept of how youths could be taught Wicca:

> You can imagine my delight when I read of "Hogwarts School of Witchcraft and Wizardry" which is basically an over-the-top, whimsical fiction of my dream. Imagination is the first step to actualization, so it thrills me that children are reading these books. Someday, perhaps there'll be a "Henbane's School of Witchcraft and Magick."[37]

But is there any real evidence that children may be venturing toward occultism due to Rowling's material? Yes (see pages 16–17 in "To Be a Child Again"). And the data is continuing to mount as Rowling's fantasy spreads from country to country.

8

Harry Hype

With the unparalleled popularity of the Harry Potter books by J.K. Rowling, a whole new generation—young and old—are adventuring into the magical world of witches and wizards....As you read through the pages of this book and go through the training methods, you will enter a world that up until now may have seemed like only fantasy.... Transforming what seems like fiction into nonfiction can look like a difficult task, but it isn't.

—SIRONA KNIGHT
The Witch and Wizard Guide

Many adult Harry Potter fans have for some reason failed to see, or refused to see, even the remotest possibility that some kids might be drawn into witchcraft by way of Rowling's fantasy. Why this is remains a mystery, especially since multiple examples of youths being influenced by the fantasy in other ways can already be seen worldwide.

A 1999 BBC story noted how interest in boarding schools had increased among British children due to Harry Potter. Britain's Boarding Education Alliance (BEA) said the books "have helped to re-invent the image of boarding schools." The BEA campaign

director added, "The books have probably done more for boarding than anything else we could have imagined…. The Harry Potter books have helped to project an image of choosing to go to boarding school as 'fun.' "[1]

Another Potter trend among young people took root in 2001, as British animal protection groups were growing concerned that the use of owls as messengers in the series might create "a surge of interest in keeping owls as pets." " 'We understand that Harry Potter keeps [an owl] in a parrot cage, which is against everything we know,' said Jenny Thurston, a trustee at the World Owl Trust at Muncaster Castle near the village of Ravenglass, England. 'That is horrendous. It will foul up people's imagination.' "[2]

Sure enough, less than a year later kids were clamoring for the bird. In fact, *The Times* of London reported, "The popularity of Harry Potter books has led to a wave of owl thefts." As of 2005, animal welfare experts were still saying, "The popularity of Harry Potter has increased demand for pet owls."[3]

Even more relevant is a 2002 story titled "Siberian Potter Fans Drink Poisonous Potion," which recounted the hospitalization of two dozen kids "poisoned after drinking a 'magic potion' inspired by the series of books about a boy wizard." It explained that "older children stole copper sulphate from a school laboratory and fed it to younger children in a Potteresque initiation ceremony."[4] Less troubling, but still indicative of Harry Potter's influence, "Magicians [illusionists] across the world have been capitalizing on the story of Harry Potter to increase interest in the art of magic and in their performances."[5]

From Boarding Schools to Witchcraft

What about emulating real-world magick as opposed to harmless stage illusion (magic)? "The Harry Potter series of adult-read

children's books has helped fuel a revival of British interest in the occult."[6] says James Woudhuysen, director of forecasting at international product designers Seymour Powell (London) and professor of innovation at De Montfort University (Leicester).

Steve Paine—a Wiccan high priest and the husband of Wiccan high priestess Kate West, an official of The Pagan Federation—made a similar observation about Rowling's books. They "are taken as fantasy entertainment. But they do encourage people to think about different forms of spirituality."[7]

Most enlightening, however, was a 2003 interview with Nigel Bourne, The Pagan Federation's media officer:

> *Host:* Do you think that with this impetus that you've been given by this sort of…by, as we mentioned at the very beginning, you know, "Buffy the Vampire Slayer," with "Harry Potter," which has opened up this whole new world to kids particularly, I think…
>
> *Nigel:* Yes.
>
> *Host:*…and indeed older kids as well (Nigel laughs), do you think, to be honest, it's something that you can really—and I don't mean this in too materialistic a way—can cash in on, to really kind of tell the world—
>
> *Nigel:* Yes. Oh I think there has—
>
> *Host:* —what you're all about, and actually attract even more people?
>
> *Nigel:* Yes. It would be very, very easy, at this moment in time, to "sell" paganism.[8]

Anecdotal evidence suggests that a similar thing is happening across the United States. For example, in Laurel, Maryland, the owner of a New Age supply store reported that the "Harry Potter

phenomenon has brought customers to his store."[9] And when Allan and Elizabeth Kronzek, authors of *The Sorcerer's Companion*, asked child fans of the series which topics most interested them, many respondents wanted more information on "spells, charms, and curses."[10]

Also, innumerable bookstores and mega–shopping centers are displaying *real* occult volumes (nonfiction) near the Harry Potter books. This trend and its effects were even detailed by a 13-year-old, whose essay appeared in witchvox's March 2002 series "When Your Parents Disapprove" and was posted in the "Young Pagan Essays" forum:

> You're 12 years old, and have stumbled upon the book *Teen Witch* by Silver Ravenwolf at this very odd and interesting section of Borders called "Magickal Studies." Next to *Teen Witch* is the book *Wicca: a Guide for the Solitary Practitioner* by Scott Cunningham. You have never heard of this term before—"Wicca," but naturally you're a huge fan of "Charmed" and "Harry Potter," so you immediately open to around the middle of this interesting book, *Teen Witch*. What's the first thing you see? Spells! Tons of them! "Oh cool! Now I can be a real Witch!" you say, as you take this fascinating book to the checkout line. You get home, and you start reading this book. Soon enough, you learn that Witchcraft isn't a cool fad, but a religion. Still, you are amazed and want to learn as much as you can. You purchase more books at Borders, including Cunningham's. You read constantly, especially on the Internet, frequently visiting your favorite site "The Witch's Voice." Soon enough, your mom (who thought you were just reading fiction

books similar to Harry Potter) learns that you are actually reading real, authentic books, focused on teaching Witchcraft. This second-person story must be one of the most common stories shared by all teenage Witches in their first stage of learning.[11]

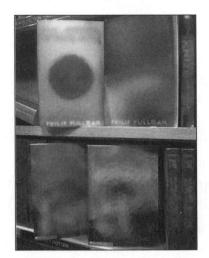

Two prominent displays at a Borders bookstore in Southern California. On one shelf located deep in the "Children's" section (left), an entire row of Harry Potter volumes (lower shelf) was displayed beneath another row of Philip Pullman's His Dark Materials trilogy books (top shelf). This is no surprise, given J.K. Rowling's hearty endorsements of Pullman's work (see p. 166) and the publisher they have in common, Scholastic Books.

Just two aisles away in the same store, on the back side of the children's section, were a number of nonfiction books advocating real-world occultism for teenagers (right). In this row of books from left to right were *Teen Astrology; Elements of Witchcraft; The Book of Wizardry; Teen Witch: Wicca for a New Generation;* and *Tarot Kit for Teens* (including a deck of tarot cards). These kinds of displays are now commonplace. (Photos: Richard Abanes; cover images have been blurred to honor copyright restrictions.)

Hooked on Magick

In a word, Harry Potter is motivating an unknown number of kids to obtain material on real-world witchcraft. Sometimes this information is actually packaged to imitate the courses offered at Hogwarts. One such book is *The Witch and Wizard Guide* (2001)

by Sirona Knight, a Wiccan who has written extensively on neo-paganism.[12] An advertisement for her volume, which targets children and teens, brazenly uses Harry Potter's popularity to lure young buyers:

> A complete guide to doing the magic in Harry Potter using modern Wiccan Techniques. Learn divining techniques such as tarot, runes, "witching," and crystal scrying....This guide contains a history of witches and wizards, how to make potions, and defense against the dark arts.[13]

Knight covers subjects directly taken from Rowling's books, capitalizing on their phraseology and openly explaining her desire to attract young Harry Potter fans (see quote at beginning of chapter). Several amazon.com reviews joyfully link Knight's book to the Potter series, taking special note of how Knight employed Potter terminology (see note 14 for text of reviews).[14] A similar book, *The Real Witch's Handbook*, takes advantage of the series as well. The following advertisement for the volume appeared at witchcraft.org:

> Harry Potter, Sabrina: The Teenage Witch, Buffy the Vampire Slayer, Charmed—it seems we can't get enough of all things magical or "witchy" at the moment. The result of all this interest is that Wicca has become the fastest growing religion in the UK.[15]

Rowling has nothing but ridicule for critics who worry that Harry Potter might be leading some children into occultism. During an interview on *Dateline NBC*, for example, she said such concerns were "utter garbage," then joked,

If that's what my books were doing, I would by now have met one child who would have come up to me covered in pentagrams and said, "Can we, you know, go and sacrifice a goat later together, will you do that with me?" It's never happened, funnily enough.[16]

But evidence linking Harry Potter to a growing youth interest in occultism continues to increase. Of course, it would be unrealistic to think that *every* young Harry potter fan will definitely get curious about occultism. But it is equally improbable, as many neopagans have noted, to assume that none of them will.

Adults: Harmful or Helpful?

No one who has legitimate concerns is saying kids are going to start covering themselves with pentagrams—or begin sacrificing goats. More important Rowling herself is missing the whole point. In reference to her cavalier attitude, Robert Knight (Director of the Culture and Family Institute) observes,

> Rowling dispatches legitimate concerns about *influence*. In the same way, defenders of "slasher" movies full of sex and violence say, "I've never heard of a kid seeing a film and then going right out and raping and murdering." This ignores the obvious, which is that kids, particularly those on the edge, are deeply affected by what they see and hear. Besides, some kids *do* go right out and copy what they have seen, like the teens who went on a killing spree after seeing the film *Natural Born Killers*. To say that kids won't immediately become witches after reading or viewing *Harry Potter* does not mean that many children won't take an unhealthy interest in witchcraft and the occult. It just might not materialize instantly.[17]

Rowling is overlooking a lot, especially given the way some adults are boldly nudging children toward occultism. Consider the popular "Harry Potter Links" Web site (sirlinksalot.com) for Rowling's fans. This Internet location includes a link to Harry Potter's *real* astrological birth chart by professional astrologer Barbara Schermer.[18]

The chart is at Schermer's Web site, called "Astrology Alive."[19] It links to her astrological interpretation of Harry's horoscope; a "Your Horoscope" page for fans; and real astrology books at Amazon.com (*Mythic Astrology, The Inner Dimensions of the Birth Chart,* and *Astrology, Karma & Transformation*).[20]

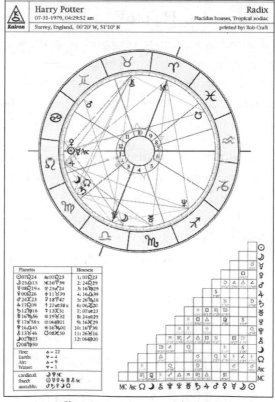

Chart courtesy of Barbara Schermer.

Not to be outdone by sirlinksalot.com, in mid-2002 Yahoo News pointed Harry Potter fans to a Discovery Channel Web site advertising the TV special *Real Magick: The Science of Wizardry*. This page in turn led Web surfers to "The Wizard's Lair," "The Sorcerer's Guide," and other "Web Links" (sites where children could learn about real magick and objects used by occultists). The last link read, "Fortune tellers, mythic beasts and true tales of witchcraft await."[21]

Another example of adults using Harry Potter to introduce children to the occult is *Beacham's Sourcebooks for Teaching Young Adult Fiction: Exploring Harry Potter*. This teacher's guide to Rowling's books not only includes chapters covering the history of real magick and occult practices, but also suggest assignments that have students researching these practices and persons via Beacham's resource Web site.[22] Here are listed *Drawing Down the Moon* by Margot Adler (a very influential Wiccan); *The Encyclopedia of Celtic Wisdom*, which "discusses subjects noted in the Harry Potter novels"; and *An Encyclopedia of Occultism*, a "reprint of a classic encyclopedia source listing information about alchemy, the Philosopher's Stone, and the real Nicholas Flamel."[23]

On a broader plane, many popular Harry Potter Web sites designed for children now turn up links to various occult/Wicca/neopagan sites, such as—

❖ witchvox.com (linked from the-leaky-cauldron.org)[24]

❖ astrologyalive.com (linked from cybersleuth-kids.com, for children K through 12)[25]

❖ workingwitches.com and pantheism.net (linked from quick-quote-quill.org)[26]

The distance between Rowling's fantasy world and real-world occultism is just too short. This issue might be less significant if Rowling's story occurred in a place far removed from our reality—in a world largely disassociated from the world in which we live (for example, in Narnia or Middle-earth). But Harry Potter takes place in the here and now, just a few hours from London. Unlike Narnia or Middle-earth, Hogwarts is a parallel world rather than another world (per J.K. Rowling);[27] Harry Potter is a fictional tale with a *non*fictional backdrop, and it can be accessed by any child at any bookstore or library.

This is only one of the many differences separating Harry Potter from both The Chronicles of Narnia and The Lord of the Rings (see chapter 9). Another important dissimilarity between the older classic works and Harry Potter is the morality offered in the latter. It is moral relativism, pure and simple.

Rowling over Morality

Countless articles have applauded the morality of Harry Potter. Rowling herself says, "I think they're very moral books." Most reviewers, such as Wheaton College literature professor Alan Jacobs, agree: "Rowling's moral compass throughout the three volumes is sound—indeed, I would say, acute."[28]

In fairness, it is true that Harry and his companions demonstrate some praiseworthy characteristics. They display loyalty and courage, reject materialism, eschew race and class distinctions, and hold an aversion to blatant evil (for example, murder, hatred, torture). The "good" characters in Harry Potter also show great compassion for the weak, downtrodden, and hurting.

At the same time, Rowling's "moral compass" is hardly "acute." Her morals and ethics are at best unclear and inconsistent; at worst, they are totally confused. The mixed message in

Harry Potter is partly due to the way Rowling's "good" characters unrepentantly do what "bad" characters typically do.

Harry and other "good" characters *habitually* lie, steal, cheat, ignore laws, break rules, and disrespect authority. Each one bases his or her actions not on any objective moral standard, but on their own subjective feelings. They are the embodiment of moral relativism and its companion, situational ethics.

Relativism is "the doctrine that knowledge of truth is relative and dependent upon place, and individual, and experience." This philosophy usually translates into an "if it feels right do it" mode of living—regardless of any external restrictions or moral standards. The result is convenient, flexible, ethics.[29]

Like the morality of Wicca (see chapter 2), Harry Potter reflects what has become both acceptable and popular in our society. Right and wrong, good and bad, righteous and evil—pop culture has lumped all of these concepts together in the realm of "Subjective Interpretation." As the computer junkies in the 1995 film *Hackers* put it, "There is no right or wrong, only fun and boring."

The Good, the Bad, and the Ugly

Rowling's "good" characters perfectly demonstrate relativistic thinking: "By and large they go with their conscience," the author says. This sounds great. But the approach routinely leads to *unrepentant* "bad" behavior. The result is not a world of consistent morality, but a realm of moral ambiguity in which Harry learns to "balance his sense of what's right and his sense of what's necessary."[30]

Unfortunately, Rowling's boy-wizard oftentimes defines as "necessary" many things that are not necessary at all—they are simply things he wants to do. Whether it entails breaking rules, disobeying laws, or lying is inconsequential. Throughout all the

books thus far released, Harry typically calls his own shots, so to speak, making decisions based on what he feels.[31] He resorts to cheating, various wizard crimes, and rule-breaking—yet he remains a hero. Oddly, most of the time Harry's unethical deeds are not just excused, but rewarded! Rarely does he suffer any negative consequences for his poor choices. And when he is "punished," it usually amounts to not much of a lesson.

More than anything else, however, lying seems to be his primary means of negotiating life.[32] But adults in the series voice little concern. This is understandable given the philosophy expressed by the fantasy's most honorable wizard, Dumbledore. He believes "that the truth is *generally* preferable to lies."[33]

Dumbledore's perspective is not surprising since he, too, lies. On page 353 of *Prisoner of Azkaban*, for instance, we learn that when he first became headmaster, he lied to his staff, the school's students, their parents, and the citizens of a nearby town so young Lupin (a werewolf) could attend Hogwarts.

How did Lupin repay the favor? He disobeyed the rules, wandering off school grounds as a wolf and nearly causing the deaths of innocent people. Lupin explained to Harry how easily he dismissed his guilt:

> I sometimes felt guilty about betraying Dumbledore's trust....He had no idea I was breaking the rules he had set down for my own safety and others' safety....But I always managed to forget my guilty feelings every time we [James, Sirius, and Peter] sat down to plan our next month's adventure.[34]

In this same book, readers find out why Harry seems so bent toward rule-breaking. His father, James, also "didn't set much store by rules." In reference to Sirius Black (Harry's godfather)

and James, Professor McGonagall recalls, "Black and Potter. Ringleaders of their little gang. Both very bright...but I don't think we've ever had such a pair of troublemakers."[35]

Lupin, who was a close friend of James's, reveals that Harry's father and two other Hogwarts students (Sirius Black and Peter Pettigrew) secretly and illegally became *animagi*—in other words, wizards who can turn themselves into animals. They were supposed to register with the Minister of Magic, but remained unregistered, again contrary to wizard law.[36]

Also in Book III, Harry inherits a magical "Marauders Map" from teen troublemakers Fred and George Weasley. It shows every corridor in Hogwarts and displays moving figures that reveal the whereabouts of teachers and students. The boys stole it from a drawer marked "Confiscated and Highly Dangerous."

To activate the map, George taps it, saying, "*I solemnly swear that I am up to no good.*" As Fred gives it to Harry, he sighs about the map's makers, "Noble men, working tirelessly to help a new generation of lawbreakers."[37] Fred and George, in fact, are tirelessly disobedient themselves. Although depicted as good kids, they customarily disobey their parents, violate school ordinances, and lie, all the while expressing gleeful satisfaction over their antics (see *Prisoner of Azkaban*).

In Book IV, for example, it is revealed that for years the twins have been simply ignoring their mother's instructions by continuing to invent dangerous magical gag-gifts. It is all depicted quite humorously. They also ignore their father's request to not gamble on the Quidditch World Cup game. Ultimately, a defeated Mr. Weasley capitulates to his sons, pleading, "*Don't* tell your mother you've been gambling." Fred cheerfully responds, "Don't worry, Dad....We don't want it [their money] confiscated."[38]

Adult "Role Models"

Mr. Weasley himself seems to be the source of his children's tendency toward rule-breaking and lying. Although a Minister of Magic employee, he regularly circumvents wizard laws. His job is to prevent wizards from illegally bewitching "things that are Muggle-made" (appliances, books, clothes). By doing so he protects Muggles from objects that might prove to be harmful.

To capture wizards and witches who have broken this law, Mr. Weasley conducts raids and confiscates their unlawfully bewitched property. But Mr. Weasley is "crazy about everything to do with Muggles" and has a shed full of Muggle objects. His son Ron explains, "He takes it apart, puts spells on it, and puts it back together again. If he raided *our* house he'd have to put himself under arrest." Mr. Weasley even lies to his wife about the extent to which he has bewitched his Muggle car.[39] His illegal/unethical practices go on and on.[40]

Rubeus Hagrid (Hogwarts Keeper of the Keys and Grounds), another "good" character, is even less inspiring as a role model. He often breaks school rules, ignores wizard laws,[41] bends to the dictates of the children, and is a drunk. This last trait of Hagrid's is most troubling. He often turns to alcohol and gets wasted (rather humorously) when either depressed *or* joyful.[42]

Rowling explains, "[His name] is another old English word, meaning—if you were *hagrid* (it's a dialect word)—you'd had a bad night. Hagrid is a big drinker—he has a lot of bad nights." Moreover, "Rubeus" means red. So Rowling is making a play on words: "Rubeus Hagrid" = "red-[faced] drunk."[43]

The only characters that seem to care about discipline and following rules and laws are the dislikable Dursleys, nasty Rita Skeeter (a reporter), Snape (a mean professor), and Argus Filch (the school caretaker).[44] In actuality, then, Rowling's good characters are not particularly "good" models. Why then do they still

appear extraordinarily good in the story? It is a literary illusion created by Rowling's radical redefinition of good and evil.

Redefining Good; Recasting Evil

Harry is not alone in exhibiting less than admirable behavior.[45] Yet he and his friends remain exemplary heroes. Why? Because Rowling has obscured their *mildly* evil deeds behind the *horrendously* evil deeds of her book's "bad" characters. She has made Voldemort and his Death Eaters so repulsive that the immoral and unethical deeds of Harry and his band take on an appearance of benevolence, fun, and virtue.

Those who stand *against* Voldemort are good. Those who stand *with* Voldemort are bad. Exactly what each character does in order to fight Voldemort becomes less important than the fact they are standing against him. This morality is not only flawed, but also simplistic. And it allows for all kinds of "bad" things (lying, stealing, cheating) to be done by "good" characters (Harry, Dumbledore, Mr. Weasley) without those characters having to show remorse for their conduct.

Rowling further downplays the unseemly deeds of her "good" characters by elevating two virtues *above all others*: bravery and courage. As she herself has stated, "If the characters are brave and courageous, that is rewarded."[46] What everyone is failing to recognize, however, is that Rowling's "evil" characters are brave and courageous, too. Her evil characters also show perseverance, loyalty (in the face of persecution), and a willingness to make sacrifices for their cause.[47]

Of course, Voldemort's method of operation may drastically differ from Harry's, but the two characters to some degree share a similar way of determining their course of action—subjective self-interest. Voldemort wants what he wants, as does Harry. The main differences between them lie in the rules they break, the

falsehoods they tell, and the goals they pursue. But even their powers and spells are essentially the same (see chapter 9).

This is why the "Harry-Potter-is-a-battle-between-good-and-evil" argument is, in truth, a mischaracterization. Although often used as a defense of Rowling's works, it has little to do with the books because they do not, in fact, contain a true "battle between good and evil." The war in Harry Potter is a conflict between *horrific* bad (Voldemort and his followers) and a *milder* admixture of "good" and "bad" (Harry and his companions).

The latter group seems admirable only because it is set against the deep wickedness of the former group. Bestselling fiction author Michael O'Brien feels that such a moral universe is woefully lacking and inconsistent:

> Harry's faults are rarely punished, and usually by the negative authority figures in the tale. The positive authority figures actually reward Harry for his disobedience when it brings about some perceived good. His lies, his acts of vengeance, and his misuse of his powers are frequently ignored. The message of "the end justifies the means" is dominant throughout. Lip service is paid to a code of ethics—never really spelled out—but in fact the undermining of those ethics is reinforced at every turn.[48]

Adult Harry Potter fans are asking, What good qualities might kids pick up from Harry and his pals? But few if any are asking, What *bad* qualities might children pick up from Harry and his pals? To sum up what we've seen, the answer to this second question is obvious:

❖ Disobedience is not very serious, especially when you either disagree with the rules you are breaking or you do not see any reason for their existence.

❖ When possible, try getting around consequences or punishment, either by lying or by using "connections."

❖ Obedience should be forsaken in favor of your own gut feeling, even if it means disobeying those who have the authority to make the decision about what should be done.

❖ Sometimes it is acceptable to use deception or conceal information so you can achieve your own desire (even if it means deceiving a spouse).

❖ Ethics and morality are not only random, but also situational, and you should feel free to re-create morality to suit you as your circumstances change.

❖ The end justifies the means by which you pursue your goals.

It is true that unrighteous deeds play a part in fairy and fantasy tales—but there is usually an implied understanding that the characters involved are either 1) "evil" characters, or 2) "good" characters undergoing a deep struggle over their actions. In some cases, these "good" characters are behaving "badly" only because they are somehow being deceived or bewitched (such examples occur in both The Chronicles of Narnia and The Lord of the Rings).

In Harry Potter, on the other hand, morality is inconsistent and confused. Heroes act according to situational ethics, moral relativism, and an "end-justifies-the-means" philosophy. Both good and bad deeds are rewarded—as long as the one being "bad" is on the side of "good," which Rowling defines for the reader as anyone who stands against Lord Voldemort.

Rowling's magickal universe is a topsy-turvy world rife with occultism, but devoid of any firm rules of right and wrong. As former astrologer Marcia Montenegro remarks, "There is no moral

center in Harry Potter. Good and evil are depicted as being two sides of the same coin, which is the occult worldview"[49] (see chapter 2).

Teach Your Children Well

Caution and discernment are needed when it comes to giving J.K. Rowling's books to children. The series contains 1) real-world occultism and 2) inconsistent moral messages. A guiding hand will go a long way in helping young Harry Potter fans avoid problems stemming from the tale's real-world magick and exaltation of various unethical and immoral actions:

> Are we committed to discussing these issues with our children? Are we willing to accompany them, year after year, as their tastes develop, advising caution here, sanctioning liberality there, each of us, young and old, learning as we go? Are we willing to sacrifice precious time to pre-read some novels about which we may have doubts? Are we willing to invest effort to help our children choose the right kind of fantasy?[50]

No one, of course, is better equipped than a parent to judge what is and what is not appropriate for a child. Parents of vulnerable or at-risk children may have to intervene to turn their children's interests in healthier directions. Children in this category include those who are 1) already showing deep fascination with occultism, 2) especially susceptible to peer pressure, 3) hanging around with a "bad crowd" of kids, 4) *preoccupied* with imaginary worlds, and 5) often *obsessed* with a book or movie.[51]

Unfortunately, many parents are now being told that there are no problems at all with Harry Potter. Some misguided individuals have gone so far as to say that the series is nothing less than

full-blown Christian literature, written by a Christian author, whose goal was to embed the Christian gospel in her fantasy. This is a terribly confused position fed by misinformation and disinformation.

Sadly, an immense number of people seem to have jumped on this bandwagon: biased news journalists, uninformed Potter fans, Christian scholars who are self-conscious about looking narrow-minded, well-meaning Christians alarmed by society's materialistic and nonsupernatural mind-set, and even some religious leaders.

This innovative Harry-Potter-is-really-Christian interpretation of Rowling's fantasy, along with issues relating to the topic of entertainment in general, will be the subject of part three.

Part Three

That's Entertainment

The brightest minds in the country devote their great talent, and use sophisticated psychological techniques, to influence your children to purchase products—or rather, to want products—regardless of whether or not they are good for your kids....They see children's minds as a kind of cash cow. "If you own this child at an early age, you can own this child for years to come," explained Mike Searles, president of Kids-R-Us....Wayne Chilicki, a General Mills executive, agrees:..."We believe in getting them early and having them for life."

Advertisers infuse their pitches with messages that prey upon the emotional weaknesses and insecurities of children. "Advertising at its best is making people feel that without their product, you're a loser," explained Nancy Shalek, president of the Shalek Agency. "Kids are very sensitive to that....You open up emotional vulnerabilities, and it's very easy to do with kids because they're the most emotionally vulnerable."

—GARY RUSKIN
"Why They Whine: How Corporations
Prey on Our Children"
Mothering magazine,
November/December 1999

9

The Potter Wars

[Rowling's books are] the most over-praised, over-publicized and marketed books ever printed. They are not precisely bad books—just not very good books....[Potter's popularity] suggests a psychological need, a community of feeling with readers "into it" around the world. A kind of cult, in fact, boosted by the peer pressures of child consumers.[1]

—JACK MARKOWITZ
business columnist,
The (Pittsburgh)*Tribune-Review*

Not everyone is a Harry Potter fan. Even some of Rowling's fellow fiction/fantasy writers have had less than high praise for the boy-wizard saga. Distinguished literary critic and award-winning author A.S. Byatt, for instance, said Rowling's series "is written for people whose imaginative lives are confined to TV cartoons, and the exaggerated mirror-worlds of soaps, reality TV and celebrity gossip." And celebrated novelist Colleen McCullough, author of *The Thorn Birds*, has matter-of-factly remarked: "[Rowling] is such a lousy writer."[2]

But tastes vary in the world of literature. As with art, what appeals to one person may be unappealing to another. There is

certainly room for divergent opinions on whether or not Harry Potter is "good" from a literary standpoint. Much less debatable are the answers to several other questions previously discussed in these pages.

Do the books contain a plethora of real-world occult references? Might the books cause *some* children to grow curious about magick and occultism? Is the morality in the books acute or askew? Are Witches/Wiccans using Harry Potter to attract children to other books that positively present real-world occult practices and beliefs?

Recently, another question has been added to the still-boiling pot of Harry Potter controversies: Is the magical series a "Christian" work written by a committed "Christian" whose deliberate goal is to present "a modern interpretation of the gospel" (that is to say, a symbolic representation of it)?[3]

Some Christian scholars, ministers, and teachers are answering: "Yes." As author John Granger has said, "By theme, by plot, and by design, the Potter books are meant to 'baptize the imagination' in Christian imagery and doctrine, oftentimes as bald and bold as Lewis's Narnia and Tolkien's Middle Earth."[4]

But such a view is as imbalanced and misguided as the position taken by those individuals who call Rowling a practicing witch and say her novels teach Satanism. Both are distortions of the truth. Both are based on misinformation and poor research. These well-meaning advocates of the "Harry-Potter-is-really-Christian" view have simply gone to an extreme in the opposite direction of the worst anti-Potter critics.

Saying that Harry Potter is a "Christian" story full of "Christian" symbolism on the level of Lewis's Chronicles and Tolkien's trilogy does a great disservice to *all* of these works. First, it cheapens what Lewis and Tolkien achieved. Second, it contradicts what Rowling herself has said about Harry Potter. Third, it

lulls people into a false sense of security about Harry Potter, leading them to believe there are few if any problems with it.

Nevertheless, assorted Christians have been advancing this new approach to Harry Potter, and in so doing, claim to be revealing the fantasy's "hidden key." Its most notable proponent is John Granger, author of *Looking for God in Harry Potter*.[5]

Harry Potter Is Really Christian?

According to *Looking for God in Harry Potter*, Rowling's fantasy is resoundingly consistent with Christianity. Harry is a "Christian hero," says Granger. Moreover, the very reason why Rowling's work is so popular is because she "is a Christian novelist of the Inkling School [see chapter 6] writing to 'baptize the imagination' and prepare our hearts and minds for the conscious pursuit of the greater life in Jesus Christ."[6]

Sharing this perspective are various authorities, including Francis Bridger, a theologian and principal of Trinity College in Bristol, England (*A Charmed Life: The Spirituality of Potterworld*); and John Killinger, a minister and professor of religion at Samford University in Birmingham, Alabama (*God, the Devil, and Harry Potter: A Christian Minister's Defense of the Beloved Novels*).[7] Unfortunately, their assertions are plagued by a myriad of flaws that can be distilled down to two main issues:

1. The plainest reading of Harry Potter reveals that it is not a depiction of anything Christian, but instead, is a depiction of the magick worldview. (This has been confirmed by Witches, occultists, and neopagans.)

2. Rowling herself has explained both her work and her faith in ways that clearly contradict the assertions being made by the "Harry-Potter-is-really-Christian" group of supporters.

The second issue is the most problematic. For example, some have said that the name "Albus Dumbledore" means "white or pure soul." Albus means "white" and Dumbledore means "bee," which "is a traditional symbol for the soul."[8] But Rowling disagrees. She apparently named this Harry Potter character using the Old English for "bee" because Dumbledore likes music and she "imagined him walking around humming to himself."[9]

Consider, too, comments that have been made about the character Ginny Weasley, who is featured in *Chamber of Secrets*. It is claimed that the name Ginny "should be read 'Virginia' or 'virgin innocence,'" because it really means "virgin innocence, purity."[10]

But the author says "Ginny" does not stand for Virginia, but is short for "Ginerva,"[11] which invalidates the Virginia = virgin notion. This is only one of many misunderstandings that have been exposed by Rowling's own explanations. The following is a partial listing of the dozens of interpretation errors in the Harry-Potter-is-really-Christian idea:

❖ *"Harry Potter"*—"The Cockney and French pronunciations of Harry's name tell us what his name means....Arry with a long 'A' suggests the word 'heir.'...If Harry means 'Heir-y,' then what is our Harry 'Heir to' or 'Son of'?...The answer to that is in the biblical use of the word 'Potter.'...Potter can be used as a synonym for 'God'—and thus Harry Potter means 'Heir to' or 'Son of God'....Harry Potter is 'son of God.' "[12]

Rowling's explanation—" 'Harry' has always been my favorite boy's name, so if my daughter had been a son, he would have been Harry Rowling. Then I would have had to choose a different name for 'Harry' in the books, because it would have been too cruel to name him after my

own son. 'Potter' was the surname of a family who used to live near me when I was seven....I always liked the name, so I borrowed it."[13]

✧ *"Severes Snape"*—"I read in the Rev. Francis Bridger's *A Charmed Life* that snape is 'an English word meaning "chide" or "rebuke," and hence the whole name means 'severe rebuke.' "[14]

Rowling's explanation—"Many of the names are taken from maps—for instance, Snape, which is an English village."[15]

✧ *"Goblet of Fire"*—"I think the title was changed [to *Goblet of Fire*] so the tournament would have a more Trinitarian feel (the Triwizard Tournament)—and so the title would point to the overarching meaning of the book."[16]

Rowling's explanation—"I preferred *Goblet of Fire* because it's got that kind of 'cup of destiny' feel about it, which is the theme of the book."[17]

✧ *"Sorcerer's Stone"*—"*The Philosopher's Stone* [the book's title in the UK], then, is about Harry and Christ."[18]

Rowling's explanation—"The book is really about the power of the imagination. What Harry is learning to do is to develop his full potential."[19]

One of the most serious hindrances to the Harry-Potter-is-really-Christian theory is its reliance on "symbols" and "symbolism." A 2002 review declared, "Granger's work invites the reader to go back to Rowling's novels and see Christian symbols previously missed."[20]

In reality, however, these symbols were never truly "missed." They were noticed long ago by most fans, but were never interpreted as Christian—let alone exclusively Christian. In fact,

these same symbols have been read in many alternate ways.[21] Everyone, it seems, wants to wave Harry Potter as some sort of banner that represents *their* particular worldview or beliefs:

✧ *Vedic astrologers* say that Harry Potter reflects an astrological "rags to riches" story.[22]

✧ *Secularists* praise Harry Potter as being either "a tribute to the wonders of science and technology" or "a nontranscendent neo-Stoicism."[23]

✧ *Jewish Kabbalists* assert that Harry Potter mirrors things "in the history of Kabbalah."[24]

✧ *New Agers* claim that Harry Potter is an attempt to familiarize children "with the realm of 4th density and the behind-the-scenes hyperdimensional controllers who exist there, continually interacting with and manipulating their 3rd density puppets."[25]

✧ *Homosexuals* see "much of the basic Potter plot" as being "identical to the traditional coming-out story....Mr. Dursley keeps noting that wizards and witches dress in purple, violet, and green clothing—all colors associated with homosexuality."[26]

A brief glance at what some have called the uniform symbology of Harry Potter reveals no uniformity at all. Some symbols, although they *could* be used within a Christian paradigm, also could be used within an occult paradigm (see note 27 for a chart of symbols).[27]

This is not to say that Harry Potter contains *no* elements that are consonant with Christianity. It does. As English professor Ken Jacobsen has noted, "The overarching theme of the novels is the power of love to conquer death, a central theme of the New

Testament to be sure."[28] Other aspects of Harry Potter compatible with Christianity would be references to immortality,[29] blood as being life-giving, and rites/rituals.[30]

But all these themes and elements can be found in countless stories. Bram Stoker's *Dracula,* for example, is built entirely around the concepts of immortality (both physical and spiritual), the life-giving power of blood, and "various quasi-religious rituals."[31] Is *Dracula* a Christian novel?

Moreover, as Jacobsen also observed, Rowling "draws together elements from many cultural, mythological, literary, and religious traditions—e.g. Greco-Roman, Egyptian, Celtic, Gnostic, Hermetic, etc.—not just Christianity." In other words, she is all over the symbolist map, using elements taken from Christianity, occultism, pagan lore, mythology, humanism, and "pop psychology."[32]

Nothing suggests that these non-Christian elements should be either dismissed or painstakingly re-interpreted just so Harry Potter can be considered "Christian." Even if at the end of the series Harry were to vanquish Voldemort by dying and rising again in three days to become Hogwarts's headmaster, it still would not mean that Rowling is a Christian seeking to veil the gospel in her fantasy. It would just mean that she had borrowed yet another popular myth found in many cultures; namely, the dying and rising savior story—the one that C.S. Lewis said was the only myth to become fact.

Not Another Inkling

In truth, the actual key to rightly interpreting Harry Potter as either Christian or non-Christian has little to do with what Rowling has said in her books. The symbolism, as we have seen, is far too broad to presume an exclusively Christian meaning.

More important is what Rowling has said about her spirituality. Is she writing as a Christian? Has she expressed "Christian" intentions? Does her faith come into play?

This raises the most serious obstacle to the Harry-Potter-is-really-Christian theory. Any true Christian who is writing a veiled gospel story would have to be a fairly solid believer—someone who publicly professes faith in Jesus Christ as Lord and Savior (for example, Lewis and Tolkien).

The importance of a profession of faith for any "Christian" writer cannot be overstated, because an author always writes from within his or her own paradigm (or worldview). Harry-Potter-is-really-Christian advocates make it a point to stress that Rowling "is a Christian (Church of Scotland)," and that her books undeniably express "the traditionalist background and philosophy she shares with C.S. Lewis and J.R.R. Tolkien."[33] But what do we really know about Rowling's faith?

Has Rowling ever acknowledged Jesus as her personal Lord and Savior in any interviews or writings (as Lewis and Tolkien did, many times)? No. Has she ever made particularly favorable comments about "the church" in general (either her own or all of Christendom)? Not really. Has she ever declared an abiding trust in the Bible? Hardly.

In her books, for instance, Rowling has only made a few church-related or religious allusions—none inspiring. First, there is the Hogwarts Death Day party for ghosts, which is attended by a group of deceased "gloomy nuns." Second, the word *transfiguration* (used by Christians for Jesus' partial unveiling of his glory to his disciples) is used comically in Harry Potter for magically turning one object into another. Third, a reference to the founding of Hogwarts mentions "an age when magic was feared by common people, and witches and wizards suffered much persecution [the medieval witch hunts]," and elsewhere we have Harry writing an

essay titled "Witch Burning in the Fourteenth Century Was Completely Pointless—Discuss."[34]

Finally, and most interestingly, we have Nicholas Flamel, a pivotal hero in Sorcerer's Stone. He is introduced via a book the schoolchildren are reading, which was written in the 666th year of his life—the number of the anti-Christ (or "Beast") of Revelation 13:18. This character supposedly gained eternal life by creating the Sorcerer's Stone.[35]

Confessions of Faith?

As for Rowling's interview responses, they also leave much to be desired. When asked, for example, whether she believed in "prophecies in real life" (something basic to biblical predictions about the nation of Israel, Jesus' first advent, and his second coming), she answered, "No, I don't."[36]

Moreover, Rowling has never detailed her concept of God, view of Christ, understanding of salvation, or definition of "Christian." I could find no public references by her to "Jesus Christ"—except once when she used it as an emotional exclamation that most Christians would see as taking the Lord's name in vain (see note 37).[37]

Her only remark of any theological import has been, "I do believe in God. But there's no pleasing some people." She made a similar comment on Dateline NBC after being asked, "I'm just curious about your belief system—God, heaven?" Rowling simply replied, "Well, I do believe in God."[38] But she ignored the issue of "heaven" altogether, choosing instead to let the interview go in another direction.

Her vague remarks about "God" are significant because in England, although "many Britons will profess a belief in God, not so many of them would label themselves 'Christian' (which

implies active and regular attendance at church services)."[39] This could be true of Rowling who, when asked in an interview whether she was a "churchgoer," superficially answered, "Well, I go to more than weddings and christenings." She remained quite reserved in supporting the "church," saying, "I have some problems with conventional organized religion. Some problems. But, but, yes, it's a place I would go to in a time of trouble. It probably is a place I would go to in a time of trouble." The interviewer then asked, "But the institutional side of it, you know, the rules?" She replied, "I have certain problems with some aspects of that. Yes I do."[40]

But perhaps even more relevant are Rowling's ongoing endorsements of another author who is an outspokenly hostile critic of Christianity and religion: Philip Pullman (see chapters 1 and 6). Rowling, in fact, agrees with Pullman that "in the Narnia books the children are never allowed to grow up, even though they are growing older."[41]

As far back as 1999, during a child-packed appearance in Washington, DC, she recommended for nine-year-olds "anything by Phillip Pullman." Then, in July 2000, she told the BBC that Pullman was "wonderful." She also suggested in late 2000 that reading Pullman's books would be a good way for her fans to occupy their spare time.[42]

One week later, she declared, "Philip Pullman is a writer I very much admire. I think he can write most adult authors off the page....I think he's amazing." And more recently, in 2003, she commented, "I think he's wonderful. Phillip Pullman is a fantastic writer." This remark was made at "Royal Albert Hall, London, with 4,500 children in the hall and millions more online,"[43] according to her interviewer.

Recommending Philip Pullman is an odd thing for a "Christian" to do, especially one whose opinions and suggestions

can so powerfully influence children. How many kids have taken Rowling's advice and are now enjoying the anti-God, atheistic, anti-church novels of Pullman?

Rowling in Magick

"After she began writing the Potter books, Rowling researched wizardry more thoroughly." In fact, she herself has said, "Through reading I know a ridiculous amount about magic. Some of the spells in my books are ones people have genuinely believed in."[44]

Rowling has indeed done her homework, as anyone can see from her deft presentation of occult information. She displays a highly developed, vast, and intricate knowledge of occultism, its history, and nuances. (Some of it is not even commonly known, except by occultists and scholars of religion and occultism.)

The author has half-jokingly noted that she possesses an "abnormal amount" of knowledge about magick,[45] so much so that the accuracy of her books has caused many real Wiccans to conclude that she is a witch, or at least a sympathetic observer of the occult.[46] During a July 2000 interview, for instance, she said Wiccans feel her books clearly show she is "wholeheartedly on their side." She also has noted, "Practicing wiccans think I'm also a witch."[47]

It seems obvious that, rather than springing from any "Christian" roots, Harry Potter has grown from the occult-enriched soil of Rowling's fertile imagination. Without reservation she has talked about her lifelong, hobbylike fascination with "magic, wizards, and mystical stuff," admitting that she has "always been interested" in it.[48]

Although Rowling does not "believe" in witchcraft, she has repeatedly expressed sympathy for some aspects of occult and

magick. For example, she feels the number seven is "a magical number, a mystical number."[49] This is one reason why she decided to write seven Harry Potter books. Her notion about "7" is a fairly common belief found throughout the occult world. Interestingly, one promoter of "7" as a vehicle of power and magic was the occultist Helena Blavatsky (see page 127)—alluded to in the Potter series in anagram form.

Also notable is a 1999 comment by Rowling: "The Scholastic [book] cover looks the most like the way I had fantasized. It looks like a spell book because of the colors and the style of illustrations."[50] This highlights Rowling's deep knowledge and appreciation of occultism. She is comparing the appearance of her fantasy volume to a common piece of witchcraft paraphernalia: a spell book, also known as a *grimoire*.

Grimoires, which take many forms, are books containing instruction on divination, spiritism, and magick. A personalized grimoire (one holding private thoughts, magickal experiences, dreams, divination experiments) is often called a spell book because it usually contains spells. Why would Rowling be overjoyed that her books resemble a real-world occult object? Such things certainly will not direct children to Christ or the Bible— or any kind of Christian imagery.

Tolkien vs. Rowling vs. Lewis

J.R.R. Tolkien and C.S. Lewis were bold Christians who held a deep and abiding faith in Jesus, the Bible, God, and the church. Their spiritual convictions fill every nook and cranny of their fiction, in which the spiritual references and allusions to Christianity are both blatant (Lewis) and subtle (Tolkien *and* Lewis).

Baylor University professor of theology Ralph Wood has said of The Lord of the Rings, "The Gospel resounds in its

depths....Tolkien's world is thoroughly theocentric. It is inescapably God-centered." And of the Chronicles, Wood notes, "If in reading *The Lion, the Witch, and the Wardrobe*...we fail to see that Aslan is a Christ-figure, we have missed the real point of the book."[51]

Everyone knows that The Chronicles of Narnia and The Lord of the Rings express their authors' Christian faith (although not in strict allegory) because both Lewis and Tolkien 1) admitted as much,[52] and 2) used symbols and allusions that, given their specific fantasy context, cannot be interpreted otherwise.

Tolkien "was a devout Catholic who infused his work with profound Christian convictions." Lewis proclaimed his faith even more boldly. A *Field Guide to Narnia* explains that his "symbolic world of Narnia, even though fictional, points to the real....Lewis guides us, through the Narnia stories, in seeing our world with a thoroughly Christian understanding. His invented world of Narnia also illuminates what is revealed of God in the natural order. It speaks of God, Christ (in Aslan) and nature."[53]

Next to Tolkien

Joseph Pearce, author of *Tolkien: Man and Myth*, notes that "Tolkien has no time for the amoral relativism that is so prevalent in much of what passes as modern entertainment."[54] Herein lie just some of the many deep differences between Tolkien's Frodo Baggins and Rowling's Harry Potter. Frodo defeats evil by fidelity to truth, integrity, and resisting magic; Harry defeats evil via deception, rule-breaking, and use of the same magic ("power") employed by evil.

In Rowling's world, Harry and his friends use some of the very same tactics employed by Voldemort and his Death Eaters, even down to the same spells they cast. In Tolkien's world, if Frodo or

Sam or Aragorn had acted in the same way as Harry Potter and his friends, the results would have been disastrous for Middle-earth!

Tolkien, unlike Rowling, shows that evil *cannot* be defeated by use of power shared by evil or by wrongdoing. The Lord of the Rings demonstrates that conquering evil depends *primarily* on humility, courage, love, and self-sacrifice (in other words, human virtues). Brian M. Carney, journalist for the European *Wall Street Journal*, described the chasm separating Tolkien and Rowling:

> Harry is good because he's nice, and we can't help sympathizing with him, since Voldemort killed his parents and all. This is very straightforward stuff, and there's little to argue with in it. But there's also little to argue for. Tolkien delves deeper....In short, Tolkien is doubtful of man's ability to resist the temptation of absolute power. That is one of the great themes of the book. Thus Tolkien's ring is most dangerous to its wisest and most powerful characters—princes and wizards who can be made to believe that they will wield absolute power benevolently....Even Frodo, the hobbit ring-bearer in Tolkien's tale, is not immune to the temptation to use the ring, and when the moment comes for him to destroy it, he cannot bring himself to cast it away. This kind of moral complexity is simply absent from Ms. Rowling's books....
>
> In Tolkien's world the temptation of evil is one that all, or nearly all, of his characters must confront....[The Lord of the Rings] presents a serious rebuttal to the idea that good ends justify using evil means....It is time to shake off our moral complacency. "Harry Potter" will not help. For all its charms, it comes close to moral fatuousness by reducing good

and evil to naughty and nice. Tolkien did much more—showing the ethical challenges we all face, as individuals and as nations.[55]

The Lord of the Rings also presents magic as a seductive and dangerous force that does not rightly belong to humans (or hobbits). In Rowling's world, however, wizards are human, and their powers are tapped and increased via practices that have real-world occult parallels. This contrast grows even starker when one considers how Tolkien's magic bears hardly any resemblance to actual occult practices in our world.

So while a fan of Rowling's work could easily emulate the occult rituals pictured in her series, a reader of Tolkien's books would be hard-pressed to copy anything within them. Therefore, it is not inconsistent to view his work as acceptable while at the same time rejecting Harry Potter (see note 56).[56]

Compared to Lewis

Lewis, like Tolkien, depicts things such as magic, power, and morality in a biblically sound way. For instance, Lewis presents power/magic not as a single force that is good or evil depending only on who uses it and how they use it. He shows that rightness or wrongness of any "power" (or magic) is grounded in the authority—legitimate or illegitimate—from whom that power/magic flows.

In Narnia, good power/magic comes from Aslan because he has authority to exercise control over all things (as their Creator). Bad power comes from anyone else (for example, the White Witch), because they are using power/magic by usurping the rightful authority. In Harry Potter, however, all power is the same power.

Closely linked to Lewis's presentation of power/magic is his solution to evil. The good characters in the Chronicles defeat evil not by learning witchcraft, but by becoming servants of the ultimate good authority: Aslan. But as previously mentioned, the "good" characters in Harry Potter just use the same spells used by the enemy. In Rowling's world, evil and good are even trained at the same school.

It should also be noted that Rowling's fantasy is utterly dependent on magic(k). But magic in the Chronicles appears quite sparingly and in a highly stylized manner that disconnects it from the real world. In fact, when magick does invade the real world in Lewis's stories, it is a dark and destructive force.[57]

Harry Potter, however, depicts magickal arts as things that any child can access by way of a library, a bookstore, or the Internet. This is a major distinction, as one newspaper columnist observed: "Lewisian magic seems a bit pale and remote compared to Rowling's; it is far easier to imagine a Harry Potter fan thinking: 'Wow, that sounds like fun! If only I could find a way to...' "[58]

Another area where Rowling's aims are shown to be far lower than Lewis's is in the ultimate meaning of their books. According to award-winning journalist Alan Cochrum, the Potter books seem to have no grander purpose than to "provide a rollicking good time."[59] And to obtain this grand payoff, Rowling offers an endless stream of crass jokes, violent antics, and just about every other distasteful ploy used by today's R-rated films and "Mature" computer/video games:

> Rowling's voice speaks to children, rather than at them. They thus encounter the chicken-blood-and-brandy diet of baby dragons, vomit-flavored candy, and (mildly) off-color jokes, along with occasional drunkenness and violence.[60]

Harry Potter, of course, does indeed contain the marks of a clever mind: howling letters, a sport played on flying brooms, moving staircases, and demonic entities that suck out one's soul. But there is more (or perhaps less) to the books:

> Charming details are mixed with the repulsive at every turn. Ron seeks to cast a spell that rebounds on himself, making him vomit slimy slugs; the ghost of a little girl lives in a toilet; excremental references are not uncommon; urination is no longer an off-limits subject; rudeness between students is routine behavior. In volume four especially these trends are much in evidence, along with the added spice of sexuality inferred in references to "private parts" and students pairing off and "going into the bushes.[61]

Rowling's low-brow approach to entertainment is plain to see. Her characters, both good and bad, spout profanities (either explicitly or implicitly).[62] During a sporting event we see an unruly throng of leprechauns flying into the air in order to form a giant one-fingered salute to an opposing team. A salamander is blown up with a firecracker.[63]

References to "boogers" are plentiful. Hockey is played with the head of a decapitated ghost. Students squeeze yellowish-green "pus" out of magical *bubotuber* plants. And, as if unable to resist, Rowling has Ron Weasley in his astrology class saying to a girl, "Can I have a look at Uranus too?"[64]

Another Message Entirely

In a word, the spirituality, personal morals, and bold testimony of Lewis and Tolkien sharply divide their works from the Potter books. Unlike Rowling, the other two authors demonstrated in

various interviews, as well as in their books, that their main goal was to communicate the Christian gospel to the world in both veiled and unveiled ways.

Rowling, however, has merely tapped into the less admirable aspects of the human soul and psyche. Sometimes this means appealing to even the most destructive traits in us. Revenge is a good example. It is practically exalted in the books.

Harry, for instance, is incessantly pitted against his cousin Dudley, a rotten-to-the-core brat who torments our boy-wizard hero. How does Rowling handle the scenario? During a 1999 interview she revealed that Harry "wants to get back at Dudley. He's a human boy, and we the readers want him to get back at Dudley. And, in the long term, trust me, he will." Revenge, sadly, is something Rowling seems to relish. During one appearance at a K through 12 school, she told the many children in attendance, "The great thing about becoming a writer is you can get revenge on everyone."[65]

This attitude is presented beautifully in Harry Potter, where Hagrid performs an illegal spell to give Dudley a painful pig's tail. But this is not even done because Dudley has done something to Hagrid. It is done to punish Mr. Dursely for insulting Dumbledore. Revenge is taken on Dudley to more gravely hurt the father.[66]

Equally revealing is a scene where Harry finds a wizarding book titled Curses and Countercurses: Bewitch Your Friends and Befuddle Your Enemies with the Latest Revenges. Harry tells Hagrid he is looking for a way to curse Dudley. But rather than seeking to show Harry a better way, Hagrid says, "I'm not sayin' that's not a good idea, but yer not to use magic in the Muggle world except in very special circumstances."[67]

This is vintage J.K. Rowling, as is the scene where Ron expresses delight over Professor Snape's limp from an injury, saying, "I hope it's really hurting him." And then there is the

scene in which Harry uses an invisibility cloak to physically assault rival classmates who have been taunting him.[68]

Such a juvenile and patently negative approach to interpersonal conflict merely reflects what Rowling has expressed as her own mind-set, which she shared with millions of children during an online chat. She said if she could be a real witch for just one day, she would fly around "and probably get revenge on a few people."[69]

Does this sound like Tolkien? Does it reflect Lewis? Revenge is not a factor in The Lord of the Rings, where Frodo shows nothing but kindness and love to the evil and dangerous Gollum. And revenge finds no home in the hearts and minds of Aslan and his followers. Both Tolkien and Lewis impart lessons that are immeasurably deeper than "Isn't it fun to get revenge?" For these two men, morality and integrity were "dealt with as important and significant concerns."[70]

Tolkien illustrates right and wrong (good and evil) not only through the choices his characters make, but also how those choices affect others. He raises issues involving the consequences of disobedience, the merits of self-sacrifice, the detrimental effects of sin (pride, greed, lust), and the need to fulfill one's responsibilities for the benefit of others, even at one's own risk.

And the kind of morality lessons Lewis seeks to put across to readers can best be seen in the eventual results of Edmund's disobedience—the sacrificial death of Aslan (see chapter 6). Ultimately, the once malicious and traitorous Edmund is transformed into Narnia's King Edmund the Just. Christ, as a true Lion King, is exalted, and Lewis's story does indeed prepare readers for the gospel.

Like Night and Day

The same cannot be said about Rowling. The questions are simple, Do her books primarily advance the same kind of

Christian themes fleshed out by Tolkien and Lewis? Does she deal so expertly and directly with God, divine sovereignty, human virtue, Christ, biblical values, Christian morality and ethics, integrity, and faithfulness?

No—according to Rowling herself, who said that Harry Potter is primarily "about the power of the imagination. What Harry is learning to do is to develop his full potential." That's about it. She adds, "What I'm saying is that children have power and can use it, which may in itself be more threatening to some people than the idea that they would actually learn spells from my book."[71]

Rowling has explained her inspiration, purpose, and message again and again, declaring that the magick in Harry Potter and its "good vs. evil" plot is just a vehicle for her overarching thesis: Children have power that they need to find, hone, and use. Since the release of her first book, she has been telling everyone this is the central theme of her fantasy (see note 72 for explanations).[72]

Giving young readers a vicarious sensation of empowerment over adults is what Harry Potter is all about. And by guiding her little fans along such a route, Rowling hopes to enable them to have enough courage to step out on their own and discover their own notions of right and wrong.

Secular Potter supporters have made similar observations about what the books communicate. In his "Wild About Harry (Potter)" article, Lawrence University history professor Edmund Kern pointed out that Harry is "governed by rules of his own making."[73] Kern—who teaches courses entitled Religion, Magic, and Witchcraft in Early Modern Europe—thinks this is a fabulous approach.

So, too, does James Morone (political science professor, Brown University), who glowingly wrote in *The American Prospect* that the children in Harry Potter "make their own choices

whether or not the adults approve."[74] Morone, a Harry Potter fan, adds the following observations:

> Harry always does precisely whatever the adults warn him not to do....He and his friends flout every rule— yet in the end, they save the day. The books cheerfully celebrate a kind of children's chaos....The series' manifesto might be "Hey, you can't respect every regulation." Harry's classmate Hermione "had become a bit more relaxed about breaking the rules," writes Rowling near the end of *Sorcerer's Stone*, "and she was much nicer for it."...
>
> Forget punishment. These kids break the rules, save the day, and get rewarded for bravery....The adults misbehave right alongside the kids.[75]

These messages and themes are not C.S. Lewis. They are not J.R.R. Tolkien. And they are certainly not Christian. So is Rowling really trying to do what Tolkien and Lewis did? She answered this question herself when she said, "I've read both of them—both of them were geniuses, I'm immensely flattered to be compared to them, but I think I'm doing something slightly different."[76]

With direct reference to Tolkien's trilogy, she noted, "I think—setting aside the obvious fact that we both use myth and legend—that the similarities are fairly superficial." As for Lewis's Narnian tales, she commented, "Really, C.S. Lewis had very different objectives to mine. When I write, I don't intend to make a point or teach philosophy of life."[77]

Rowling is not doing with her works what Tolkien and Lewis did with their works, nor is her inspiration coming from the same creative reservoir into which Tolkien and Lewis dipped their pens. The other two authors received their impetus from the

depths of the Christian faith they unreservedly shared during interviews and passionately expressed through their lives. They knew, and told others, that their works were Christian in content and ultimate meaning. Rowling, however, has expressed to the world completely different messages—and none of them involve Christ.

Toil and Trouble

In 2000, USA Today noted that thanks to the Potter series, a bespectacled, orphaned son of a murdered witch and wizard has become "the soul mate of millions of children around the world." Also significant are the findings of a New York research group: "Half of all Harry Potter readers are over age 35 and a quarter are over 55. That leaves the remaining 25% being the children that we all think dominate the target market."[78]

This should give pause to anyone making the often heard argument that Harry Potter has reinvigorated children's reading habits. In fact, it is quite possible that Harry Potter has not affected children's reading habits very much at all. How is this possible? Apparently, despite the hundreds of millions of Harry Potter books that have been purchased, overall book sales actually *plunged* in 2003.

And the market is not growing. Six years after Harry Potter's initial installment, most people (including children) are simply not reading any more than they did before it came out. Even Barbara Marcus of Scholastic Children's Book Group (the U.S. publisher of Harry Potter) said that although everyone thought the series was going to radically change the reading habits of children, it's happened only "to a small degree, but not to the level we've hoped."[79]

So what are kids reading? Mostly Harry Potter—over and over and over. It is not uncommon to hear stories of children reading the same Potter books dozens of times, but virtually nothing else (though this does not apply to every child). And sadly, the Potter movies may ultimately discourage some children from further reading if they become overconsumed with the fantasy's high-tech silver-screen images.

Media literacy expert and communications professor Diane Penrod warns that "it is entirely plausible that for many youngsters a Harry Potter movie filled with incredible computer-generated graphics of fantastic special effects will be far more entertaining and impressive than reading the series."[80]

For Christians, this is all very troubling because of how the movies and books depict occultism (small-"w" witchcraft), unbiblical values, and unethical and immoral behavior most attractively—all beneath a deceptively whimsical mask. For non-Christians, Harry Potter presents a problem only to those parents concerned about their child either becoming curious about occultism or emulating the bad habits of the story's "good" characters (drunkenness, lying, profanity).

In the end, it is the responsibility of every parent to safeguard the hearts, minds, and souls of their children. Such a responsibility, of course, goes far beyond just the books they read. It extends to the movies and the TV shows they watch. We'll take an in-depth look at these forms of entertainment in chapters 10 and 11.

10

Marketers
and Moneymakers

Every day, we're bombarded with information and images from a wide variety of media, including television, radio, newspapers, magazines, books, and the Internet.[1]

—"An Introduction to Media Literacy"
Team Media Literacy

Kids are no longer kids. They are little gold mines. In 2004 teenagers spent $169 billion.[2] Product marketers, PR firms, and global merchandisers love them. But teens are not the only ones now categorized as "consumers" by big corporations. Pre-schoolers to pre-teens now draw the attention of conglomerate executives, even more since 1998 when research by the University of Georgia disclosed that U.S. children aged 4 to 12 were spending up to $4.1 billion a year and saving $500 million in their piggy banks.[3]

Today, children and teens actually make up a more important buying sector than adults. They represent *four* consumer groups:

1. primary buyers

2. buyers who, through peer pressure, influence other buyers (that is to say, their friends)

181

3. buyers who, through "pester-power,"[4] get their parents to lay down big money

4. future buyers

Advertisers now routinely hire researchers and child psychologists to provide in-depth information on child development, emotions, and social needs: "Using research that analyzes children's behaviour, fantasy lives, art work, even their dreams, companies are able to craft sophisticated marketing strategies to reach young people."[5]

Anyone need only look at the ongoing Harry Potter phenomenon. It remains a textbook example of how the tentacles of big corporations, through the power of the media, can create a buying frenzy that is unstoppable as well as inescapable. And yet in the end everyone is left thinking it all came about because of the greatness of the product itself or the uninfluenced free-will choices of consumers.

Creativity Loves Publicity

The multibillion-dollar Harry Potter industry began coalescing in June 1997, when the English publisher Bloomsbury released *Harry Potter and the Philosopher's Stone* in the UK. The publicity machine at Bloomsbury ("famous for its public relations skills"[6]) simultaneously kicked into high gear via reporter Anne Johnstone of *The Glasgow Herald*. (Johnstone had earlier been sent a manuscript of Rowling's book and adored it.)[7]

The Scottish newspaper ran a heart-rending story about Rowling (who is also Scottish), describing her as a penniless "lone mum." Johnstone explained how the new author "landed in Edinburgh with a baby under one arm and a dog-eared manuscript

under the other. Apart from the proverbial battered suitcase, she owned nothing else."[8]

Days later, the *Sunday Times* of London ran an almost identical story about Rowling—a poor, "unemployed single mother" whose dream of having a book published had been realized. But this version hinted at unnamed sources that had said a U.S. publisher was seeking publishing rights, offering amounts possibly "as high as $500,000"[9] (an unrealistically high amount). A media buzz had started.

These stories paved the adult marketing road for Rowling, while the marketing path for kids was smoothed by Bloomsbury's decision to hide their new author's gender by use of "J.K." instead of Joanne: "The use of the author's initials instead of her full name was a marketing ploy designed to make her work acceptable to boys, who actively choose not to read books by women."[10]

But an even better use of publicity came during the book's first week of release, when Scholastic Books in the United States acquired the publishing rights to Rowling's fantasy for an impressive $100,000. Newspapers in England and Scotland ran stories almost back-to-back about the new UK author who had finally hit the big time (even though the initial printing was only 1000 copies).

From Britain to America

Thus began a major PR campaign to drive sales. Rowling's personal rags-to-riches journey sounded even more thrilling than the tale told in her books. As she herself said, "It was a Cinderella story for the press; broke, divorced mother writes in cafés while her daughter naps beside her, and finally strikes it lucky."[11]

As Christmas approached, Bloomsbury secured for Rowling an appearance on *Blue Peter*—"the BBC's most prestigious children's programme to an audience averaging around 4 million viewers."

This show, more than anything else in those early days, "created the word of mouth and promoted the pester-power that by Christmas 1997 had the book soaring up the bestseller lists."[12]

But nothing was happening in America—no newspaper stories, no TV coverage, no magazine articles. Even back in Britain, as of November 1997, Rowling's book had sold only about 30,000 in the United Kingdom. The UK press, however, kept churning out human-interest articles on Rowling.

The same inspiring tale hit newsstands again and again, "all captioned along the lines of 'penniless single mother Joanne Rowling.'" This was the best advertising she could have received. The UK was captivated by articles like "From the Dole [Welfare] to Hollywood" and "Coffee in One Hand, Baby in Another—A Recipe for Success."[13]

However, Rowling still maintains "there was no advertising for the books, but the books continually climbed the charts. She says the children were the ones who told each other about it." Similarly, her agent, Christopher Little, told 60 Minutes that "the demand came from nowhere but the playgrounds."[14]

America's playgrounds, however, would not see Harry until September 1998, a full month after Rowling's second book—Harry Potter and the Chamber of Secrets—had been released in England. This lag time gave Scholastic ample opportunity as a "media company"[15] to let everyone in the United States know that the greatest book to ever hit American shores was just around the corner. And the publicity worked.

U.S. kids, deprived for more than a year, were salivating for the much talked about Potter books from across the sea. Helping feed their obsession were Amazon.com, Barnesandnoble.com, and other Internet outlets that pushed the as-yet-unobtainable commodity hard. (Interestingly, the first dozen or so reviews of the novel on the American amazon.com Web site are not even

from U.S. kids. They are from English fans, dating to February 1998—another good marketing idea that came from somewhere.)

Finally, Scholastic released *Harry Potter and the Sorcerer's Stone* in America. Three months later it showed up on the *New York Times* bestseller list, in December 1998.[16] Real "Pottermania," however, did not begin till early 1999, after Scholastic used its immense influence to turn Harry Potter into a brand name.

According to the business and finance publication *Selling to Kids*, Scholastic chose to release the second Harry Potter book three months ahead of schedule (in June 1999), then "leveraged the excitement to announce September debuts for *The Prisoner of Azkaban* (Book III) and the paperback edition of Book I."[17]

Scholastic subsequently took out advertisements in the *New York Times* and *USA Today*, and booked "a major appearance for Rowling on the 'Rosie O'Donnell Show.' Those channels provided broad reach to adults who were reading the books themselves and bringing them home to kids."[18]

With the release of *Goblet of Fire* (Book IV) at midnight on July 8, 2000, "Pottermadness" gripped the world. Of course, it had been fed by a pre-release publicity blitz that "leaked" all kinds of eyebrow-raising secrets about "no advance copies, no reviews by newspapers and no sales before today. Every retailer had to sign a strict embargo agreement." The security itself "contributed to the story's mystique."[19]

Consumer-behavior expert Britt Beemer said, "There is more wizardry in the marketing of the book than there even is in the book itself." Potter's appeal, according to Beemer, stemmed "70 percent from marketing and 30 percent from content." In the words of Stephen Brown—professor of marketing research at the University of Ulster (Northern Ireland)—"The Harry Potter phenomenon has been very astutely marketed."[20]

But today's ongoing frenzy has not been generated merely by the marketing efforts of a lone publisher. Hollywood has played a major role in the hype of Harry.

Make Way for the Big Boys

As early as 1998, Warner Brothers was looking at involvement with Harry Potter, finally deciding to snatch up movie rights in late 1999.[21] Warner Brothers, of course, is only one subsidiary of the phenomenally huge conglomerate AOL Time Warner. Its corporate fingers touch virtually everyone nearly every day. And Warner Brothers used its reach to achieve one goal: make "J.K. Rowling" and "Harry Potter" household names by the release date of the first picture in November 2001.

The key was to get Rowling's books into everyone's hands as soon as possible. An article in *Jump Cut: A Review of Contemporary Media* rightly observed that Harry Potter became a fantasy that was "produced as a commodity, driven by an industry that continuously raises the stakes for a film's survival in terms of expected returns." Warner Brothers pulled out all the stops. And as the *Jump Cut* article also noted, "At this point, it is hard to separate literary success from marketing campaigns that surround the whole project."[22] What we do know is that once Warner Brothers bought the movie rights to Harry Potter, a deluge of publicity kept the boy-wizard's popularity level rising with unprecedented speed.

In addition to the innumerable points of contact with the public that were made available through Warner Brothers's sister company America Online, the production studio was able to draw publicity help from AOL Time Warner TV stations and magazines: CNN, TNT, TBS; *Time, Entertainment Weekly,* and *People.*

For example, soon after Warner Brothers picked up Harry Potter, *Time* ran a cover story titled "Wild About Harry"

(September 20, 1999). That was only the beginning. Martin Lindstrom, an expert in brand marketing, complained that by late 2001 virtually no one could escape all things Potter:

> I've been in the brand business for more than a decade, and I can't recall another brand that was so widely exposed so quickly and so intensely. Never. Not even Coca-Cola, Disney, or Microsoft has achieved such powerful visibility in the retailing environment across the globe.[23]

In other words, "by the time of the film's release, the marketing muggles had ensured that only those in a comatose state had not heard of Harry Potter.... The film attracted crowds in the first few days of its release as a result of two years of marketing." James Oakley, a professor of marketing at Purdue, remarked, "The Harry Potter story is an amazing study in marketing. They've taken a book and built an enormous franchise."[24]

For such a triumph, J.K. Rowling's books ended up winning two awards in October 2001—awards no one seemed to notice. Both were presented at the Marketing Week–Chartered Institute of Marketing Effectiveness Awards ceremony. First, the fantasy series won the "Fast-Moving Consumer Goods Award" in the "non-food and drink" category. Second, Rowling took the event's "Grand Prix Winner of Winners" trophy. All winners, according to CIM spokesperson Ray Perry, were rewarded for showing that "effective marketing creates business success."[25]

In the eyes of Rowling, Scholastic, and Warner Brothers, marketing is deadly serious business. Consider what's at stake in light of Scholastic's Form 10-K filed in May 2004 with the U.S. Securities and Exchange Commission. This filing shows that Scholastic's *"Children's Book Publishing and Distribution* segment

revenue grew by $168.7 million, primarily from higher *Harry Potter* revenues, which increased approximately $125 million, substantially due to the June 21, 2003 release of *Harry Potter and the Order of the Phoenix*."[26]

Rowling's world of wizardry has now invaded all forms of entertainment. And the marketing of it has been so complete and so successful that the ICFAI Center for Management Research included a Harry Potter "case study" in its November 2004 catalog:

> The case examines how the Harry Potter series of books led to the creation of a multi-billion dollar business for various companies...the creation, as a brand is examined in detail. The case then describes the various marketing and promotional activities taken up by Harry Potter's author and publishers in the UK and the US. Thereafter, the case examines how Warner Brothers (which acquired its worldwide licensing and movie rights), turned the brand into an immensely successful marketing property. The case also explains the reasons why Warner Brothers and JK Rowling were very protective about the brand and what precautions they took to ensure that the brand's image does not get diluted.[27]

But Rowling's fantasy tales account for only a small portion of youth entertainment. Far more influential than any single boy-wizard is the flood of images from Hollywood that children must filter through their young minds. They include depictions of occultism, raw violence, and mature sexual themes. How might these images affect kids? How are they being used to market all manner of ideas and behaviors to children? How are they being used by corporations to sell, sell, sell?

The Temptation Tube

"No parent in his or her right mind would allow a stranger to enter their household and teach their kids for 3 hours a day," says Dr. Victor C. Strasburger of the University of New Mexico's School of Medicine. "Yet that's precisely what the media do, and what they teach kids is potentially more harmful than good."[28]

Television is by far the most pervasive and invasive influence on children. Very few kids today live TV-free or even TV-limited. There are "more households with TV sets than with indoor plumbing," and two-thirds of all of these households have three or more TVs.[29] Moreover, as far back as 1999 "two-thirds (65%) of children 8 and older" had a TV in their bedroom, and by 2003 they had been joined by "a third (36%) of children six and under."[30]

What does this all mean? According to Gary Ruskin of the consumer watchdog organization Commercial Alert, children and teens "are in the crosshairs of the entertainment and advertising industries." He adds, "These industries have enlisted sophisticated psychological research techniques, the most potent devices of media influence and persuasion, and increasingly the most brazen means of delivering their commercial messages to vulnerable and impressionable children."[31]

Simply put, television is a dream come true for corporations. It is a vehicle for advertisement delivery that is unparalleled in range and effectiveness. The main targets, of course, are teens and tweens (ages 8 to 12)—and even pre-schoolers (ages 2 to 5), who actually "have difficulty distinguishing between advertising and reality in ads, and ads can distort their view of the world." As Canada's Media Awareness group has pointed out, "Young children are especially vulnerable to misleading advertising and don't begin to understand that advertisements are not always true until they're eight."[32]

One vulnerability exploited by corporations is known as the "bandwagon effect." In her article "The Trouble with Harry: A Reason for Teaching Media Literacy to Young Adults," writing and communications professor Diane Penrod explained the phenomenon in connection to Rowling's fantasy:

> If news reports, advertisements, and word-of-mouth reflect that *everyone*—or seemingly everyone—is watching, reading or buying Harry Potter, then inexperienced media consumers become easy targets for these powerful messages. Children and teens are particularly susceptible to bandwagon fallacies because their range of experiences with media messages and real life interactions are limited. The bandwagon effect is particularly successful with those who have a lack of self-esteem and want to be like others. To many young minds, if everyone is seeing the movie, purchasing the book, or buying Harryphernalia, the possibility of being left out of this consuming frenzy may play upon his or her self-worth. Without solid media literacy skills to dismantle bandwagon-messaging techniques, adolescents remain especially susceptible to feeling like the odd one out if they do not purchase the latest item or see the hottest movie or buy the latest fashion.[33]

"Today the average child watches more than 40,000 television commercials per year." It is no surprise that "advertisers spend more than $12 billon per year on advertising messages aimed at the youth market."[34] This saturation of young minds with commercials (along with product promotions presented through popular TV shows) has contributed to several problems now endemic among children and teens: eating disorders, obesity, excessive drinking and smoking, illicit drug use, even gambling.

The corporate world not only touches youth, but also molds and shapes them to accept whatever products are being pushed, whether alcohol, junk food, soft drinks, cars, condoms, or clothes. But to accomplish this goal, corporations also must portray the world for children in a certain way. Gary Ruskin of Commercial Alert also made this observation:

> Advertising doesn't just sell products, but a worldview in which products are the means and ends of life. The effects are usually what the advertisers expect and hope for. Name a problem that affects young people today, and chances are that it relates to something that ads are telling them to do.[35]

And the corporations seem to be succeeding in their efforts. According to a survey conducted by the Child Welfare League of America, "More than 55% of teens said that TV has more influence on their outlook on the world, the nation, and local events than any other medium."[36] Sadly, this has helped lead to a society full of young people whose concepts of the world are highly flawed, especially when it comes to the two most often depicted themes on TV: sex and violence.

According to a 2003 Kaiser Family Foundation survey, 38 percent of kids from 10 to 12 said their peers received "a lot" of information about sex, AIDS, alcohol, drugs, and violence from TV, movies, and other entertainment media.[37] Media influence actually won out over fathers as a source of information about such issues, and equaled the influence of mothers, teachers, and schools!

In his insightful article "Children and the Media," Dr. Victor Strasburger cited the thoughts of one concerned Federal Communications Commissioner, who asked, "There is no question

that television is a powerful teacher; the only question is, what is it teaching?"[38]

This question is not a comfortable one, given some of the programming that children are watching. Disturbing, too, is the evidence that suggests "television's influence on children and adolescents is related to how much time they spend watching television. As a result, with prolonged viewing, the world shown on television becomes the real world."[39] What is this "real world" like?

Sex in the Cities

The Nielsen ratings for the week of December 13 to 19, 2004, revealed a troubling fact about ABC's provocative show *Desperate Housewives:* It was the most popular broadcast-network TV program for kids aged 9 through 12![40] What exactly is this show about? The Parents Television Council summarizes:

> Mary Alice Young commits suicide. Mary Alice then narrates the series, introducing us to her friends:...[a] harried mother of four young children whose husband is frequently on business travel;...[a] single mother raising a young teen daughter;...[a] married woman having an affair with her seventeen-year-old gardener; ...[a] seemingly perfect wife and mother who just found out her husband wants a divorce....
>
> Sex is the biggest content problem on this series. Previous episodes have included nudity and sexual situations between Gabrielle and her teenage gardener, as well as discussions of male anatomy and sexual function.[41]

Other programs often watched by children and teens are even worse. Comedy Central's *South Park*, which airs at 8:30 PM

Central Time, features endless strings of the worst obscenities and harshly perverse scenes: for example, the December 1, 2004, episode that featured a "Whore-Off" in a county-fair setting while the entire town (including children) looked on in amazement and cheered.

Adult "cartoons" like *South Park* now pepper the TV listings of basic cable—and they air as early as 9 PM in some places (for instance, *The Ren & Stimpy Adult Party Cartoon* on Spike TV; *Drawn Together* on Comedy Central; and *Futurama* on Cartoon Network). The Cartoon Network, which airs kiddie cartoons all day, actually switches at 11 PM to a block of "mature" cartoons known as "Adult Swim." But its Web site advertises all of the cartoons together, telling Web surfers—no matter how young they may be—that the adult cartoons exist "very nearby if you have a TV set and a clock."[42]

Closer to reality are a wide variety of shows on numerous stations that depict strong sexual content as well as explicit violence. CBS, for instance, aired a shocking episode of its *Without a Trace* crime drama on November 6, 2003. The episode "crossed all lines of decency with scenes of graphic teen sex orgies." The network then re-aired it on December 31, 2004. The series is a "Nielsen-ranked Top 10 show watched by hundreds of thousands of children."[43]

And, of course, we have *Sex in the City*, which may be the most talked-about sex-based show in history. (It's now in syndication on TV.) It airs surprisingly early on TBS: 6 PM PST. The program incessantly features bawdy story lines about the sexual exploits of three New York women and how their sexual encounters affect them.

Sex in the City is only one of many popular shows watched by teens that offer high sexual content (others include *That '70s Show* and *Friends*).[44] MTV, which could well be the most popular

network for children and teens, brazenly markets sex to kids (see appendix B). The problem with such programming was expertly revealed in a study of 1792 adolescents (ages 12 through 17) by the American Academy of Pediatrics:

> Watching sex on TV influences teens to have sex. Youths who watched more sexual content were more likely to initiate intercourse and progress to more advanced noncoital sexual activities....Basically, kids with higher exposure to sex on TV were almost twice as likely than kids with lower exposure to initiate sexual intercourse.[45]

What are the chances of a child or teenager being exposed to such mature themes on TV? Surprisingly high:

> In a sample of programming from the 2001–2002 TV season, sexual content appeared in 64% of all TV programs. Those programs with sexually related material had an average of 4.4 scenes per hour....1 out of every 7 programs includes a portrayal of sexual intercourse.[46]

This saturation of TV shows with sex-related images and dialogue, say researchers, "may create the illusion that sex is more central to daily life than it truly is and may promote sexual initiation as a result."[47] In other words, rather than art imitating life, life (at least adolescent life) ends up imitating art.

According to behavioral scientist Rebecca Collins, kids do not even have to be exposed to sexual images to be influenced. "Exposure to TV that included only talk about sex was associated with the same risks as exposure to TV that depicted sexual behavior."[48] More frightening, however, is the way that television is affecting youth violence and aggression.

Violence Begets Violence

In addition to the 15,000 "sexual references and innuendoes" that children see on TV each year, they also view "10,000 acts of violence."[49] According to the American Psychiatric Association, by age 18 a U.S. youth "will have seen 16,000 simulated murders and 200,000 acts of violence."[50] This is despite the evidence from literally hundreds of studies proving beyond any doubt that seeing so much violence within an entertainment context dramatically affects the behavior of children and teens.

First, violent entertainment desensitizes youth to images and actions that should be naturally disturbing to them. It's also addictive.[51] So, in order to keep drawing children back to programming, producers must supply more graphic violence as a way of going beyond the previously set level of psychological–visual stimulation. This results in a lack of sensitivity in the real world to real violence and harm done to others.

Second, violent entertainment can affect some children and teens so significantly that they act out aggression in an unhealthy way, participate in antisocial behaviors, or both. By 2003, for instance, educators were "frequently" reporting that they had seen "kids imitating dangerous stunts and violent behaviour that they've seen on TV." This same year an extensive survey of 5700 students (grades 3 through 10) by the Canadian Teachers's Federation found that "51 per cent of Grade 7 to 10 kids said that they had personally witnessed the real life imitation of some 'violent act' from a movie or TV show."[52]

Copycat, Copycat

TV-inspired acts of violence or aggression usually fall into two main categories: 1) stunts gone awry and 2) premeditated crimes. These actions can also be broken down into two other groupings:

1) acts that *accidentally* lead to injury or death and 2) acts that *intentionally* harm or kill someone. All of it is copycat-based.

Consider the five-year-old boy who burned his mobile home down and killed his younger sister in an attempt to imitate the pyro-antics of MTV's *Beavis and Butt-head.* Three girls trying to imitate the same cartoon also ended up burning a house down.[53] And then there was the three-year-old boy who "picked up the family cat and swung it around his head like a Teenage Mutant Ninja Turtle hero wielding a weapon. When his mother tried to intervene, the boy said, 'It's just like [the turtle] Michelangelo.' "[54]

Even seemingly harmless programs like *The Tonight Show* have caused problems. Following a 1979 episode in which Johnny Carson was "hung" by a professional stuntman, the parents of 13-year-old Nicky Defilippo found their son "hanging from a noose in front of the television set, which was still on and tuned to the station" that had broadcast the show.[55]

Such accidents are common among younger children, who usually cause harm accidentally through stunts gone awry. Teens and tweens, however, can also premeditate actions and intentionally cause harm, with teens being more prone to such behavior. This difference is mostly because older kids understand that TV is unreal and must *choose* to duplicate the pain or injury they know will result from their actions (although they seem to not fully grasp its permanent nature or legal consequences). They have more understanding of what *might* happen—and in some cases, of what they deliberately *want* to happen.

But children younger than eight, according to the American Academy of Pediatrics, "cannot uniformly discriminate between 'real life' and 'fantasy/entertainment.' They quickly learn that violence is an acceptable solution to resolving even complex problems, particularly if the aggressor is the hero."[56]

Predictably, the cases involving TV-inspired aggression, dangerous stunts, or both gone wrong are numerous. Those resulting from viewing World Wrestling Federation (WWF) matches, for instance, have led not only to injuries but several deaths. A seven-year-old "killed his younger brother with a 'clothesline' move...he had seen his wrestling heroes perform on TV." A four-year-old "jumped up and down on a fifteen-month-old baby and killed him after their babysitter left to buy cigarettes. The babysitter had put on a WWF video to entertain the children while he was gone."[57]

MTV's *Jackass*, more than any other TV program, has encouraged children, teens, and youths in their early 20s to engage in all kinds of violent and destructive stunts. Many youngsters have suffered terrible injuries (severe burns, broken bones, internal injuries)[58] and even death (see note 59 for accounts)[59] by trying to repeat stunts seen on this, as well as other programs.

In January 2001, for instance, 13-year-old Jason Lind was rushed to a hospital in critical condition with severe burns. The boy was trying to mimic what he had seen on *Jackass*, which featured the ultra-hip host setting himself ablaze (while wearing a special suit). Police labeled it a "copy cat" stunt.[60]

Lind's story is only one of many. Teens and young college kids worldwide have become enamored with the show. And to make matters even worse, the program was actually made into a film titled *Jackass: The Movie*. Now, *Jackass*-like stunts are so popular that there are now dozens of non-MTV sites developed by teens dedicated to recording their own antics on home video. Consider the following:

✤ *The American Jackass*, where kids can submit home videos of dangerous stunts as "the chance to show the world the jackass you really are"[61]

❖ *CKMS Vids*, which features videotaped "*Jackass*-style stunts performed by high school students"[62]

❖ *Live Now, Die Later*, which is billed as "stupid pranks from a group of teenage boys in the UK"[63]

❖ *Original Life*, which offers "bone-breaking stunts, death-defying leaps, ridiculous pranks and general acts of misconduct and hilarity"[64]

The most alarming form of copycat behavior, however, occurs when children or teens emulate criminal activity, including deliberately harmful behaviors seen on TV. Fortunately, this is the least common type of TV-inspired violence. Still, Leonard Eron, senior research scientist at the University of Michigan, estimates that "television alone is responsible for 10% of youth violence."[65] There is an immense list of tragedies linked to kids copying what they have seen on TV.

A New Danger

There is clearly a problem presented by the current mix of TV, kids, and violence—especially in the United States. As of 2001, America had "the highest rate of youth homicide and suicide among the world's 26 richest nations." And the 2003–2004 school year in America saw 48 deaths inside schools, "more than in the past two school years combined and more than in any year in the past decade."[66]

But this scenario gets even worse in light of a growing fad among youths. They are videotaping their own crimes, effectively casting themselves as stars of their own violent productions.[67] This practice is best exemplified by the brutal and vicious attacks taped by a group of well-to-do Las Vegas teens dubbed the "311

A group of teens in Great Britain videotape their *Jackass*-like stunts and make them available for viewing on the Internet at a Web site they call "Live Now, Die Later" (www.LNDL.net). In this series, the boys set various parts of their body on fire. Other videos made available to anyone visiting their site include footage of them jumping off roofs into trees, crashing themselves into bushes using shopping carts, falling from great heights, and hitting or kicking each other as hard as they can to see the effects of such brutality. Interestingly, anyone accessing their site also is presented with a "pop-up" ad that lists the other top worldwide *Jackass*-like sites on the Internet. (Photos: Richard Abanes; permissions granted by Lee Doyle and LNDL.net Web site.)

Boyz." Not only did they nearly kill one teenager, but they did it all in hopes of making a profit:[68]

> Teens in Jacksonville, Fla., recorded themselves trashing million dollar homes. Teens in Los Angeles were laughing so hard they could barely hold the camera as they shot people with a paintball gun. And then there was the act in which one teen videotaped another as he sucker-punched a complete stranger....But in this [Las Vegas] case, the peltings were also meant for profit. Fueled by backyard wrestling tapes and reality TV, lawyers say the teens simply saw dollar signs.[69]

Clinical psychologist Ken Druck commented, "I don't know why it's a shock to us that these kids would try to find a way to turn violence into entertainment. It's all around them." Many other reasons probably exist for why teens might want to participate in such "entertainment," but a 1996 University of California study uncovered what could be a prime reinforcing factor for violence: In TV shows, "perpetrators of violent acts go unpunished 73 percent of the time....Forty-seven percent of violent situations present no harm to the victims and 58 percent depict no pain."[70]

In its position paper titled "Psychiatric Effects of Media Violence," the American Psychiatric Association explained the detrimental effect of such depictions:

> The most effective way of reducing the likelihood of young viewers imitating violent behavior is to show such behavior being punished. Ignoring consequences of violence (including the pain of victims, the victims' families, *and* the families of perpetrators) or depicting the consequences unreasonably sets in motion a destructive encoding process....The violent behaviors and attitudes thus encoded, aggression is now all the more likely in personal situations.[71]

Equally troubling is the stunning lack of parental guidance for kids in regard to TV. For instance, the previously mentioned Canadian survey (see page 195) found that nearly half of the children polled said "no household rules" existed about "which TV shows they can watch, and two-thirds report that no one dictates which video or computer games they can play, or for how long....Kids who experience little supervision of their media use are more likely to regard media violence as benign."[72]

Children cannot be trusted to always make responsible choices about TV. This is because most children "are unable to sift through the images presented in media, psychologists say, and are particularly vulnerable to the suggestions in images that are close to their own lives."[73] The result will often be copycat behavior, as child development experts have pointed out:

> Not only are images much more compelling than words to children, but youngsters' brains have not developed the capacity to weigh the potential of long-term consequences of an action, even when those consequences are spelled out....Over the last 40 years, an extensive body of research has accumulated drawing a strong connection between exposure to images of violence in media—from cartoons to music videos and video games—and aggressive, violent behavior in children and teenagers....
>
> While few psychologists say that exposure to violence in media alone will create a violent individual, most agree that when children also see violence in their home or community and have little close interaction with a parent or other adult, it increases their tendency to resort to violence themselves....Children learn by imitating what they see around them, trying things out that look interesting and adapting them to fit themselves. And that includes violence and idiotic stunts.[74]

Not even cartoons can be trusted today since they have been engulfed by a rising tide of "mature" themes, especially violence. This is undeniably true of the new Japanese *anime* cartoons that have gained popularity in America via the WB and Fox networks

and the Cartoon Network (for example, *Digimon*, *Batman Beyond*, and *Dragon Ball* Z).

These recent additions to children's programming were covered in "Violence Finds a Niche in Children's Cartoons," a 2001 *New York Times* article. Gone are the days of Wile E. Coyote crashing himself into a cliff while chasing the Road Runner, or Jerry Mouse getting the best of Tom Cat. Things are now much more realistic and sadistic:

> A pug-nosed thug kicks in an elderly storekeeper's face. Then he punches a young heroine in the eye and cracks her in the small of the back with a heavy bar stool. Her limp frame collapses to the ground as he stands over her with his gun drawn and pointed at her head. Two young boys are in a fistfight on a moving boxcar....A little girl karate-kicks another little girl so hard that she flies through the air. Her head smashes into a cement post. She is knocked cold.[75]

Such cartoons are so violent that Nickelodeon has refused to air them. " 'It's more violence for violence's sake than I've ever seen,' said Cyma Zarghami, Nickelodeon's executive vice president and general manager." They only confirm earlier studies that revealed "more children's shows than adult shows contain violence."[76]

Simply put, today's youth is violent. The younger generation is slowly, yet systematically, being desensitized to violence and trained to meet life's challenges with aggression. The result will be a more violent adult population in years to come.[77] As child

psychologist Dr. George Gerbner puts it, "The roles [young people] grow into are no longer home-made, hand-crafted, and community inspired."[78] Instead, they are developing a worldview based on television and not their own experience.

David Proval, who plays Richie Aprile on HBO's successful series *The Sopranos,* has rightly observed, "Kids are influenced by what they see on television and in films. We have a medium so well-tuned and so powerful that it is, in many ways, reality to them. They see and rely on these representations." Jim Henson, creator of The Muppets, put it most succinctly: "Television is basically teaching whether you want it to or not."[79] Exactly what is being taught and how those lessons are affecting children will be the focus of chapter 11.

11

Time for a Reality Check

We live in a media-saturated society. Young people in the United States have access to more forms of information and entertainment than any culture in the history of the world.

—DAVID CONSIDINE, PHD
Media Literacy Program,
Appalachian State University

Children often do things that leave adults speechless. Even normally level-headed children make some terrifically bad choices at times—usually in connection to something dangerous or risky. Why does this happen? Recent medical research suggests that it may be due in part to how a child's brain develops. Even the adolescent brain, as the National Institute of Mental Health has said, is "a work in progress."[1]

Brain studies have shown that children, especially adolescents, respond to situations using a part of the brain called the *amygdala*, which is where fear and simple "gut reactions" are processed. But it is another area of the brain entirely—the prefrontal cortex—that "controls such things as planning, organization, and emotional control—all those civilized behaviors that preteens and teens are famous for lacking."[2]

Unfortunately, the prefrontal cortex develops more slowly than the amygdala. This may partially explain how and why kids

thoughtlessly do risky things they *know* are wrong or dangerous. There is a kind of knowledge–response disconnect.

Parents and police are left asking in great frustration, *"What were you thinking?"* The truth is, they were not thinking at all. They were *feeling.* This may also be why almost everything an adolescent faces invariably becomes traumatic: puppy love, failure at sports, interpersonal conflicts. Apparently, teens truly do respond to life more with their hearts (amygdala) than their heads (prefrontal cortex).

Herein lies the reason why media images so powerfully affect young people. They are designed to evoke emotions. Be it a TV show, a movie, a commercial, or a video game—the objective of its images is always to make a person feel something: anger, sadness, joy, delight, fear, lust. Emotion is the goal. That's entertainment!

The problem is that children and teens can actually be shaped not only by their emotions, but also by the entertainment that pulls those emotions out of them, especially in this age of high-tech wizardry. In the 1994 book *Making Connections*, educators Renate and Geoffrey Caine argue that kids are having their entire worldview molded because they

> live in a world of vast media and technological input that entertains and influences them in both conscious and unconscious ways....[It] influences the makeup of their personalities and values, and ultimately influences how they see and interact with their world.[3]

The influence on children and teens through these entertainment forms is undeniable. Kids are feasting on not only sex and violence (see chapter 10), but also spirituality. This is a key point to remember, given the prevalence of TV occult dramas (*Medium* on NBC and *Point Pleasant* on Fox), adventures (*Buffy the Vampire Slayer*), and comedies (*Charmed* and *Sabrina: The Teenage Witch*).

Thanks to the Silver Screen

Since Hollywood's earliest days, a niche for the "horror" film has always existed. Early silent flicks like *Nosferatu* (1922) paved the way for later classics such as *Frankenstein* (1931) and *The Mummy* (1932). These pictures opened the door for not only an increasing number of scary films in the 1950s and 1960s, but also for science-fiction movies.

But such productions (especially the supernatural ones) were infrequent when counted against the total number of movies coming from Hollywood. Moreover, they were restrained in their depiction of gore, violence, and sexuality, and real-world occultism.[4] Then in 1968, everything changed with the release of Roman Polanski's Academy Award–winning *Rosemary's Baby*.

This was the first picture in America "to provide a popular illustration of occult traditions."[5] It also elevated the horror/supernatural/occult film genre to a whole new level of reality that would eventually be expertly expressed in *The Exorcist* (1973) and *The Omen* (1976). These latter movies rendered gore and real-world occult themes far more realistically than anything that had ever been seen before.

But such themes still put occultism in an ominous light. Not until the mid-1990s did another kind of film begin to emerge. In addition to the usual portrayals of occultism and witchcraft as negative (1958's *Bell, Book, and Candle* being a rare early exception), films appeared in which both themes were being cast in a positive light: *The Craft* (1996) and *Practical Magic* (1998).

Most people have dismissed such films as innocent fun, but occultists and knowledgeable observers of the religious landscape have commented on their proselytizing value. In an article on Wicca produced by the Ontario Consultants on Religious Tolerance, for instance, it was stated that *The Craft* "probably generated a great deal of interest in Wicca (a.k.a. The Craft) among teenagers."[6]

Long before this observation was ever made, *New Worlds of Mind and Spirit* (a Wiccan/neopagan publication) had already declared as much:

> *The Craft* created a surge of interest in magick, the occult, and Witchcraft. New students and interested seekers are flocking to bookstores, people are looking for or establishing covens. There is an intense interest in Wicca reminiscent of the late sixties.[7]

TV shows positively portraying occult beliefs, practices, and rituals also have enjoyed popularity. And like their big-screen counterparts, they have contributed to the current interest in occultism and witchcraft among children and teens. *The X-Files*; *Charmed*; *Sabrina: The Teenage Witch*; *Buffy the Vampire Slayer*; and other shows have all been linked to this rising fascination. Well-known Witch, Phyllis Curott comments that

> Hollywood is very sensitive to where the audience is. They're creating product that reflects what's happening at the grass roots level—they're responding to the market. They know there's an audience. And, in fact, ratings are huge. Teenage girls and young women who are a big part of this market share have found the Goddess! And that is very empowering and liberating....These shows (*Charmed, Sabrina, Buffy the Vampire Slayer* and *Practical Magic*) are showing witches as good, strong and independent young women who use their power to help people—who show them working together. All of those are steps in the right direction.[8]

A recent *New York Times* article on Wicca in America supports Curott's assertion, noting how Witchcraft is "gaining an ardent following among teenagers, mostly girls, who are in part captivated by the glossy new image of witches portrayed on television

shows and in the movies."[9] Wiccans themselves are helping out with this, according to Pat Devin, who worked as a consultant for the movie *The Craft*.

Devin—a high priestess, the Public Information Officer of Covenant of the Goddess, and an elder priestess of the Dianic Feminist Separatist Tradition—revealed that some of the magick in *The Craft* is "fairly authentic" and that she herself "created some reasonable sounding chants."[10] Interestingly, Devin wanted no "real" Wiccan deities named in the movie (for example, Hecate) because she felt it would be unsafe.

"I don't want a bunch of teenagers invoking Hecate when they don't know what they're doing," she said. "It's disrespectful and believe me if she shows up and you don't know what to do, you don't want her there." Devin also admitted that "young people getting involved with magic, with occult practices, who don't know what they're doing can and do get themselves into hot water—it happens all the time."[11]

Paranormal Perceptions

Devin's cautionary remark only echoes what some Christians have been saying for years with regard to the effect movies can have on some children. Equally worrisome are the effects that literature, including magazines, can have. For example, after the teen publication *Bliss* published a report on paganism that included information on The Pagan Federation, this UK neopagan group "received more than a thousand letters in one month."[12] The organization's spokesperson Andy Norfolk had this to say about the surge of inquiries:

> Some of the increase in interest is because some of the films and books show young glamorous women using magic to beat evil. These fantasies provide a role model for some young women who would like to

emulate their heroines and so start to find out about contemporary paganism.[13]

Kids (as well as adults) are learning about spirituality from films. Professor Cynthia Freeland, author of *The Naked and the Undead: Evil and the Appeal of Horror*, says "films about the super-natural—an ever-growing genre in Hollywood—are almost exclusively watched by teenagers and young adults."[14]

Hollywood's shift from making supernatural films primarily for mature audiences (for example, 1980's *The Shining* and 1983's *Poltergeist*) to producing graphic horror or occult-oriented works for younger crowds has taken years. But, says Lynn Clark, author of *From Angels to Aliens: Teenagers, the Media, and the Supernatural*, today it must be recognized that "whatever is distinctive about the most recent films to engage supernatural themes is their central appeal to teens and preteens."[15]

Kids now are even gaining access to older R-rated films. These movies, which are often aired during family/daylight hours on TV, run the gamut from gruesome slasher/"splatter" films (such as those in the *Friday the 13th* and *A Nightmare on Elm Street* collections) to horrifying occult-based movies like *The Exorcist*. (In fact, *The Exorcist*—one of the most shocking and visually disturbing films of all time—aired on the SciFi channel virtually uncut on Sunday, January 23, 2005, during the mid-afternoon.)

The media, at the very least, is desensitizing the public, particularly youths, to occultism; not only its horrible side, but also its more "benign" side, which is often presented as the religion known as Wicca. Of course, not every teenager is going to convert to Wicca just because of "Buffy," *The Craft*, or Harry Potter. But such forms of entertainment could play a significant role in drawing some children into the occult.

The Internet, too, helps expose children to occultism. For example, the "Yahooligans" Web site (Yahoo's "Web Guide for

Kids") includes a main "horoscope" link nestled between links for "News" and "Reference." Other Web sites that children can access go far beyond horoscopes, delving into the depths of serious hardcore occultism.

According to the general secretary of The Association of Teachers and Lecturers in England, "Youngsters can very easily visit a choice of hundreds of websites on witchcraft, Wicca magic, casting hexes and bloodletting techniques, without any adults having control as to what they read." This comment came on the heels of a year 2000 British teachers's poll of 2600 11- to 16-year-olds that found "26% were 'very' interested in the occult and another 28% 'fairly' interested."[16]

UK newspapers subsequently ran several stories on the concerns of teachers and others who were "worried that nobody is monitoring the effect this fascination with the occult is having on its teenage followers." Britain's Association of Teachers and Lecturers also called for classes geared toward warning kids about occultism, adding, "This goes beyond reading a Harry Potter story. This represents an extremely worrying trend among young people. Parents and teachers should educate children and young people about the dangers of dabbling in the occult before they become too deeply involved."[17]

Even for less susceptible viewers (stable children, mature adults, or teens who would never dabble in magick), the barrage of occult films, books, and magazines might at the very least reinforce the false notion that occultism is harmless and unworthy of any "serious moral objections."[18] But viewing the occult as so innocuous would be a mistake. So, too, would it be erroneous to think that no children will copy what they see at the movies— whether it is violence, or sexuality, or spirituality. As we have seen, even when it comes to something as tame as Harry Potter there is reason for concern.

Movie Ratings

Harry Potter, of course, should not be singled out. What holds true for Rowling's fantasy holds true for any movie. Such is to be expected—as previously shown, kids copy what they see. Surprising, however, is Hollywood's irresponsible attitude, evidenced by the fact that children's fantasy and "family" films are not the only movies being directly marketed to kids.

Movie studios have boldly pitched "Restricted" (R-rated) films to under-17 children—the very ones from whom such movies are supposed to be withheld. A 2000 U.S. Federal Trade Commission report on 44 R-rated pictures revealed that as many as 80 percent of them had been marketed to children under 17.

One studio admitted that its goal was to completely target teens and "make sure that everyone between the ages of 12 and 18 was exposed to the film." It also was discovered that "Hollywood routinely recruits tweens (some as young as nine) to evaluate its story concepts, commercials, theatrical trailers, and rough cuts for R-rated movies."[19]

Another tactic used by Hollywood to get kids hooked on more explicitly adult forms of entertainment can be seen at any nearby video–DVD store. Producers are now taking teen-oriented pictures, adding "raunchier scenes," then removing the voluntary ratings (movie ratings are strictly voluntary). These unrated versions "are released on video and DVD with 'Director's Cut' or 'Uncensored' labels."[20]

This only points to the fact that the entire movie rating system is flawed. Some movies that probably should get an R rating based on profanity, crudeness, suggested sexuality, or nudity often get a non–R rating just because they do not use a certain swear word more than one time. But other movies get an R rating just because there may be one or two scenes of violence—even though the film overall is an inspiring saga (for example, *The Last*

of the Mohicans or *Schindler's List*). Here are some things parents may not know about ratings:[21]

❖ G is not only rarely used but usually avoided by studios. It hearkens back to films such as those from the old Disney days of *Charlie, the Lonesome Cougar* (1967) or *The Sound of Music* (1965). The Internet Movie Database lists only 1428 films as G-rated.

❖ PG, which suggests parental guidance, can include some rather mature themes, profanity, and even flashes of breasts and the buttocks (for example, Franco Zeffirelli's *Romeo and Juliet,* 1968). A child of any age can purchase a ticket to a PG film and enter without a parent or guardian.

❖ PG-13 is any film that pushes the "PG" limit for sexuality, nudity, violence, profanity (including the f-word),[22] and gore. It is arguably a vague rating, with some movies being *soft* PG-13s and others being *hard* PG-13s. Children can still enter all these films unaccompanied.

❖ R, the most common rating for movies, requires a child to be accompanied by a parent or guardian. The rating indicates that the movie is "adult" in nature, but that does not necessarily mean it is bad. The rating system, as previously noted, is not fair. But generally speaking, an R-rated film (depending on its genre) could contain liberal amounts of one or more of the following: explicit sexual situations, mature themes, violence, profanity, extended nudity (including full frontal), and gore.

Unfortunately, children and young teens are regularly watching some of the most violent and sexually explicit PG-13 and R-rated films being released. And, like TV, theatrical movies have inspired

far too many copycat acts that have landed youths in jail, in the hospital, or in the cemetery (see note 23 for examples).[23]

Whether at the theater or at home on DVDs, movies also present parents with another problem. Film openings are now made into "events" that, like the Harry Potter movies, are tailor-made for selling "not only a movie, but toys, clothes, videos, record albums, computer games."[24]

This is accomplished through something called "four-walling"—a film studio saturates society with all things relating to a movie prior to that movie's release. It is all designed to make the public extraordinarily aware of a film's opening weekend— you simply cannot avoid exposure.

But such an "out there" marketing technique can also help parents identify which movies their kids might be most interested in seeing. They can in turn find out more about the film. So from a parental perspective, "four-walling" at least gives adults a kind of heads-up.

Developing Media Literacy

In conclusion, nothing in this chapter is meant to be a blanket condemnation of either marketing or television. Some commercials are hysterically funny, cute, or poignant—and certainly helpful. And there are many good TV programs. In fact, I very much enjoy TV (including numerous commercials). Few things make me happier than taking in a Monday-night football game with the guys or watching a Food Network special with my wife (not to mention those reality shows like *The Amazing Race* and the ubiquitous *Survivor*).

But to benefit from these shows and other kinds of programming, both adults and children must develop *media literacy*—

the ability to read, analyze and critically evaluate information presented in a variety of formats (television, print, radio, computers, etc.). Being media literate means that you are able to recognize the arguments and techniques used to present information or persuade an audience to accept an opinion, buy a product, or watch a program.[25]

Professor David Considine, instructor of media studies and literacy at Appalachian State University, lists five main principles that can be taught to children to help with media literacy:[26]

1. "Media Are Constructions," meaning that everything we see on TV and in the movies has been "carefully edited, selected, sequenced, and targeted." A perfect example of a "construction" would be any of the so-called reality-TV shows. They are not reality. They are *unscripted* shows that lead viewers down a planned route of entertainment by use of intense video editing and selective casting of certain types of people.

2. "Media Have Commercial Motives" is self-explanatory. Any for-profit company associated in any way with media presentation of any kind is going to have dollar signs as a main motive.

3. "Each Medium Has Its Own Language, Codes, and Conventions." In other words, the way something is produced (how it is shot with a camera, what kind of film is used, the sound levels) is crafted to elicit a response.

4. "Audiences Negotiate Meaning," or rather, people interpret things they see differently, even though the media industry targets certain groups.

5. "Media Contain Values and May Have Social Consequences," which refers to how TV programs and commercials communicate values, morals, and priorities—whether or not such things are *specifically* mentioned.

Making sure that kids understand these principles will go a long way toward ensuring their media literacy—which according to the White House's Office of National Drug Control Policy "can empower youth to be positive contributors to society, to challenge cynicism and apathy, and to serve as agents of social change."[27]

TV can be a positive thing for adults *and* children. But boundaries must be set for kids—which includes teenagers, who cannot even see TV's influence on them. A Kaiser study showed that 72 percent of kids 15 to 17 years old "believe that sexual content on TV influences the behavior of kids their age 'somewhat' (40%) or 'a lot' (32%). Just one in four (22%), however, think it influences *their own* behavior to this degree."[28]

The key is to make sure that TV is used to enhance a child's growth and to supplement other vehicles of learning and development: family interaction, outside play, reading, and school. This is an across-the-board concept applicable to all ages—except for children under two years old. In 2003 the American Academy of Pediatrics recommended that children that young not be allowed to watch television at all![29]

More questions remain about movies and books in general. And it seems that there is a never-ending list of questions concerning the whole Harry Potter controversy, fantasy in general, and related issues surrounding contemporary culture, religion, and censorship. I hope to answer in my final chapter at least some of the most common questions linked to these crucial topics.

12

Does Anyone Have a Question?

Limit your child's use of TV, movies, and video and computer games to no more than 1 or 2 hours per day. Do not let your child watch TV while doing homework.

Get into the habit of checking the content ratings and parental advisories for all media.... Watching and listening yourself are the best ways to decide which movies, shows, games, or CDs are suitable for your child.[1]

—AMERICAN ACADEMY OF PEDIATRICS

There is no end in sight to the controversies surrounding Harry Potter, fantasy, the occult, TV programs, movies, and witchcraft books. In the meantime, however, all of us can take a few steps toward finding a little personal peace of mind by eschewing emotionalism and sticking as close to the facts as possible.

This approach, unfortunately, has not been common throughout various groupings—namely, the religious, literary, and educational. Debates have raged out of control about not only witchcraft and the occult, but also religious freedom, First Amendment rights, and censorship.

Opposing viewpoints have sparked emotional arguing, mean-spirited insults, irresponsible speculations, ugly rumors, misrepresentations of fact, malicious news articles, and a significant level of disinformation. Persons on all sides of the debate have been guilty of fruitless bickering, which has produced far more heat than light.

In this closing chapter, I wish to simply answer some of the questions I have heard asked most often during the last several years. I have attempted to be as impartial and fair as possible, using straightforward reasoning and the facts as I have uncovered them through my research, some of which I have presented previously in this book. Ultimately, you the reader will have to weigh the evidence and go with what seems reasonable to you.

Harry Potter

Shouldn't everyone (including Christians) be allowed to read Harry Potter without being condemned?

Of course! No one should be condemning anyone. It would be wrong to criticize Christians for reading Harry Potter if that is what they want to do. Reading fantasy books, seeing R-rated movies, and watching adult-themed sitcoms on TV (such as *Will & Grace*) fall under the category of Christian "freedoms"—issues over which Christians are not to judge each other. Such things, in and of themselves, are not the issue.

The true issue is determining if various activities are beneficial, harmful, or neutral. Regarding Harry Potter, the issue is threefold:

1. Does Harry Potter contain positive presentations of real-world occultism?

2. Does Harry Potter glamorize unethical behavior (in addition to presenting some laudable virtues like loyalty and bravery)?

3. Does Harry Potter contain enough real-world occultism and unethical behavior to adversely affect some children?

All three of these questions, I believe, have only one valid answer: yes. The applicable Scripture, then, would be, " 'Everything is permissible for me'—but not everything is beneficial" (1 Corinthians 6:12).

Why is *Harry Potter* so popular?

Some Christians have declared that Harry Potter's success is directly due to its being a veiled "Christian" story that appeals to everyone's unconscious need for God. But this is not a reasonable claim. A variety of far more plausible explanations have been given—and none of them have anything to do with religion.

First, Harry Potter is filled with the kind of gross imagery and crass humor that juveniles find entertaining: vomit candy, pus and booger references, assorted profanities, "Uranus" jokes, and a dash of bloody violence.

Second, "Harry Potter is a classic ugly duckling story, one of the great archetypes in literature. Misfit, rejected, even abused, Harry one day finds all that changed."[2] Both kids and adults can identify with this.

Third, according to one reviewer, Harry Potter is popular "because this character has the ability to uncover the eternal child we all have buried inside. A teenager's identity crisis set amidst an epic adventure, the stories appeal to everyone who's ever wanted to beat the odds and become a hero."[3]

Fourth, corporate marketing and creation of the brand name "Harry Potter" have contributed greatly to the public's clamor for the series.

Doesn't Harry's popularity prove he is an admirable character and worthy of emulation as a "good" role model for kids?

First we must ask, Who is defining "good"? J.K. Rowling defines as "good" in her stories anyone who stands against Voldemort (or horrific evil), regardless of whatever else they may do. This is not an adequate definition or representation of "good." In fact, such a depiction of "good" actually blurs the lines between good and evil, effectively numbing young children to various forms of what might be termed lesser evil: lying, stealing, cheating, swearing, drunkenness, and disobeying authority (basically, all of the things Harry and his pals do).

Second, it is a mistake to think that our culture exalts only those icons that are good models for children. Entertainment is rife with plenty of less-than-ideal celebrities and with TV and movie characters that ridicule the values many people would consider "good": for example, Beavis and Butt-head, Freddy Krueger from the Nightmare on Elm Street series, and Johnny Knoxville from MTV's *Jackass*.

Obviously, not everything popular that the entertainment world gives us is "good." (Interestingly, many children have said that one of the reasons they like little Harry so much is because he and his friends are often so bad![4])

How can anyone condemn Harry, since he and other "good" characters show Christlike agape love (sacrificial love) through-out the books?

The Greek term *agape* when used by Christians is not just an emotional feeling for persons whom we love or for those who love

us—even if that love leads to sacrifice. Love for those who love us reflects *phileo* love (or reciprocal love).

It is *phileo* that we see in both the sacrifice of Harry's mother for her son and in Harry's life-risking deed during the Triwizards' Tournament (see *Goblet of Fire*), when he attempts to save a friend from captivity. Such deeds are admirable, to be sure. But they do not qualify as *agape*. Why? Because many people would make great sacrifices—perhaps even of their life—for a close friend or loved one. This is a natural, albeit difficult, response that both "good" *and* "evil" people demonstrate.

Agape, however, is a very different kind of love. It is the extraordinary capacity to sacrifice for enemies—or at the very least, for people with whom we have little or no relationship. The apostle Paul explains the difference: "Very rarely will anyone die for a righteous man, though for a good man someone might possibly dare to die. But God demonstrates his own love [*agape*] for us in this: While we were still sinners Christ died for us" (Romans 5:7-8).

The defrocked priest played by Gene Hackman in *The Poseidon Adventure* (1972) displayed such love when he sacrificed his life for fellow passengers whom he barely knew. Would Harry have made such an extra-sacrificial effort for Malfoy, Professor Snape, or a stranger? That is doubtful. Not once do we see Harry display any concern for characters other than those that show concern for him.[5]

Harry certainly was not showing *agape* love when he used his invisibility cloak to get back at fellow students who had been taunting him (see *Prisoner of Azkaban*). Christ taught, "If you only love those who love you, what special credit is that to you? Even evil people love those who love them. And if you only do good to those who do good to you, so what? Evil people do the same thing" (Luke 6:32-33, author's paraphrase).

The true Christian definition of *agape*, biblically speaking, is sacrificial love that does not take necessarily into account the value to oneself of the other person being loved. It reaches out to those who may have little or no particular value to oneself—even an enemy. This is not what we find in Harry Potter.

If Harry Potter is so "satanic" just because it has witches and magic, then doesn't that mean a lot of other fantasy stories and fairy tales also are "satanic" ("Hansel and Gretel," for example, and "Sleeping Beauty")?

First, the most articulate and reasonable critics of Harry Potter have never said that the novels are "satanic." The religion known as Satanism does not appear in Harry Potter, nor do the teachings of Wicca. Second, Wicca and Satanism are themselves vastly different. Third, it is the magick and occultism in Rowling's volumes that are problematic (see chapters 7 and 8). It is this *real-world* occultism that separates Harry Potter from most other fantasy works and fairy tales (see chapters 3 and 4).

Why should anyone be worried about the "magic" in Harry Potter since it is no different than the high-tech devices used in science fiction?

Actually, the magick in Harry Potter is not at all like the high-tech devices we find in science fiction—which are placed into the story for the purpose of allowing things to happen that otherwise would be impossible. The main difference is that the technology in most sci-fi stories cannot be duplicated, nor does it have anything to do with occultism. In Harry Potter, however, characters go beyond such unreal "mechanical" forms of magic by delving into real-world magick and witchcraft.

It should also be noted that, although Potter fans often say that Rowling actually uses her characters to make fun of things

like divination, such a claim is not entirely true. Consider Madame Trelawney, for instance, who is Hogwarts's divination teacher. She is indeed painted as a quirky witch, whose forte is a very "imprecise" branch of magic. At the same time, though, Trelawney accurately predicts the future during a classic episode of spirit-channeling.[6]

Hermione, too, excels at arithmancy (a form of divination). And Harry is himself a clairvoyant, who accurately predicts that a hippogriff (named Buckbeak) will survive a scheduled execution.[7]

How can the Harry Potter series be condemned for occultism when its main characters do not even contact spirits, which is what the Bible really condemns?

In reality, Harry and his friends are in constant communication with spirits. These include Binns (a Hogwarts teacher), Peeves (a poltergeist, or malevolent spirit), Moaning Myrtle (a murdered Hogwarts student), and Nearly Headless Nick (Gryffindor's resident apparition). Each student dorm, in fact, has its own house-ghost. And in *Prisoner of Azkaban*, Dumbledore uses these and countless other ghosts to send messages to the students. One also must not forget the episode with Trelawney (see previous question).

Shouldn't a critic of Harry Potter also be willing to condemn A Christmas Carol by Charles Dickens? After all, Scrooge talked to ghosts too.

This question has been posed quite often. However, such an analogy is flawed in several ways.

First, Scrooge did not seek out or maintain any relationships with, nor regularly commune with, the ghosts in *A Christmas Carol*. He also did not use them to transmit messages to others. In fact, he kept pleading with the ghost of Marley to leave! In Harry

Potter, however, spirits of the dead are consistently called upon, spoken to, welcomed as friends, and used to convey messages.

Second, and far more damaging to this argument, is the fact that the three Christmas spirits that visit Scrooge are not even spirits of the dead. They are symbolic representations (or manifestations) of Christmas time spans that come into existence yearly—that is to say, Christmas past fades into Christmas present, which in turn gives way to Christmas future. This is quite different from what is depicted in Harry Potter.

Finally, at the end of A Christmas Carol, one is left with the hinted-at possibility that Scrooge's vision was just a nightmare that, like Marley's apparition, resulted from "an undigested bit of beef, a blot of mustard, a crumb of cheese, a fragment of an underdone potato."

Isn't Hogwarts School a perfect fantasy model to show how children need the guidance of wise and competent adults in order to get through life?

Actually, the mature characters in Harry Potter— that is to say, the "good" adults, including Dumbledore—serve minor purposes and are fairly incompetent as well as oblivious to the goings-on at Hogwarts. Even favorable reviews have noted as much: "Though Rowling's child heroes are imperfect...they are usually smarter and braver than adults. Some of the nicest teachers at Hogwarts, though friendly and knowledgeable, often don't have a clue to what's going on around them. Others are weak and incompetent, or complete phonies."[8] Another reviewer writes,

> Most of the adults in these books are deeply flawed. At Hogwarts the teachers drink like fish; the gentle giant, Hagrid, positively staggers through the first three books....Professor Trelawney is a New Age flake.

Professor Snape, the potions master, is a slime. Cornelius Fudge, the minister of magic, is a dithering ass. These people constantly boss the kids around. But most of the adults are knuckleheads. The kids disobey them and, as a result, save the day. In *Prisoner of Azkaban*, for example, everyone tells Harry not to leave the school grounds. Naturally, he immediately scampers out through a forbidden passage. By the end of the book we learn that Harry's father, one of Hogwarts's great mischief makers, would have been highly disappointed if his son had never found any of the secret passages out of the castle.[9]

Obviously, the adults in Harry Potter leave much to be desired in showing children the benefits of mature guidance. Part of the story's attraction is how adults, especially parents, are not central to the action. They are taken out of the way, and this appeals to a child's desire to be away from adult control (which is a natural desire). As Judith Krug of the American Library Association has said, "There's no one always telling him [Harry] what to do, and what young person hasn't at one point said, 'Oh, if they'd only leave me alone.' Or: 'I wish that I didn't have parents.' They don't mean this in a mean way. It's just that parents get in the way."[10]

Harry Potter has sparked interest in reading among children. Isn't that a positive sign? Shouldn't the books be applauded for pulling kids away from Xbox and PS2?

Just because a child is reading does not mean that *what* they are reading is good (see chapter 1). Some material is not emotionally, psychologically, or spiritually healthy. To think otherwise leaves a door open for children to read anything regardless of content, including violent, pornographic, and racist literature.

Few persons would distribute *Playboy* to children for its humor and interesting news articles, even though quite a few adolescent boys might appreciate the gesture and be happy to "read" the magazine. The same could be said for white supremacist literature. Novelist Michael O'Brien comments,

> While it is true that the Potter books are hooking a generation on reading, I must say that this is a superficial defense of the series. Will the 100 million young fans of Harry now turn to Tolkien and Dickens and Twain? Or will they go searching for more of the thrills Rowling has whetted their appetite for? There is a lot of corrupt literature out there, well-written material that may indeed stimulate a literary habit as it speeds the degeneration of moral consciousness. A discerning literacy—the true literacy—is of very great importance in a child's formation. But literacy alone can never be enough. Is an appetite for reading fiction a higher value than a child's moral formation? Is *any* book better than no book? Would we give our children a bowl of stew in which there was a dose of poison, simply because there were also good ingredients mixed into the recipe? Of course we wouldn't.[11]

The real problem today, then, is not necessarily that kids are *not* reading, but rather, the substance of what they *are* reading.

Don't most occult experts, even Christian ones, agree that the world of wizards and spells created by Rowling is not the same as the real world of occult-type practices?

No. There exists no documentation to support the contention that a majority of "experts" on occultism believe the wizards and spells in Rowling's novels are wholly different than actual

occultism. The media has repeatedly quoted only a few so-called authorities—who, in reality, are not occult experts.

The five Christian sources regularly cited as supporters of Harry Potter are 1) John Granger, who is trained in classical languages and literature; 2) Chuck Colson, who is primarily a social commentator and an evangelist to prisoners; 3) Alan Jacobs of Wheaton College, a literature professor; 4) Connie Neal, an author specializing in the area of family and marriage; and 5) *Christianity Today*, which is a social–cultural magazine that specializes in covering events relating to the Christian community.

None of these sources are "occult experts," nor have any of them received even a basic education (either academically or ministerially) in the occult field. The same can be said for the second tier of Christian authors and speakers that are regularly quoted by Potter fans and the media: John Killinger (a Presbyterian minister) and Francis Bridger (a college principal and theologian). Many true "experts" on occultism, however, have indeed voiced concerns about Rowling's books.[12]

Why is there so much concern about Harry Potter, when it is obvious that a lot of kids reading the books are not suffering any psychological or spiritual problems, or being drawn into occultism?

First, "a lot" of kids do not represent *all* kids. Just because most children may remain unaffected by Harry Potter is no reason to completely dismiss concerns that some children might indeed be drawn into witchcraft, magick, or the occult. Second, it would take many years and numerous surveys to measure with any exactitude a correlation between Harry Potter and youth occultism. Nevertheless, there are signs that some children are gravitating toward occultism because of the books.

Isn't it a bit paranoid to think that, just because some of the good characters in Harry Potter do a few bad things, children will be affected adversely?

Fantasy, no matter how imaginative it may be, teaches some form of morality—usually one that reflects the author's views. Literature, in this way, can either reinforce or alter the moral universe in a child's mind. The problem is, many children reading Harry Potter are so young (as young as six) that they still have little or no discernment about the worldview being presented to them through the books. Hence, the images and indirect lessons of the text could sway their behavior in years to come.

Children engage in seeking lessons about life from stories far more intensely than adults. Moreover, when seeking such lessons, they do so via an indirect method: rather than pondering which traits of a character they most want to adopt, they simply decide which character in total they most want to be like.

Consequently, rather than emulating just the "good" traits of a character, they end up copying a character's entire persona—good and bad traits, mannerisms, thoughts, attitudes, and behavior. A clear delineation between good and bad, therefore, must be offered in order for children to nurture within themselves a strong moral center of being.

Censorship and Entertainment

Wouldn't it be best to just ban or destroy harmful books, movies, and TV shows altogether—maybe even burn them in a public display of protest?

No. One of the greatest things about America is its freedom. And being careful to not tread on the freedom of others is something that Christians, indeed all Americans, must keep in mind.

Blanket banning of various forms of entertainment and learning can lead to harmful attitudes and intolerance. Banning and "book-burning" can also harm intellectual growth for many people who deserve to have a full scope of entertainment and learning materials from which to choose—even if we may not agree with what they want to choose.

At the same time, book-burning, like any other form of expression, also is an American freedom. And as much as someone may disagree with this form of public self-expression, it is no worse than (perhaps not even as bad as) flag-burning. True tolerance, therefore, must include toleration—though not approval—of unpopular opinions and practices, such as book-burning and the belief that certain books should be banned. (Of course, it is quite another thing when book-burners decide that they want to impose their views on others *by force* and destroy property that does not belong to them.)

How can anyone promote censorship of books, movies, or TV programs? Isn't that just like book-burning and book-banning?

This is a terrible misperception. Censorship is not book-burning. Book-burning only becomes "censorship" when the book-burners want to burn *other people's* books. Censorship, in fact, is prevalent everywhere throughout the U.S.—not only in public schools, but also in places frequented by the general public (for example, in libraries). Society enforces numerous laws to protect children from harmful material. (In convenience stores, note the plastic-wrapped, paper-covered pornography behind signs that read, "18 Years Old—No Reading in Stores.")

Censorship is merely the way a community (or segment of it) deals with certain material that it deems inappropriate for a specific location or readership—for example, racist, pornographic, or

anti-Semitic literature. Such materials are censored with little or no adverse news coverage or public outcry. English professor Gene Edward Veith makes an astute observation about this:

> Just because the government is not allowed to exercise censorship does not mean that private citizens cannot say no to objectionable material. Yet, parents who object to their children reading certain books are accused of censorship. Retail stores that refuse to sell objectionable CDs are charged with censoring them. Conversely, that the government is not allowed to prevent certain kinds of material from being published is taken to mean that libraries, schools, and bookstores have an obligation to put it on their shelves....Private citizens are free to do things that the government is not allowed to do.[13]

In other words, censorship is just treating with caution certain materials that may be harmful to a specific segment of the populace. Nevertheless, many people decry as "censorship" any attempts by parents to have some say over the books, movies, and TV shows their children enjoy. But this is inconsistent, at best, and hypocritical at worst.

If all books, movies, and TV programs about witchcraft and the supernatural are to be off-limits, then won't that mean that at least three-quarters of all children's literature will also have to be off-limits?

Again, no moderate critic of such material wants it to be "off-limits" entirely. Instead, responsible concerned parents and youth workers are just calling for caution when it comes to putting violent and sexually explicit entertainment in the hands of children

and teens, also hoping that similar care will be taken with material presenting occultism in a way that might cause kids to become curious and start dabbling in it.

Isn't restricting the entertainment that is available to children a violation of their First Amendment rights?

No. Children already are restricted from reading and purchasing materials that state and local governments have ruled as obscene, adult, and/or inappropriate. Then, children also are prevented from engaging in activities many adults are allowed by virtue of their age and maturity: voting, smoking, drinking, and driving.

Shouldn't kids just be allowed to make their own decisions about what they want to read, watch, or play?

Not completely. With regard to certain kinds of entertainment, it is just not possible for children to always decide for themselves what is best. Being a parent means guiding, leading, teaching, and sometimes—at least until a child is closer to adulthood—making decisions about what is best for a child, even concerning forms of entertainment.

Children invariably choose bad things for themselves. Recently, for example, it was found that teen smoking and drug use has not decreased significantly, even though TV ads and commercials about the dangers of cigarettes and drugs have been airing for several years. As a further example, teens have been copying the sexual practices glamorized in their favorite TV shows (for example, *Friends*).

Are Christians saying that the only good forms of entertainment are ones that present Christian teachings and have God mentioned in them?

No. A book, movie, or TV program (or video game) cannot be judged exclusively on whether or not the work mentions God

or seeks to advocate a religious worldview. Good intentions sometimes produce very anti-Christian results, while intentions not necessarily "Christian" can sometimes produce very Christian-like results. For example, Stephen King's book *Desperation* actually has a great deal of Christian teaching in it and is quite favorable toward Christianity. It also shows the beauty of one's personal relationship to God and the power of Christian prayer over evil.

How can a fantasy image that is not real convey any harmful message?

All kinds of images can be used to convey both good and bad messages. For example, in Aesop's fable "The Hare and the Tortoise," the image of that slow and steady turtle conveys a good message that centers around the value of patient and consistent work. Obviously, the race between the turtle and the rabbit never took place. Nevertheless, the moral to the story is learned.

Other images, however, convey different messages. This is especially true in advertising. Consider the Camel Cigarettes cartoon figure of Joe Cool the camel. So many adults objected to the particular message being conveyed to young people by Joe smoking his cigarette that the image was banned from magazine ads and billboards.

Aren't children able to tell the difference between fantasy and reality well enough to know that the stories, messages, and images contained in books, movies, and TV shows are not real?

As already shown, children tend to copy what they see in the media—period. Whether kids know or don't know that something is unreal is often irrelevant. Additionally, child-development experts know that many children under eight years old have a hard time distinguishing fact from fiction.[14]

For example, Bernice Cullinan, former president of the International Reading Association, has observed that most children by second or third grade can tell what is real and what is make believe, but "those six years old and younger will certainly have more trouble making such a distinction."[15] Bestselling author Michael O'Brien makes several observations on this issue:

> It is important to note that children read fiction with a different consciousness than adults. This is something that has been overlooked by those Christian leaders who have written pro-Potter commentaries. They forget that children are in a state of formation, that their understanding of reality is being forged at every turn.[16]

The crucial point O'Brien is making is that books send certain messages that children may not be equipped to properly evaluate and judge. Regardless of their maturity level, a child will not see, read, enjoy, or reflect on a piece of literature the way an adult would. This is a crucial fact that many people seem to be forgetting in determining the potential influence of not just books, but also other entertainment forms.

Christianity, the Bible, and Occultism

Where does it say in the Bible that witchcraft is wrong?

Deuteronomy 18:10-12 is the most notable Old Testament passage wherein many occult practices are condemned. They include divination, astrology, witchcraft, charms, spells, wizardry, and necromancy (communication with spirits of the dead). Other Old Testament passages contain similar condemnations.*

---

* See 2 Kings 17:17; Leviticus 19:26; Joshua 13:22; 2 Chronicles 33:6; Isaiah 44:25; 47:13-15; Jeremiah 27:9; 29:8; Ezekiel 13:9,23,29; 22:28; Zechariah 10:2.

"Magick" also is prohibited in both the Old and New Testaments. Several words are used to describe it. One such term, *kashap*, can be found in Exodus 7:11 as well as Deuteronomy 18:10, Daniel 2:2, and Malachi 3:5. It means to practice magick or sorcery, use witchcraft, or to enchant. *Kashap* in its feminine form appears in Exodus 22:18. This is the well-known verse in which God tells Israel that the penalty for being a witch is execution. Obviously, practicing magick/sorcery/witchcraft must be an extremely profane activity in the eyes of the Judeo-Christian God (see also 2 Chronicles 33:6).

Keshep, which is the corresponding noun form of the verb *kashap*, is another general term used for magick. It means magick or magical arts, sorcery or sorceries, soothsayer, spell, or witchcraft. It is sternly condemned in several biblical passages (2 Kings 9:22; Isaiah 47:9,12; Micah 5:12). Consider God's intense displeasure over *keshep* that is especially apparent in the condemnation of Nineveh in Nahum 3:4-7:

> Because of the multitude of the whoredoms of the well-favoured harlot, the mistress of witchcrafts [*keshep*], that selleth nations through her whoredoms, and families through her witchcrafts [*keshep*]...I am against thee....I will show the nations thy nakedness, and the kingdoms thy shame. And I will cast abominable filth upon thee, and make thee vile, and will set thee as a gazingstock [a spectacle]. And it shall come to pass that all they that look upon thee shall flee from thee, and say, "Nineveh is laid waste" (KJV).

There is also a strong emphasis against magick in the New Testament. Acts 8:9-24 speaks of Simon the sorcerer, or magician, who astonished the people of Samaria with his magickal arts. Although he pretended to be a convert to Christianity, the

biblical account ends with him offering the apostles money for the secret of their power—and Peter rebuking him for still being bound in his sins (verse 23). There also is Acts 19:19, which describes how Ephesian converts to Christianity gathered together and burned all of their books relating to magick.

Another passage that is relevant is Galatians 5:20, which puts magick/witchcraft alongside hatred, strife, and murder. Similarly, Revelation 9:20-21 and 18:23 describe magick/sorcery as harmful. Clearly, the art of magick—seeking to cause change in accordance with one's own will through ceremonies, rites, rituals, spells, witchcraft, or charms—is resoundingly condemned by the Bible.

Isn't it true that the word for witch in the Bible is "poisoner" of the body or mind, which would mean that the Bible is not condemning real witchcraft as people know it today?

In order to dismiss Christian concerns about witchcraft, Wiccans and other occultists (as well as the media) have often repeated a piece of misinformation that has become extremely popular. According to their argument, the word translated as *witch* in Exodus 22:18 ("Thou shalt not suffer a witch to live") actually should be translated "poisoner" (either of the body or mind). Wiccans agree that it is understandable why the Israelites would not want poisoners among them, but since witches are not poisoners, then the Bible really does not condemn witches.

Well-known witch Doreen Valiente, for instance, stated in her book *An ABC of Witchcraft* that Exodus 22:18 does not "refer to witchcraft at all." She added, "The word translated as 'witch' is the Hebrew *chasaph*, which means a poisoner. In the Latin version of the Bible called the Septuagint, this word is given as *veneficus*, which also means a poisoner."[17] Such an assertion, however, is a prime example of how people can make utterly false statements, yet have them widely repeated and believed.

First, *kashap* does not mean "poisoner." According to *The New International Dictionary of the Bible*, the word means "to practice sorcery." This is confirmed by countless language references, including *The New Brown-Driver-Briggs-Gesenius Hebrew and English Lexicon* and *The International Standard Bible Encyclopedia.*[18]

Second, contrary to Valiente, the Latin version of the Bible is not the Septuagint. The Septuagint is the Greek translation of only the Old Testament, and the word used in it for *witch* in Exodus 18:22 is *pharmakos*, not *veneficus* (which is a Latin word).

Third, the Latin version of the Bible is called the Vulgate (translated by Jerome about AD 383 to 405). And even it does not use the word *veneficus*, but rather, the word *maleficus*, which means a practitioner of magick/sorcery.

A witch, then, biblically speaking, is anyone who practices occultism in any one of a variety of forms that include divination, magick, astrology, sorcery, and spiritism. Modern-day Wiccans, as well as most neopagans, practice such arts. Their belief system, therefore, is indeed condemned by the Bible.

The notion that a "witch" is nothing but a "poisoner" may have come from a misunderstanding of the origins of the modern word for "pharmacy." It derives from the Greek word *pharmakon*, which has a meaning linked not only to the idea of a drug or poison, but also the concepts of magick or charm. These root meanings stem from the fact that "witches" have traditionally been associated with herbs and potions (which if used improperly might be poisonous). But such an association does not mean that the actual word *witch* as used in the Bible really means "poisoner."

Is it even possible for a child to convert to Witchcraft?

In April 1974, the Council of American Witches adopted a set of principles of Wiccan Belief. One principle reads, "We

acknowledge a depth of power far greater than that apparent to the average person. Because it is far greater than ordinary, it is sometimes called supernatural. But we see it as lying within that which is naturally potential to all." Another principle says, "This same creative power lies in all people."

According to witches, everyone has the potential to be a witch—even children. All they need to do is embrace the principles of Wicca and tap into their magical powers within. This is why Wiccans today are actively seeking to convert them (contrary to their claims) via witchcraft books that target teens and children. Noteworthy is how some of these same books are capitalizing on the popularity of Harry Potter and its fantasy brand of witchcraft (see chapters 7 and 8).

Interestingly, any child can convert to Witchcraft without his or her parents even knowing it. Wicca is a religion that can easily be practiced in secret with little paraphernalia or outward show of conversion. It can be a fairly solitary religion, or a belief system that is practiced with others. This is one reason why so many teenagers, especially girls, are now turning to Wicca. A significant number may already be practicing Wiccans without their parents' consent or knowledge.

Why are Christians still upset over Harry Potter when so many Christian leaders have said the books are just fine?

Novelist Michael O'Brien answered this question very well in a recent interview:

> I'm surprised by the promotion of the Potter series in certain Christian circles, even among some Catholic academics. Perhaps this is due to their naiveté about the power of fantasy. Possibly it's an over-reliance on individual reason, as if to say, "I am so intelligent, and

my child is so intelligent, that we can enjoy the irrational and the corrupt without being affected by it, and therefore it's not really corrupt." This *non sequitur* is based on the mistaken belief that the imagination can be safely contained within an airtight compartment of the mind. I'm guessing here, but I suspect there is also a certain fear at work in their adamant and not always objective reaction to criticism of the Potter series. Is their overreaction caused by a fear of anti-intellectualism? A fear of "fundamentalism"? Perhaps even a fear of loss of credibility among other academics? I'm not certain. At the very least it indicates a lack of understanding about the integral relationship between faith and culture, between imagination and the world of action.

Consistently, the pro-Potter advocates extract details from the books that point to some kind of "morality" in the series, actually more a set of "values"—to use the modern term—than genuine morality. Their approach is, I think, rather revealing. Any serious scholar should know that empirical "evidence" for any theory can be found by dipping selectively into a large body of source material, and that this can be highly misleading. When a scholar operates from an *a priori* need to find supportive data for his gut attraction, truth gets lost in the process. And this is the crux of the problem for all of us: Regardless of whether we are impelled by a gut attraction or a gut repulsion to the world of Harry Potter, we must ask ourselves if we are thinking according to principles, or…articulating impressively as we let ourselves be driven by feelings.[20]

How can Christians object to the violence, death, sexuality, and occultism in a book, movie, or television program when the Bible is filled with all kinds of violence, adultery, evil, and descriptions of horrible wars?

Drawing an analogy between entertainment forms and the Bible is terribly flawed. Moreover, such an analogy springs from the same source as the anti-Christian rhetoric filling newspaper stories and other media reports.

First, Scripture was not written to be a source of "entertainment," nor is it meant to be a tool for stimulating a child's imagination. In other words, the mature themes in the Bible are not presented for fun or amusement.

Second, the literature category of a series like Harry Potter is fantasy/fiction, whereas the Bible is historical narrative. The Bible tells the story of the ancient nation of Israel (Old Testament) and the life of Jesus of Nazareth (New Testament). It is absurd to compare deliberate fantasy with what is written in the Bible (although atheists and agnostics certainly see the Bible as fiction). One might as well place Harry Potter next to a History Channel documentary on the Nazi Holocaust. It is mixing categories.

Third, the Bible does not contain gratuitous references to violent deeds. The same cannot be said for many of today's books, movies, and TV shows.

Aren't Christians the last people who should be complaining about anything, since they are the ones who are actually hurting society with their narrow-minded bigotry?

There may indeed be some individuals who call themselves Christians who also exhibit a lack of sophistication about certain issues. However, labeling all Christians as narrow-minded bigots seems more of an attack against the Christian religion than an

argument against legitimate concerns relating to various forms of entertainment. Persons who ask a question like this commonly ignore some very beneficial aspects of the Christian faith:

❖ Christian shelters for the homeless

❖ Christian foster parents who open their homes to abused children

❖ Christian-built orphanages

❖ Christian hospitals

❖ Christian-owned and operated food centers for the poor in our inner cities

❖ Christian organizations, like Samaritan's Purse, which send relief aid and supplies to war-torn and disaster-stricken regions in the world

No one, though, seems to be asking a number of other questions (which, of course, would be politically incorrect): Have occultists built any hospitals, homeless shelters, or orphanages throughout the world? How often do Wiccan covens go as a group into the inner cities to feed the poor? When has any atheist or agnostic organization donated its resources or started programs to help starving or poverty-stricken people in foreign countries? Did anyone see any relief teams of witches or neopagans traveling to Asia to help tsunami victims in 2004 and 2005?

Appendix A

What's So Bad About Occultism?

Our answer to the question posed by this appendix's title depends on our perspective. Christians, of course, view occultism as problematic because it clearly is prohibited by the Bible.*

These passages, however, mean very little to persons who do not happen to be Christian or who do not believe in the reliability of Scripture (for example, skeptics, atheists, agnostics, occultists, people of other faiths).

But regardless of whether or not a person is Christian, there are a variety of *non*religious reasons to avoid occultism, especially when it comes to youth involvement. These reasons are important and should be kept in mind by all parents, whatever faith (or *non*faith) they happen to espouse.

First, occult practices are notorious for failing. Consequently, they may be little more than a waste of time, energy, and money. Divination, psychic readings (including telephone hotlines), ESP, and occult prophecies are very unreliable ways to get good information about the world, our lives, others, and the future.

---

* See Exodus 7:11; 22:18; Leviticus 19:26; Deuteronomy 18:10-12; Joshua 13:22; 2 Kings 17:17; 2 Chronicles 33:6; 1 Samuel 15:23; Isaiah 44:25; 47:13-15; Jeremiah 27:9; 29:8; Ezekiel 13:9,23,29; 22:28; Zechariah 10:2; Acts 16:16-18; among many other places.

Consider famed psychic Gordon-Michael Scallion, who claims to average nearly 89 percent accuracy with his predictions.[1] But out of 66 predictions he made for 1995, only a few came to pass, and all of those were so vague that it would have been difficult for them not to come true (for example, UFO sightings will increase, herb sales will soar, media programming on metaphysics and the world of the spirit will expand).[2]

The renowned psychic Edgar Cayce (1877–1945, a.k.a. the Sleeping Prophet) has an equally dismal record. His failed predictions include the complete geographical annihilation of Japan, America, and the Arctic sometime between 1958 and 1998; the destruction of New York City, Los Angeles, and San Francisco within "one generation" of 1941; the appearance of the mythical continent of Atlantis by 1968/1969; and worldwide devastation via a "pole shift" in the year 2001.[3]

Astrologers have not fared any better at predicting the future. Consider the results from the following studies that have been done on this form of divination:[4]

✧ A 1979 advertisement in *Ici Paris* offered a free horoscope reading, and those who responded were asked to judge how accurate they and their friends found it to be. Of the first 150 replies, 94 percent said it was accurate, along with 90 percent of their friends and family. It was later revealed that the respondents all received the same horoscope reading—that of a notorious mass murderer.

✧ In 1982 the Australian Skeptics organization compared the horoscopes from 13 different newspapers for the same week and found that they gave a wide variety of *differing* predictions for the *same* astrological sign. After rating the predictions for such topics as health, luck, relationships and finance, the researchers concluded that "most signs had a fairly even spread so, for instance, you could find one

paper telling you it would be a lucky week and another saying the opposite."

✣ In 1989, in response to a $100,000 TV challenge to any psychic or astrologer who could prove the truth of their claims, an astrologer cast the charts of 12 people after being given their birth information. Then he interviewed the 12 and attempted to match them to their horoscopes. He did not get a single one right.

✣ In 1994 six astrologers and psychics were challenged by the Melbourne *Sunday Age* to predict the winner of the Melbourne cup. Not one of them came close.

Second, many occult practices involve entering an altered state of consciousness (ASC) wherein one's normal everyday awareness (or consciousness) is replaced by an alternate (or altered) awareness. During an ASC persons cannot separate fact from fiction and function under a confused sense of reality. An ASC is induced when anything interrupts or brings to a halt "the normal patterns of conceptual thought without extinguishing or diminishing consciousness itself."[5] (A hypnotic trance, for instance, is an ASC.)

Third, teen and young-adult occult involvement is sometimes accompanied by violent or criminal behavior or both.[6] Occult involvement has actually been identified as one of the early warning signs of potential violence in a child. This is according to many authorities on the subject, including Dr. Reid Kimbrough, psychologist and executive director of The Justice Group.*

Since 1997, Kimbrough has been conducting seminars nationwide for law-enforcement personnel and educators concerned

---

* Kimbrough's credentials are impressive: 20-year veteran police officer; master of arts degree in psychology/professional psychology; doctorate in behavioral science, with emphasis in psychology; consultant to the U.S. Department of Justice; behavioral scientist; police psychologist; adjunct faculty member of the Tennessee Law Enforcement Training Academy.[7]

about youth and school violence. His "Children at High Risk for Violent Behavior" course includes material that explains occultism's link to youth violence. Warning signs may include 1) a student listening to music which has death or suicide in its lyrics; 2) possessing paraphernalia such as skulls, black candles, or a Satanic Bible; 3) preoccupation with a Ouija board or tarot cards, drawing satanic symbols on themselves or property; and 4) wearing black clothing.[8]

Others also see a link between occultism and juvenile violence. Consider, for example, the important volume *Chasing Shadows: Confronting Juvenile Violence in America* by Gordon Crews, PhD (associate professor and head of the Criminal Justice Department, Jacksonville State University) and Reid Montgomery Jr. (Associate Professor, College of Criminal Justice, University of South Carolina). The authors' assertions about occultism's link to youth problems, along with those of Kimbrough, are far from reactionary or sensationalistic. They, like other knowledgeable persons, present a balanced assessment of how youths respond to various types of stimuli received at critical junctures in their emotional and psychological development.

Of course, just because a teenager wears black does not mean he or she is into occultism. There are usually many signs present. Staying connected with one's child is the answer, as is helping a child navigate those difficult years when they are trying to break free of childhood restrictions—which is often done by deliberately seeking to go contrary to mainstream society.

Norvin Richard, professor of philosophy at the University of Alabama, agrees. He believes youths who gravitate toward occultism could be looking for a value system that opposes the values of previous generations. "I think one could say those who dabble in the occult have lost faith in ordinary senses of good and evil," he has stated. "They've lost faith in the principles and the sources of those principles that are more conventional and they're looking for direction elsewhere."[9]

Appendix B

Helpful Resources

MTV is blatantly selling raunchy sex to kids. Compared to broadcast television programs aimed at adults, MTV's programming contains substantially more sex, foul language and violence—and MTV's shows are aimed at children as young as 12. There's no question that TV influences the attitudes and perceptions of young viewers, and MTV is deliberately marketing its raunch to millions of innocent children.

—Parents Television Council, 2005
"MTV Smut Peddlers:
Targeting Kids with Sex, Drugs and Alcohol"

On February 1, 2005, an Associated Press article titled "Study: MTV Delivers a Diet of 'Sleaze'" revealed the results of a study launched by the Parents Television Council. According to the PTC, the programming on the youth-driven MTV network is far worse in content than the most adult programs aired on major networks: "During one week last March, the watchdog Parents Television Council said it counted 3,056 flashes of nudity or sexual situations and 2,881 verbal references to sex."

In light of the fact that MTV's main viewers are as young as 12 years old, this study shows how carefully parents must monitor the

entertainment options now accessible to their children. The following resources should be helpful.

- ❖ Al Menconi Ministries, 760-591-4696, www.almenconi.com

- ❖ American Academy of Pediatrics, 847-434-4000, www.aap.org (under "Media" topic)

- ❖ Center for Media Literacy, 800-226-9494, www.medialit.org

- ❖ Coalition for Quality Children's Media, 505-989-8076, www.cqcm.org

- ❖ Commercial Alert, 503-235-8012, www.commercialalert.org

- ❖ Decent Films, www.decentfilms.com

- ❖ Entertainment Software Rating Board, www.esrb.org/index.asp

- ❖ Kaiser Family Foundation, 650-854-9400, www.kff.org

- ❖ Kids Net, 202-291-1400, www.kidsnet.org

- ❖ Media Awareness Network, 613-224-7721, www.media-awareness.ca

- ❖ Media Watch, 831-423-6355, www.mediawatch.com

- ❖ Movie Guide, 800-577-6684, www.movieguide.org

- ❖ National Institute on Media and the Family, 612-672-5437, www.mediafamily.org

- ❖ New Mexico Literacy Project, 505-828-3129, www.nmmlp.org

- ❖ Parents TV, 213-629-9255, www.parentstv.org

- ❖ Studio O'Brien, www.studiobrien.com

Notes

Documents published by major news sources such as *USA Today*, *Newsweek*, the *Chicago Tribune*, the *New York Times*, the *Los Angeles Times*, and the British Broadcasting System (BBC) are available online at their well-known and easily accessed Web sites. Therefore, no Internet addresses are given for these citations.

More difficult to find documents, however, have their current URL listed (as of February 2005). But notes that refer to documents stored in large Internet databases (for example, the archive of interviews with and articles about J.K. Rowling kept at the Harry Potter fan site www.quick-quote-quill.org/index2.html) do not have the specific URL listed; instead, they include only the main Web page, from which a search can be done.

To Be a Child Again
1. David McCord, "Books Fall Open," in *One at a Time* (Boston: Little, Brown, 1977), p. 343.
2. There are several computer/video games based on Rowling's works and Tolkien's trilogy (for example, "Harry Potter & the Sorcerer's Stone"; "Harry Potter: Quidditch World Cup"; "The Lord of the Rings: The Two Towers"; and "The Lord of the Rings: The Battle for Middle-earth").
3. "Locals Protest at 'Occult' Potter," *BBC News*, Dec. 19, 2001; "Australian College Bans Potter," *BBC News*, July 2, 2003; Anthee Carassava, "Harry Potter and the Clergy's Ire," *New York Times*, Jan. 17, 2003.
4. WisdomWorks, "New Study Looks at Effect of Harry Potter on Teens," press release, May 16, 2002, www.gospel-net.com/cgi-bin/newspro/viewnews.cgi?search. This poll also found that only 1 percent of Harry Potter readers and viewers were *less* interested in witchcraft as a result of the series. Most (86 percent) said that reading or viewing Harry Potter had made *no difference* at all to their general interest in witchcraft. The data was gleaned from research conducted by the Barna Research Group, Ltd., of Ventura, California. This study includes the perspectives of 612 teenagers who were surveyed by phone between March 14 and March 25, 2002.
5. WisdomWorks, www.gospel-net.com/cgi-bin/newspro/viewnews.cgi?search.

Chapter One: Fantasy's Fall
1. Jack Zipes, *Sticks and Stones* (New York: Routledge, 2001), pp. 5-6.
2. See Tom Engelhardt, "Reading May Be Harmful to Your Kids," *Harper's Magazine*, June 1991, pp. 55-62.
3. Margaret R. Marshall, *An Introduction to the World of Children's Books* (London:

Gower, 1982; 1988 edition), p. 13. Margaret R. Marshall is former chairman of the Children's Libraries Section of the International Federation of Library Associations.

4. Zipes, p. 7.

5. Donna Jo Napoli, as quoted in Alyson Ward, "The Terrible Tale of the New York Dark Side of Children's Literature," *Fort Worth Star-Telegram*, Sept. 21, 2004.

6. Engelhardt, pp. 57-58.

7. Jeff McQuillan, "Seven Myths About Literacy in the United States," *ERIC/AE Digest*, August 1998, www.ericdigests.org/1999-2/seven.htm; adapted from Jeff McQuillan, *The Literacy Crisis: False Claims, Real Solutions* (Portsmouth, NH: Heinemann, 1998); also available at http://library.adoption.com.

8. Patrick Clinton, "Literacy in America," *Book Magazine*, Sept./Oct. 2002, available at www.bookmagazine.com.

9. For example, a 1999 survey found that on a daily basis, kids aged 2 to 18 spend only about 44 minutes reading for fun, in comparison to 2 hours, 46 minutes watching TV (Kaiser Family Foundation, "New Study Finds Kids Spend Equivalent of Full Work Week Using Media," Nov. 17, 1999, www.kff.org/entmedia/1535-pressrelease final-doc.cfm). And from 1983 to 1998 more than 10 million children "reached the 12th grade without having learned to read at a basic level" (William J. Bennett, et al., "A Nation Still at Risk," *Policy Review*, July-Aug. 1998, www.policyreview.org/jul98/nation.html).

10. Mary Anne S. Moffitt and Ellen Wartella, "Youth and Reading: A Survey of Leisure Reading Pursuits of Female and Male Adolescents," *Reading Research and Instruction*, Winter 1992, pp. 1-17.

11. Jim Vaccaro, "The Journey to Literacy," *The Book & the Computer*, June 12, 2000, www.honco.net/100day/02/2000-0612-vaccaro.html.

12. Clinton, www.bookmagazine.com.

13. Jack Markowitz, "Rowling's Spell Grows on Parents, Wall Street," *The Tribune-Review* (Pittsburgh, PA), Dec. 26, 2004, http://pittsburghlive.com/x/tribune-review/trib/newssummary/s_286951.html.

14. Diane Penrod, "The Trouble with Harry: A Reason for Teaching Media Literacy to Young Adults," *The Writing Instructor*, Dec. 2001, available at writinginstructor.com.

15. Zipes, pp. 8-9.

16. David Denby, "Buried Alive: Our Children and the Avalanche of Crud," *The New Yorker*, July 15, 1996, p. 48.

17. Denby, pp. 51-52. He wrote, "What's lost is the old dream that parents and teachers will nurture the organic development of the child's own interests, the child's own nature. That dream is largely dead. In this country, people possessed solely by the desire to sell have become far more powerful than parents tortuously working out the contradictions of authority, freedom, education, and soul-making."

18. Nick, "Who Is Harry Potter?" Aug. 18, 2004, www.veritaserum.com/editorials/?view=7.

19. Zipes, p. 172.

20. Zipes, p. 171.

21. These despised critics include several reviewers who have made commendable contributions to the literary world: Oxford-educated Anthony Holden (an award-winning journalist and biographer); Roger Hutton (editor of *The Horn Book*, a 75-year-old children's literary digest); and Harold Bloom (literary critic and Yale scholar). Holden skewered Rowling's work as "not particularly well-written," while

Sutton said it was "critically insignificant," adding that, as literature goes, the series is "nothing to get excited about" (Anthony Holden. Quoted in Sarah Lyall, "Wizard vs. Dragon: A Close Contest, but the Fire-Breather Wins," Jan. 29, 2000, *New York Times*. Roger Sutton. Quoted in Elizabeth Mehren, "Wild About Harry," July 28, 2000, *Los Angeles Times*).

22. Harold Bloom, "Can 35 Million Book Buyers Be Wrong? Yes," July 11, 2000, *Wall Street Journal*. Bloom, as quoted in Jamie Allen, "Harry and Hype," July 13, 2000, CNN Online.

23. For example, "In an interview with the Rome-based Zenit news agency, Massimo Introvigne, a sociologist of new religious movements, said that Catholic critics of the Potter series represent a new and 'dangerous form of fundamentalism,' and inferred that their approach could lead to a 'Catholic version of the Taliban regime'" (Michael O'Brien, "The Potter Controversy: Or Why That Boy Sorcerer Just Won't Go Away," July/August, 2003, *Saint Austin Review*, available at http://studiobrien.com /site/index.php). Similarly harsh comments have been made in various forums, especially online. Consider "Dunking Harry Potter" by David W. Jansing, who said, "The American Christian Taliban, for want of anything more worthwhile to get upset about, insists that Harry Potter, an intelligently written series of books that encourages young people to read beyond their reading level, is an adverse influence and should be banished from our shores" (www.bartcopnation.com/dunking.html).

24. A *London Review of Books* article, for instance, referred to stupid "born-again" Christians (Wendy Doniger, "Spot the Source: Harry Potter Explained," *London Review of Books*, reprinted in *The Guardian*, Feb. 10, 2000, available at www.guardian.co.uk). And a *Jewish World Review* article titled "Casual Censors and Deadly Know-Nothings" called Rowling's critics "barbarians" whose attacks amounted to "ignorance parading as piety" (Suzanne Fields, "Casual Censors and Deadly Know-Nothings," *Jewish World Review*, Dec. 7, 1999, available at www.jew ishworldreview.com).

25. Zipes, p. 173.

26. James E. Higgins, *Beyond Words: Mystical Fancy in Children's Literature* (New York: Teachers College Press, 1970), p. 2.

27. Approximately 90 million copies of this novel have been sold.

28. Aileen Jacobson, "Horrors! He's A Hit," *Chicago Tribune*, Dec. 16, 2004.

29. Diana West, "The Horror of R.L. Stine," *American Educator*, Fall 1995, p. 39. One need not read very far into Fear Street for evidence supporting West's assertion. In Stine's *Cheerleaders: The New Evil*, we find the cheerleader Corky letting out "a horrified wail" as she sees a "bright red gush of blood spurting from Rochelle's neck." A screwdriver has plunged into Rochelle's body it has been allowed to full from high up in the gym bleachers: "The blood poured out over Rochelle. The hairbrush fell from her hand. She slumped forward until her head hit the floor" (Stine, p. 49). Three pages later we read that Bobbi had "been trapped in the shower....locked inside. Then scalding hot water shot out of the showers. Unable to escape, Bobbi had suffocated in the boiling steam. Murdered" (Stine, p. 52). In Stine's *Broken Hearts* we find this lurid scene: "He stared at the bloody wound in her side. Stared at the puddle of blood at his feet....The blood red swirls floated angrily in Dave's eyes. Blinding him. Suffocating him. So much blood. Such a big, red wound. And so much blood. Puddles and pools" (p. 141).

30. Both quoted in West, p. 40.

31. Donna Hartmann, "R.L. Stine Still Gives Us 'Goosebumps,'" Oct. 31, 2004, *Bradenton Herald,* www.bradenton.com/mld/bradenton/entertainment/10052554.htm.

32. One excerpt reads, "And then the heads. Human heads. Hair caked with dirt. Skin loose, hanging from their skulls. They stared at me with pleading eyes, faces twisted, mouths hanging open in pain. 'Take me with you,' one of them called in a dry whisper" (R.L. Stine, *Headless Halloween,* Goosebumps Series 2000, #10, excerpt available at http://scholastic.com/goosebumps/books/other_titles.htm).

33. Michael O'Brien, *A Landscape with Dragons* (San Francisco: Ignatius Press, 1998), p. 67.

34. Since 1997, Stine has also released two more sets of horror stories for children: The Nightmare Hour and The Nightmare Room.

35. R.L. Stine, interview of unknown origin, n.d., www.cognivision.com/timecapsule 61/timecapsule61/team_10_literature.htm. This interview—the "Literature" choice made by sixth and seventh graders at the Leonardo da Vinci Intermediate School (IS 61 in Queens, New York)—was included in their "time capsule" class project. As of 2005, Stine had produced nearly 200 Fear Street/Goosebumps books (as well as 20 more spine-chilling horror novels for young adults), was planning a TV miniseries, and had a Goosebumps television show already running (FOX-TV). A Fear Street movie tentatively titled *Let's All Kill Jennifer* (Disney) also is in the works (see "Exclusive Interview: Robert Zappia," www.halloweenmovies.com/site/interview_rz.htm).

36. J.K. Rowling, as quoted in Mark McGarrity, "A Wizard of Words Puts a Spell on Kids—'Potter' Author Visits School in Monclair," Oct. 14, 1999, *The Star-Ledger,* available at www.quick-quote-quill.org/index2.html; J.K. Rowling, interview with Judy O'Malley, "Talking with J.K. Rowling," *Book Links,* July 1999, available at www.quick-quote-quill.org/index2.html; and "Potter Author's Content Warning," Sept. 29, 2000, *BBC News,* available at www.quick-quote-quill.org/index2.html.

37. Quoted in MacNeil/Lehrer Productions "Pulp Fiction" news segment, Feb. 13, 1997, www.pbs.org/newshour/bb/education/february97/goose_2-13.html.

38. See Georgette Brown, "Good vs. Evil—But Which Is Which?" *Sun Herald,* Feb. 28, 1997, available at www.sunherald.com/mld/sunherald/. In this article, Brown refers to an opinion piece ("Illiteracy Should Cause Goosebumps") by the father of an eight-year-old boy. The father expressed his belief that Goosebumps was "no big deal" because at least his son was reading. (The *Sun Herald* is a Mississippi Gulf Coast newspaper.)

39. Quoted in MacNeil/Lehrer, www.pbs.org/newshour/bb/education/february97/ goose_2-13.html.

40. West, p. 41.

41. Steve Russo, "Real Answers with Steve Russo," www.24sevenvideos.com/gb.html.

42. Russo, www.24sevenvideos.com/gb.html.

43. Sam Coates, "God Is Cut from Film of Dark Materials," *The Times* (London), Dec. 8, 2004, available at www.timesonline.co.uk.

44. Peter Hitchens, "This Is the Most Dangerous Author in Britain," *The Mail on Sunday,* Jan. 27, 2002, p. 63, http://pers-www.wlv.ac.uk/~bu1895/hitchens.htm.

45. Philip Pullman, *The Golden Compass* (New York: Alfred A. Knopf, 1995; first edition), p. 30; Philip Pullman, *The Amber Spyglass* (New York: Alfred A. Knopf, 2000; first trade paperback edition, 2002), p. 33.

46. The antichurch scope of Pullman's trilogy was described very well in a 2002 *Ex-Libris* review: "The Church…is an all-encompassing institution, meddling with every

aspect of day-to-day life. Representatives of the Church are two-faced hypocrites who mutilate children, severing them from their souls, in the name of preserving them from sin, and who reject advances in physics on the grounds of heresy" (William H. Duquette, "Philip Pullman, C.S. Lewis, and J.R.R. Tolkien," *Ex-Libris Reviews*, Jan. 1, 2002, www.wjduquette.com/exlibris/ex20020101.html#Pullman).

47. Pullman, *Amber Spyglass*, pp. 31-32.

48. Pullman, *Amber Spyglass*, p. 441; Philip Pullman, *The Subtle Knife*, (New York: Alfred A. Knopf, 1997; revised trade paperback edition, 2002), p. 50.

49. Pullman, *Amber Spyglass*, pp. 410-411.

50. Pullman has said, "I see no sign of God anywhere....No sign of God—a living God. So I have to consider myself an atheist. But because of my upbringing I'm a Christian atheist, and I'm a church atheist. I know the Bible and the hymn book and the prayer book very, very well, and they form a deep and inescapable part of my nature....But I find it impossible to believe" (Philip Pullman, as quoted in Heather Lee Schroeder, "Author Pullman Finds It Impossible to Believe," *The Capital Times*, Oct. 13, 2000, www.madison.com/tct/books/topic/children/index.php?ntid=4667&ntpid=). He also has stated: 1) "I'm caught between the words 'atheistic' and 'agnostic.' I've got no evidence whatever for believing in a God. But I know that all the things I do know are very small compared with the things that I don't know. So maybe there is a God out there. All I know is that if there is, he hasn't shown himself on earth" (Philip Pullman, "A Dark Agenda?" interview by Susan Roberts, Nov. 2002, www.surefish.co.uk/culture/features/pullman_interview.htm); and 2) "Atheism suggests a degree of certainty that I'm not quite willing to accede to. I suppose technically you'd have to put me down as an agnostic" (Philip Pullman, as quoted in Helena de Bertodano, "I Am the Devil's Party," *The Sunday Telegraph*, Jan. 29, 2002, available at www.telegraph.co.uk).

51. Philip Pullman, "Carnegie Medal Acceptance Speech," 1996, www.randomhouse.com/features/pullman/philippullman/speech.html.

52. Philip Pullman, "Philip Pullman's Answers to Questions About Science and Religion," interview with the Readerville Forum, Feb. 2001, www.geocities.com/the_golden_compass/rvreligion.html.

53. Pullman, *The Subtle Knife*, p. 50.

54. Pullman, in "A Dark Agenda," www.surefish.co.uk/culture/features/pullman_interview.htm.

55. Philip Pullman, interview with Radio 4's *Desert Island Discs*, Oct. 2003, as quoted in "Top Author Attacks Religion," available at www.freethinker.co.uk; Pullman., as quoted in Bertodano, available at www.telegraph.co.uk.

56. Philip Pullman, interview with the BBC, http://news.bbc.co.uk/cbbcnews/hi/chat/hotseat/newsid_1777000/1777895.stm#question9.

57. Philip Pullman, "Chris Weitz, NewLine, 'The Times', and How to Read," www.philip-pullman.com/pages/content/index.asp?page ID=102.

58. Pullman, interview with Schroeder, www.madison.com/tct/books/topic/children/index.php?ntid=4667&ntpid=.

59. Pullman quoted in "Top Author Attacks," available at www.freethinker.ro.uk.

60. This historical fact has been highlighted in many places and by many authors, both secular and religious. For example, a *Science and Theology News* review of Alister McGrath's *The Twilight of Atheism: The Rise and Fall of Disbelief in the Modern World* (Doubleday, 2004) observed, "The 20th century witnessed unprecedented social and

political experiments with atheism. In Germany, China, the Soviet Union and their satellites, officially atheistic political regimes rose to power with uniformly disastrous consequences. In consolidating their power, these regimes of 'liberation' went on killing sprees that eclipsed even the most egregious of the religions they opposed. Their physical assaults on traditional power blocs within their respective countries were accompanied by intellectual assaults on traditional ways of looking at the world" (Karl Giberson, "From the Bastille to Berlin: The rise and fall of atheism," *Science and Theology News*, www.stnews.org/archives/2004_june/books_from_0604.html).

61. Pullman quoted in "Top Author Attacks," available at www.freethinker.ro.uk.

62. Philip Pullman, "The War on Words," *The Guardian*, Nov. 6, 2004, http://books.guardian.co.uk/review/story/0,,1343733,00.html.

63. Pullman, "Chris Weitz, New Line," www.philip-pullman.com/pages/content/index.asp?PageID=102; Philip Pullman, as quoted in Angelique Chrisafis, "Pullman lays down moral challenge for writers," *The Guardian*, Aug. 12, 2002, http://books.guardian.co.uk/news/articles/0,6109,773058,00.html.

64. A 2004 survey of libraries throughout the entire Orange County Public Library system in Southern California revealed that His Dark Materials is categorized in that location as either "Teen," "Older Teen," or "Young Teen" (Richard Abanes, informal survey, Dec. 2004, Orange County, CA). Moreover, countless Web sites list the trilogy as being for children. Amazon.co.uk, for instance, lists it for kids 9 to 12 (www.amazon.co.uk), and Scholastic Books has placed the trilogy in its "Children's Book Zone" (www.scholastic.co.uk/zone/book_philip-pullman-reviews.htm).

65. Pullman, Carnegie Medal Acceptance Speech, www.randomhouse.com/features/pullman/philippullman/speech.html. To make matters worse, New Line Cinema (the same film company that produced the exquisite movie version of The Lord of the Rings) will be making His Dark Materials into a series major motion picture to be released in 2006. But even Hollywood cringed at the prospect of launching such an anti-Christian movie. In 2004 it was announced that "references to the church are likely to be banished in his film…[and] the 'Authority,' the weak God figure, will become 'any arbitrary establishment that curtails the freedom of the individual'" (see Coates, www.timesonline.co.uk).

66. Additional suggestions on how to pick good books for children are found in *An Introduction to the World of Children's Literature* by Margaret R. Marshall, which recommends adults should select children's books that

   • introduce children to their own cultural heritage
   • enlarge the mind and the imagination
   • offer experience in the creative and scientific inquiry process
   • encourage an appreciation of beauty and human achievement, motivation, and aspiration
   • allow the discernment of good vs. bad, right vs. wrong

67. Mary Sheehan Warren—English teacher, reading specialist, and Director of Curriculum for Aquinas Academy in Maryland—writes that a child's "undeveloped intellect is unable to objectively appraise the worth of what he digests, so that his malnutrition—even poisoning—may continue undetected. The life-supporting sustenance that the young mind seeks is what a truly civilized society is composed upon, and what God calls His people to recognize and affirm: Truth, Goodness, and Beauty (Mary Sheehan Warren, "Food for the Soul: Truth, Goodness, and Beauty

in Children's Literature," www.catholic.net/rcc/Periodicals/Faith/11-12-98/
Childrens.html). Warren additionally gives some helpful counsel with regard to
exactly what a parent needs to look for when evaluating children's literature:

- *Truth*: "A text should be examined for its presentation of the Truth. What are
  the underlying assumptions of the story?...Is the dignity of the human person
  properly addressed?...Does it laugh at what is considered to be sacred? Does it
  appropriately portray what is right?...Is there mutual respect, especially
  among the characters who might be considered to be 'ideal' by the reader? Are
  both fathers and mothers considered to be important?"
- *Goodness*: "Goodness can be offered to the child reader in two different ways:
  By affirming all things that are good; and by demonstrating what things are
  not good and why....Most of children's literature still seems to be a joyful
  recognition of the good that is found in this world. Unfortunately, the parent
  or teacher must first decide if Goodness is really what is being praised within
  a plot. Our culture today has developed a hideous tendency to describe vices
  as virtues."
- *Beauty*: "Simplicity of plot, richness of description, and nobility of character
  not only expose the child to Beauty, but also help to expand his capacity to
  imagine and to create beauty himself. He can observe how language, when
  expertly crafted, can excite many feelings, and he can become inspired to
  invent such happy pretend worlds for himself."

68. Nicholas Tucker, "Books That Frighten," in Virginia Haviland, ed., *Children and
Literature* (New York: Lothrop, Lee & Shepard Co., 1973), p. 106.
69. Tucker, p. 106. Some scenes from J.K. Rowling's series, for example, may fall into this
category. Consider the following excerpts from *Harry Potter and the Goblet of Fire*:

> [Wormtail] pulled a long, thin, shining silver dagger from inside his
> cloak. His voice broke into petrified sobs....He stretched his right hand
> out in front of him—the hand with the missing finger. He gripped the dag-
> ger very tightly in his left hand and swung it upward.
>
> Harry realized what Wormtail was about to do a second before it hap-
> pened—he closed his eyes...but he could not block the scream that
> pierced the night....He heard something fall to the ground, heard
> Wormtail's anguished panting...as something was dropped into the caul-
> dron....
>
> He saw the shining dagger shaking in Wormtail's remaining hand. He
> felt its point penetrate the crook of his right arm and blood seeping down
> the sleeve of his torn robes....[Wormtail] fumbled in his pocket for a glass
> vial and held it to Harry's cut, so that a dribble of blood fell into
> it....Wormtail, sobbing and moaning, still cradling his mutilated arm,
> scrambled to pick up the black robes from the ground.

70. Tucker, p. 108.
71. O'Brien, *A Landscape*, p. 67.
72. Jan Mark, "Another World?: A Sampling of Remarks on Science Fiction and
Fantasy—The Story of Golem," in Barbara Harrison and Gregory Maguire,
Innocence & Experience: Essays & Conversations on Children's Literature (New York:
Lothrop, Lee & Shepard Books, 1987), p. 184.
73. Lillian Smith, *The Unreluctant Years* (Chicago: American Library Association, 1953;
1991 ed.), p. 4.

74. "The Fantasy Myth," *Home School Helper*, www.bjup.com/resources/articles/hsh/0403b.html.

Chapter Two: Abracadabra Adventures

1. This statement was pulled from an advertisement for a lecture series titled "True Magical Practices and Harry Potter" (August 4, 2000). It was delivered at The Gnostic Society Center in Hollywood, CA. See http://gnosis.org/gnostsoc/gnostsoc past.htm.

2. Data obtained by the Gallup Organization shows that belief in biblical authority has "fallen to an all-time low," with 2001 statistics showing that only 27 percent of the those polled believe the Bible contains "the actual Word of God in all instances." In 1963, the figure was 65 percent (see note 3); cf. Cathy Lynn Grossman, "Charting the Unchurched in America," *USA Today*, Mar. 7, 2002.

3. *Emerging Trends*, as quoted in Terry Mattingly, "Buying St. Nostradamus," http://tmatt.gospelcom.net/column/2001/10/10/.

4. "Belief in the Beyond," *USA Today*, Apr. 20, 1998, as quoted in Matt Nisbit, "New Poll Points to Increase in Paranormal Belief," *Skeptical Inquirer*, online edition, www.csicop.org/articles/poll/index.html.

5. Mircea Eliade, *Occultism, Witchcraft and Cultural Fashions* (Chicago: University Press, 1976), p. 10.

6. Although no one knows exactly how many neopagans or Wiccans live in America, recent estimates by Witches place the number of adherents to "the Craft" at about 200,000 (see "CoG: Commonly Asked Questions," www.cog.org/wicca/faq.html #MANY; cf. Catherine Edwards, "Wicca Casts Spell on Teenage Girls," *Insight on the News*, Oct. 25, 1999, p. 15, available at www.insightmag.com). Grossly inflated numbers, however, have been offered by some Wiccans, who put the number of U.S.-based neopagans anywhere from 3 to 9 million (see Phyllis Curott, "Blair Witch Offends Witches: A Practicing Witch on the Summer's Hottest Flick," Aug. 18, 1999, chat transcript, ABC News. A transcript of this interview is now available only at the Google cache of pages. It can be accessed by entering "Blair Witch Offends Witches" in the search engine and click the "cached" link under the return "ABCNEWS.com: Chat Transcript: Phyllis Curott, a Practicing Witch"; and *Paganism: An Introduction to Earth-Centered Religions* [St. Paul, MN: Llewelleyn, 2002] by Joyce and River Higginbotham, excerpt available at www.llewellyn.com/bookstore/book.php?pn=J222).

7. Leslie A. Shepard, ed., *Encyclopedia of Occultism & Parapsychology* vol. 2, (Detroit: Gale Research, 1991), p. 1207.

8. Julien Tondriau, *The Occult: Secrets of the Hidden World* (New York: Pyramid Communications, 1972), p. 5.

9. In an attempt to better understand the highly complex and multifaceted world of the occult, sociologists have divided occultists into three separate categories:

   - *Minimal observers*, who express only a passing interest in strange occurrences such as flying saucers, land and sea monsters, and parapsychology-related phenomena. Their activities usually lack mysticism, supernaturalism, and antiscientific thought.
   - *Moderate participants*, who seek to understand mysterious causal relationships between events—i.e., they express an interest, for example, in numerology, sun-sign astrology, and palmistry.

- *Entrenched believers*, who are concerned with occult belief systems: e.g., witch-craft, Satanism, ritual magick, and other mystical traditions. They often question or contradict scientific validation of an event or relationship, and thus may see themselves as competitors to science.

10. John Michael Greer, *The New Encyclopedia of the Occult* (St. Paul, MN: Llewellyn Publications, 2003), pp. 199, 354.
11. The Pagan Federation, "Information on Paganism," www.paganfed.demon.co.uk/pathways.htm.
12. According to renowned Witch Margot Adler, *wicca* is the original Anglo–Saxon spelling for the modern English word *witch* (*Drawing Down the Moon: Witches, Druids, Goddess-Worshippers and Other Pagans in America Today* [Boston: Beacon Press, 1979], p. 11).
13. Craig Hawkins, *Witchcraft: Exploring the World of Wicca* (Grand Rapids, MI: Baker Books, 1996), p. 21. Hawkins is a nationally-recognized expert on Wicca.
14. Hawkins, pp. 29, 31, 32, 49, 76-77.
15. Vivienne Crowley, quoted in Edwards, www.insightmag.com.
16. Starhawk, *The Spiral Dance* (San Francisco: HarperSanFrancisco, 1979; 1989 ed.), p. 76.
17. Susan Greewood, *Magic, Witchcraft, and the Otherworld* (Oxford: Berg, 2000), pp. 182, 203, 204.
18. Edwards, www.insightmag.com.
19. It is important to remember that Witchcraft and neopaganism are not synonymous with Satanism, which is a different form of occultism.
20. Pauline Bartel, *Spellcasters* (Dallas, TX: Taylor Trade Publications, 2000), p. 154; cf. Hawkins, p. 28.
21. Hawkins, pp. 52-53.
22. Scott Cunningham, in his book *Wicca: A Guide for the Solitary Practitioner*, advises, "If you can't find a ritual to your liking or that fits your needs, create one" (pp. 174-175).
23. Shepard, vol. 2, p. 1569.
24. Such a misconception afflicts both extremes in the Harry Potter debate—that is to say, both the anti-Potter fundamentalists and the pro-Potter zealots (see chapter 8).
25. Leo Martello, *Witchcraft: The Old Religion* (Secaucus, NJ: Citadel Press, 1973), p. 12.
26. Scott Cunningham, *The Truth About Witchcraft Today* (St. Paul, MN: Llewellyn Publications, 1988), p. 23.
27. Aleister Crowley, *Magick in Theory and Practice* (New York: Dover Publications, 1976 ed.), p. 12; Charlotte Allen, "The Scholars and the Goddess," *The Atlantic Monthly*, Jan. 2001, vol. 287, no. 1, p. 18.
28. Jo Pearson, as quoted in "Bewitching the Academy," *Fortean Times* (#157), May 2002, p. 25.
29. B.A. Robinson, "Teens and Wicca," www.religioustolerance.org/wic_teen1.htm.
30. Frances Chan, "When Witches Came Out of the Broom Closet," lecture delivered at the Centre for Social Change Research School of Humanities and Human Services (Queensland University of Technology, Australia), paper presented to the Social Change in the 21st Century Conference Centre for Social Change Research, Nov. 21, 2003.
31. According to its listing at Amazon.com, the Young Wizards books are at a reading level of either children ages 9 to 12 or "young adult." Various reviews posted (e.g., from *Publishers Weekly*) recommend the novels for readers "10 & up" and similar age ranges.

32. Jean Feiwel, as quoted in Karen MacPherson, "Book Trend Casts Spell over Young Readers," *Pittsburgh Post-Gazette*, July 31, 2001, www.post-gazette.com/ae/20010731 witchbooks0731p3.asp.

33. MacPherson, www.post-gazette.com/ae/20010731witchbooks0731p3.asp.

34. Cate Tiernan, *Book of Shadows* (New York: Puffin Press, 2001), pp. 82, 130, 141, 182-183.

35. Tiernan, pp. 24, 27-30, 61, 94, 152-153, 40-43, 96-98, 119.

36. Accurate Wiccan beliefs and rituals are sprinkled liberally throughout the text. The book presents more than enough information for a teenager to actually start training as a Wiccan (see Tiernan, pp. 24, 27-30, 78, 136-137, 182-183).

37. These are two Amazon.com reviews posted by juveniles:
    - "This book is about wicca, which is something I had never heard of....It does give you a general overview of what wicca is about: magick, love, nature...just to name a few....I would recommend this book to anyone that has an interest in magic(k), wicca, love, or just a really good book" (fireyphoenix17, "One of the Best Books in the Best Series," review of *Book of Shadows* [Sweep #1], Nov. 4, 2002).
    - "This whole story is very romantic, dramatic, and all-out magickal....As a young Witch myself, I feel that Cate Tiernan stays true to the Wiccan ways, without straying into all that Hollywood 'hocus-pocus' stuff" (Joey Lowen, "Good Goddess," review of *Spellbound* [Sweep #6], Sept. 19, 2001).

38. Tiernan has consistently maintained she is *not* a Wiccan. Nevertheless, her books demonstrate an in-depth working knowledge of the Craft. Moreover, she makes several statements in *Book of Shadows*, for instance, that seek to not just explain away concerns about Wicca, but present Wiccan propaganda against Christianity (*Book of Shadows*, pp. 49-50, 102-103, 106, 116, 152, 153). One such instance is where Tiernan has a character explaining that Roman Catholicism actually borrowed the traditions of Christmas and Easter from Wicca. This is historically absurd.

39. Allen, www.theatlantic.com. Allen's article also discusses *The Triumph of the Moon* (1999) by British religion historian Roger Hutton (University of Bristol), which presents the results of his extensive investigation of Wicca and ancient paganism. He found that modern Wicca is almost entirely the creation of occultist Gerald Gardner (1884–1964), who apparently concocted his now famous tale about having learned the "ancient" religion of Wicca from a very old coven. Hutton "could find no conclusive evidence of the coven from which Gardner said he had learned the Craft."

    According to Hutton, the "religion Gardner claimed to have discovered was a mélange of material from relatively modern sources." He apparently fashioned so-called Wicca from the ideas of Charles Godfrey Leland ("a nineteenth-century amateur American folklorist who professed to have found a surviving cult of the goddess Diana in Tuscany") and Margaret Alice Murray ("a British Egyptologist who herself drew on Leland's ideas and, beginning in the 1920s, created a detailed framework of ritual and belief").

    Gardner then added his own pet notions derived from "such Masonic staples as blindfolding, initiation, secrecy, and 'degrees' of priesthood. He incorporated various Tarot-like paraphernalia, including wands, chalices, and the five-pointed star, which, enclosed in a circle, is the Wiccan equivalent of the cross." Gardner even infused his allegedly ancient faith with a few idiosyncrasies. "One was a fondness for

linguistic archaisms: 'thee,' 'thy,' 'tis,' 'Ye Bok of ye Art Magical.' Another was a taste for nudism: Gardner had belonged to a nudist colony in the 1930s, and he prescribed that many Wiccan rituals be carried out 'skyclad' (naked)."

In her article, Charlotte Allen notes, "This was a rarity even among occultists: no ancient pagan religion is known, or was thought in Gardner's time, to have regularly called for its rites to be conducted in the nude. Some Gardnerian innovations have sexual and even bondage-and-discipline overtones. Ritual sex, which Gardner called 'The Great Rite,' and which was also largely unknown in antiquity, was part of the liturgy for Beltane and other feasts (although most participants simulated the act with a dagger—another of Gardner's penchants—and a chalice). Other rituals called for the binding and scourging of initiates and for administering 'the fivefold kiss' to the feet, knees, 'womb' (according to one Wiccan I spoke with, a relatively modest spot above the pubic bone), breasts, and lips."

Many scholars also have spoken out against the Wiccan myth surrounding the so-called witch persecutions in history. It has been claimed, for example, that millions upon millions of witches were murdered during the European witch hunts, which Wiccans call "The Burning Times" (yet another Gardnerian term). In reality, the total number of witch hunt–era victims (about 1400 to 1800, with most being persecuted between 1550 and 1630) is probably around 40,000, with a high estimate being 100,000. And many of the victims were not witches—nor even women! Allen reveals, "The accused witches, far from including a large number of independent-minded women, were mostly poor and unpopular. Their accusers were typically ordinary citizens (often other women), not clerical or secular authorities. In fact, the authorities generally disliked trying witchcraft cases and acquitted more than half of all defendants. Briggs also discovered that none of the accused witches who were found guilty and put to death had been charged specifically with practicing a pagan religion" (see also Richard Abanes, *The Truth Behind the Da Vinci Code* [Eugene, OR: Harvest House, 2004], pp. 34-36).

40. H.B. Gilmour and Randi Reisfeld, "A Note from the Authors of T*Witches," available at www.scholastic.com/titles/twitches/index.htm.

41. See www.scholastic.com/titles/twitches/index.htm; www.scholastic.com/titles/twitches/whichtwitch.htm and www.scholastic.com/titles/twitches/horoscope.htm; www.scholastic.com/titles/twitches/magickarchive.htm.

The following sample texts taken from this Web site present authentic occult, Wiccan, and neopagan thought:

- *Rhyming Power:* Herbs, candles, moonlight, they're all good for spells. But the secret to a truly powerful spell…is the RHYME.
- *Powerful Places:* Some spells need atmosphere….Get outside and work with Mother Nature to make some magick under the sun or the stars, near trees or water. The energy of all living things will add their power to yours.
- *Creature Companions:*…Cats, dogs, and many small creatures understand how magick works better than us humans. They can help by adding their energy to yours and helping you focus.
- *Timing Is Everything:* Don't waste your time with untimely spells. Do you need a full moon?…Timing matters as much as the words you recite and the candles you light! Be patient and powerful and you will succeed!

42. See www.scholastic.com/titles/twitches/spellbook.htm.

43. See http://scholastic.com/aboutscholastic/. Scholastic also is one of the "leading publishers and distributors of children's books and educational materials in Canada and Great Britain" (see www.scholastic.ca/aboutscholastic/; and www.scholastic.co. uk/baskethelp.html).

44. Elaine Black, "Circle of Three #2: *Merry Meet* [Review]," *School Library Journal*, 2001, available at www.amazon.com.

45. See *Elements of Witchcraft: Natural Magick for Teens* (St. Paul: Llewellyn, 2003), p. 203.

46. "Three Is the Magic Number," www.teenreads.com/features/010605-circle3.asp.

47. A review of Circle of Three by a nine-year-old appears at www.teachers.ash.org.au. There seems to be no consistency with regard to how age-appropriateness is determined for such books. The Amazon.com editorial review, for instance, recommends the series for kids 12 and older. The *School Library Journal* review by Black (also posted at Amazon.com—see note 42) lists the series for children "grade 6 up." But according to Amazon.com, the fourth volume in the series (*What the Cards Said*) is for a reading level "Ages 9-12" (even though it is about tarot cards).

48. "Quick Picks for Reluctant Young Adult Readers," www.ala.org/ala/yalsa/booklists awards/quickpicks/2002quickpicks.htm, 2002.

49. Adapted from Josh McDowell and Don Stewart, *Handbook of Today's Religions* (San Bernardino, CA: Here's Life Publishers, 1983; 1992 ed.), p. 153. McDowell and Stewart incorrectly cite the original source for these characteristics as being W. Elwyn Davies, in *Principalities and Powers*, edited by John Warwick Montgomery. But the correct citation is W. Elwyn Davies, "Victims Become Victors," in John Warwick Montgomery, *Demon Possession* (Minneapolis, MN: Bethany, 1976), pp. 300-308.

50. J.K. Rowling, as quoted in Lindsay Fraser, "Harry Potter—Harry and Me," *The Scotsman*, Nov. 2002, available at www.quick-quote-quill.org/index2.html.

51. J.R.R. Tolkien, *Tree and Leaf* (London: Allen & Unwin, 1964), p. 44.

52. Colin Duriez, *A Field Guide to Narnia* (Downers Grove, IL: InterVarsity Press, 2004), p. 170.

53. Tolkien, p. 48; cf. Ann Swinfen, *In Defense of Fantasy* (London: Routledge & Kegan Paul, 1984), pp. 6-7. Swinfen, a novelist and teaching professor at the University of Dundee (Scotland), draws a distinction as well: "Fantasy may be said to aspire rather to the 'elvish craft' of enchantment. At its heart lies creative desire, like Dante's: 'In this world it [fantasy magic] is for men unsatisfiable, and so imperishable. Uncorrupted it does not seek delusion, nor bewitchment and domination; it seeks shared enrichment, partners in making and delight, not slaves.'...Fantasy [including the use of magic] draws much of its strength from certain 'primordial desires' for the enrichment of life: the desire to survey vast depths of space and time, the desire to behold marvelous creatures, the desire to share the speech of the animals, the desire to escape from ancient limitations of man's primary world condition."

54. James E. Higgins, *Beyond Words: Mystical Fancy in Children's Literature* (New York: Teachers College Press, 1970), pp. 22-23.

Chapter Three: Long Ago and Far Away

1. Northrop Frye, *The Educated Imagination* (Bloomington, IN: Indiana University Press, 1964; 1970 ed.), p. 101.

2. Hazel Rochman, *Against Borders: Promoting Books for a Multicultural World* (Chicago: Booklist Publications/American Library Association Books, 1993), p. 19.

3. See Bernice E. Cullinan, *Literature and the Child* (New York: Harcourt Brace Jovanovich, 1989), p. 5.
4. Some literature specialists would also place myth and legend into the folklore category.
5. Zena Sutherland and May Hill Arbuthnot, *Children and Books* (New York: Harper Collins, 1991; eighth ed.), p. 182; Rebecca J. Lukens, *A Critical Handbook of Children's Literature* (Glenview, IL: Scott, Foresman, and Co., 1976; fourth ed., 1990), p. 23.
6. John Buchan, "The Novel and the Fairy Tale," in *The English Association Pamphlet No. 79*, July 1931. Reprinted in Virginia Haviland, ed., *Children and Literature* (New York: Lothrop, Lee & Shepard Co., 1973), p. 221.
7. James E. Higgins, *Beyond Words: Mystical Fancy in Children's Literature* (New York: Teachers College Press, 1970), p. 4.
8. Other hallmarks of the fairy tale and folk tale are equally as striking. The following is adapted from Cullinan (p. 230): The plots are simple; the first few sentences quickly establish characters and setting, while at the same time the precise location of the story's events remains deliberately vague; the good characters are supremely good, and the bad characters are overtly bad; the characters are established along stereotypical socio-economic lines to assist in making them easily identifiable characters they do not behave in ways inconsistent with their overall personality traits. There is no subtlety of character. In other words, the wicked, wise, foolish, violent, disloyal, and so on, all perform throughout the story in predictable ways. The main story section succinctly establishes the main character's dilemma and pushes toward a resolution using straightforward, uncomplicated language; the ending cleanly resolves the problem, leaving no complications; and the characters "live happily ever after."
9. Nicholas Tucker, *The Child and the Book: A Psychological and Literary Exploration* (Cambridge, England: Cambridge University Press, 1981), pp. 95-96.
10. Richard Le Gallienne, "Concerning Fairy-Tales," in Richard Le Gallienne, *Attitudes and Avowals* (New York: John Lane Co., 1910), pp. 36-37.
11. Eudora Welty, "And They All Lived Happily Ever After," *New York Times* (Book Review), Nov. 10, 1963, p. BR22.
12. Sheldon Cashdan, *The Witch Must Die: How Fairy Tales Shape Our Lives* (New York: Basic Books, 1999), p. 6. Cashdan is Emeritus Professor of Psychology at the University of Massachusetts, Amherst.
13. See "Sun, Moon, and Talia," online article, Iowa State University, www.public.iastate.edu/~lhagge/sun,moon.htm. And then there is the old fairy tale "Donkeyskin," which features as a main plot element the incestuous feelings a father has for his daughter after her mother dies. He is a king who has been made wealthy thanks to a magical donkey that produces golden dung. The donkey is eventually slain—and completely skinned—at the request of the daughter, who must flee the kingdom or else marry her father. The princess then finds a prince, who marries her, and they live happily ever after. The father finds another wife and repents of his sinful lust (see Maria Tatar, ed., *The Classic Fairy Tales* [New York: W.W. Norton & Co., 1999], pp. 109-116).
  Many horrific stories can be found in early publications of fairy tales. In the Grimms' collection there is "The Juniper Tree," in which a woman decapitates her stepson, chops his corpse into small pieces, and cooks him in a stew that her husband devours.

Countless other tales in their unedited form are just as macabre and gruesome (see Maria Tatar, *The Hard Facts of the Grimms' Fairy Tales* [Princeton: Princeton University Press, 1987]).

14. Jack Zipes, *Spells of Enchantment: The Wondrous Fairy Tales of Western Culture* (New York: Viking Penguin, 1991) p. 15.

15. A legend, in this context, should not be confused with an *urban legend*, which is a story form of more recent origin (although a few long-term urban legends go back hundreds of years). An *urban legend* is a false rumor that is supposedly true. These stories quickly infect a society and usually express some kind of anxiety that is specific to a particular place, time, or group of people. Not only are such stories entirely false, but they are also deliberately fabricated by an unknown person or persons. They often take the form of something that happened to "a friend" or "a friend of a friend." One example of an urban legend is the false claim that the president of Procter & Gamble admitted to being a Satanist on a national TV talk show—usually any one of a dozen popular programs (see Jan Harold Brunvand, *Too Good to Be True: The Colossal Book of Urban Legends* [New York: W.W. Norton & Company]).

16. An excellent introduction to mythology is Richard P. Martin, ed., *Bulfinch's Mythology: The Age of Fable, the Age of Chivalry, Legends of Charlemagne* (New York: Harper Collins, 1991). Epic tales include trace elements of profound truths and beliefs still held by large segments of modern society. For example, we have Assyria's famed *Epic of Gilgamesh*, perhaps the oldest known epic. The main character is seeking immortality and endures an event strikingly similar to Noah's Flood (see Malcolm Edwards and Robert Holdstock, *Realms of Fantasy* [New York: Doubleday, 1983], p. 5). Another epic is Homer's *Odyssey*, which tells of Odysseus's arduous but adventurous journey back to Greece from the Trojan Wars. We also have the well-known tale of Sindbad the sailor, whose perilous trip home is described in the Arabian epic, *One Thousand Nights and a Night*.

17. J.R.R. Tolkien, "On Fairie Stories," in Christopher Tolkien, ed., *J.R.R. Tolkien: The Monsters, and the Critics, and Other Essays* (New York: Houghton Mifflin Company, 1984), p. 109. This essay was originally a lecture given at the University of St. Andrews on Mar. 8, 1939.

18. Edwards and Holdstock, p. 7; Tolkien, pp. 122, 132.

19. Natalie Babbitt, "The Purpose of Fantasy," in Barbara Harrison and Gregory Maguire, *Innocence & Experience: Essays & Conversations on Children's Literature* (New York: Lothrop, Lee & Shepard Books, 1987), p. 180.

20. E.F. Bleiler, *A Checklist of Modern Fantastic Literature* (Shasta Publishers, 1948), p. 3, as quoted in C.N. Manlove, *Modern Fantasy: Five Studies* (London: Cambridge University Press, 1975), p. 1.

21. Elizabeth Cook, *The Ordinary and the Fabulous: An Introduction to Myths, Legends and Fairy Tales for Teachers and Storytellers* (New York: Cambridge University Press, 1969), p. 2.

22. Cook, p. 5.

Chapter Four: Trusting Souls

1. Bernice E. Cullinan, *Literature and the Child* (New York: Harcourt Brace Jovanovich, 1989) pp. 5, 8.

2. Margaret S. Steffensen, Chitra Joag-Dev, and Richard C. Anderson, "A Cross-Cultural Perspective on Reading Comprehension," *Reading Research Quarterly*, vol. 15, no. 1, 1979, pp. 10-29. Cited in Cullinan, p. 50.

3. C.S. Lewis, "On Stories," in *Essays Presented to Charles Williams* (London: Oxford University Press, 1947), p. 100.

4. Wolfgang Iser, "The Reading Process: A Phenomenological Approach," in *The Implied Reader* (Baltimore: John Hopkins University Press, 1974), 274-294. Cited in Cullinan, p. 9.

5. Elizabeth Fitzgerald Howard, "Delight and Definition: The Nuts and Bolts of Evaluating Children's Literature," *Top of the News*, vol. 43, no. 4, Summer 1987, p. 363.

6. An example of this can be seen in a study that examined the responses of fourth- and sixth-graders to Ursula Le Guin's *A Wizard of Earthsea* (1975), a fairly advanced fantasy novel. One fourth-grader complained about the long sentences that, "they just rumbled by like a jumbled bunch of words." Other fourth-graders consistently misread the phrase "loosing the shadow," which described the character Ged unleashing the shadow of death. One student remarked, "I didn't understand that part about him losing his shadow" (Bernice E. Cullinan, Kathy T. Harwood, and S. Lee Galda, "The Reader and the Story: Comprehension and Response," in *Journal of Research and Development in Education*, vol. 16, no. 3, Spring 1983, pp. 29-38).

7. See André Favat, *Child and Tale: The Origins of Interest* (Urbana, IL: National Council of Teachers of English, 1977), pp. 38, 50. Bernice Cullinan observes, "[Children] consider it just when the scoundrel cook in 'The Pink' is forced to eat live coals for having deceived the king or when the maid-in-waiting is put naked into a barrel stuck with nails and dragged along the streets for having posed as the true princess in 'The Goose Girl.'...Fairy tales embody an accurate representation of the child's conception of morality" (Cullinan, p. 18).

8. Zena Sutherland and May Hill Arbuthnot, *Children and Books* (New York: Harper Collins, 1991; eighth ed.), p. 35.

9. James Britton, *Language and Learning* (Harmondsworth, England: Penguin Books, 1970), p. 11. Cited in Cullinan, p. 22.

10. A more mature outworking of this phenomenon is the playing of Dungeons and Dragons by adolescents and young adults (as well as some older adults).

11. Cullinan, p. 23.

12. See J. Piaget, *The Origins of Intelligence in Children* (New York: International Universities Press, 1952; tr. M. Cook).

13. Cullinan, p. 19.

14. James E. Higgins, *Beyond Words: Mystical Fancy in Children's Literature* (New York: Teachers College Press, 1970), pp. 49, 51.

15. Higgins, pp. 51-52.

16. Richard Le Gallienne, "Concerning Fairy Tales," in *Attitudes and Avowals*, (New York: John Lane Co, 1910) p. 37.

17. Lloyd Alexander, "Wishful Thinking—or Hopeful Dreaming," in Robert H. Boyer and Kenneth J. Zahorski, eds., *Fantasists on Fantasy: A Collection of Critical Reflections by Eighteen Masters of the Art* (New York: Avon Books, 1984), pp. 145-146,147,148.

18. Terry Pratchett, "When the Children Read Fantasy," *The Science Fact & Fiction Concatenation* (1994), www.concatenation.org/articles/pratchett.html.

19. G.K. Chesterton, as quoted in Pratchett.

Chapter Five: Life in Middle-Earth

1. Michael White, *The Life and Work of J.R.R. Tolkien* (Indianapolis: Alpha, 2002), p. 94.

2. Humphrey Carpenter, *Tolkien: The Authorized Biography* (New York: Ballantine Books, 1978), p. 110.

3. Quoted in Carpenter, p. 94; J.R.R. Tolkien, *The Fellowship of the Ring* (New York: Ballantine Books, 1973), p. 11.

4. J.R.R. Tolkien, letter to W.H. Auden, June 7, 1955, as quoted in Robert H. Boyer and Kenneth J. Zahorski, eds., *Fantasists on Fantasy: A Collection of Critical Reflections by Eighteen Masters of the Art* (New York: Avon Books, 1984), p. 92.

5. Quoted in Carpenter, p. 193.

6. In a 1958 letter to a Miss Webster, Tolkien confided, "I am in fact a hobbit (in all but size). I like gardens, trees and unmechanized farmlands; I smoke a pipe, and like good plain food (unrefrigerated), but detest French cooking; I like, and even dare to wear in these dull days, ornamental waistcoats. I am fond of mushrooms (out of a field); have a very simple sense of humor (which even my appreciative critics find tiresome); I go to bed late and get up late (when possible). I do not travel much" (J.R.R. Tolkien, letter to Miss Webster, Oct. 25, 1958, reprinted in Deborah Webster Rogers and Ivor A. Rogers, *J.R.R. Tolkien* [Boston: G.K. Hall & Co., 1980], p. 126).

7. J.R.R. Tolkien, *The Hobbit* (New York: Ballantine Books, 1965; 1982 rev. ed.), p. 302.

8. C.S. Lewis, *Of This and Other Worlds* (London: Geoffrey Bles, 1967), p. 111.

9. C.S. Lewis, *Time & Tide*, Aug. 14, 1954.

10. Tolkien, *The Fellowship*, p. 85.

11. Jeffrey Richards, *Daily Telegram*, Feb. 1, 1997, as quoted in Joseph Pearce, *Tolkien: Man and Myth* (San Francisco: Ignatius Press, 1998), p. 9.

12. Mark Gauvreau Judge, "The Trouble with Harry," July 12-18, 2000, *Baltimore City Paper*, online ed., www.citypaper.com/news/story.asp?id=3583.

13. J.R.R. Tolkien, letter to Robert Murray, Dec. 2, 1953, reprinted in Humphrey Carpenter, ed., *The Letters of J.R.R. Tolkien* (Boston: Houghton Mifflin, 1981), p. 172.

14. Eugene C. Hargrove, "An Essay," *Mythlore*, no. 47 (Aug. 1986). Hargrove explains, "The Maiai who became the wizards of Middle-earth—and who had the same nature as the Valar—were converted to living beings temporarily: 'For with the consent of Eru they…[were] clad in the bodies of Men, real and not feigned, but subject to the fears and pains and weariness of earth, able to hunger and thirst and be slain'" (see updated essay, "Who Is Tom Bombadil?" www.cas.unt.edu/~hargrove/bombadil.html). Hargrove is a philosophy professor at the University of North Texas.

15. J.R.R. Tolkien, unsent draft of letter to Robert Murray, Nov. 4, 1954, reprinted in Carpenter, *The Letters*, p. 202; Richard L. Purtill, *J.R.R. Tolkien: Myth, Morality, and Religion* (San Francisco: Harper & Row, 1984), pp. 110-111.

16. "Their name, as related to Wise, is an Englishing of their Elvish name, and is used throughout as *utterly distinct* from Sorcerer or Magician [emphasis added]….They were as one might say the near equivalent in the mode of these tales of Angels, guardian Angels. Their powers are directed primarily to the encouragement of the enemies of evil, to cause them to use their own wits and valor, to unite and endure" (J.R.R. Tolkien, note on letter to Milton Waldman, c. 1951, reprinted in Carpenter, *The Letters*, p. 159).

17. J.R.R. Tolkien, letter to Naomi Mitchison, Apr. 25, 1954, reprinted in Carpenter, *The Letters*, p. 180.

18. He wrote: "'Wizards' are not in any sense or degree 'shady.' Not mine. I am under the difficulty of finding English names for mythological creatures with other names,

since people would not 'take' a string of Elvish names, and I would rather they took my legendary creatures even with the false associations of the 'translation' than not at all. Even the dwarfs are not really Germanic 'dwarfs'...and I call them 'dwarves' to mark that. They are not naturally evil, not necessarily hostile, and not a kind of maggot-folk bred in stone; but a variety of incarnate rational creature" (Tolkien, letter to Murray, Nov. 4, 1954, in Carpenter, *The Letters*, p. 207).

19. Tolkien, letter to Murray, Nov. 4, 1954, in Carpenter, *The Letters*, p. 207.

20. Tolkien, letter to Murray, Nov. 4, 1954, in Carpenter, *The Letters*, p. 205.

21. J.R.R. Tolkien, letter to Michael Straight, c. Jan./Feb. 1956, reprinted in Carpenter, *The Letters*, p. 235; J.R.R. Tolkien, letter to A.E. Couchman, Apr. 27, 1966, reprinted in Carpenter, *The Letters*, p. 368; Tolkien, letter to Murray, Nov. 4, 1954, in Carpenter, *The Letters*, p. 205.

22. Tolkien, *The Fellowship*, pp. 76, 81.

23. Willis B. Glover, "The Christian Character of Tolkien's Invented World," *Criticism* (Winter 1971), no. 13, pp. 39-53. Quoted in Dan Graves, "Christian Elements and Symbols in Tolkien's The Lord of the Rings," *Christian History Institute*, www.gospel com.net/chi/morestories/tolkien.shtml.

24. Tolkien, letter to Murray, Nov. 4, 1954, in Carpenter, *The Letters*, p. 205; J.R.R. Tolkien, letter to Naomi Mitchison, Sept. 25, 1954, reprinted in Carpenter, *The Letters*, pp. 197-198.

25. Tom Shippey, *J.R.R. Tolkien: Author of the Century* (New York: Harper Collins, 2000), pp. 238-239, 242.

26. White, p. 214.

27. This observation about Galadriel was first submitted to Tolkien in a letter by his friend Father Murray. In reply, "Tolkien thanked the priest for his perceptive interpretations and agreed that he indeed had placed many of his views concerning Mary into the character of Galadriel" (Tolkien, letter to Murray, Dec. 2, 1953, reprinted in Carpenter, *The Letters*, p. 172).

28. White, p. 214.

29. Mark Eddy Smith, *Tolkien's Ordinary Virtues: Exploring the Spiritual Themes of The Lord of the Rings* (Downers Grove, IL: InterVarsity Press, 2002).

30. Kurt Bruner and Jim Ware, *Finding God in the Lord of the Rings* (Wheaton, IL: Tyndale House, 2001), p. xiv.

31. White, p. 216; John Tolkien, in *A Film Portrait of J.R.R. Tolkien* (Visual Corporation, Ltd., 1992), a video production.

32. J.R.R. Tolkien, letter to W.H. Auden, May 12, 1965, in Carpenter, *The Letters*, p. 355.

33. J.R.R. Tolkien, letter to Camilla Unwin, May 20, 1969, reprinted in Carpenter, *The Letters*, p. 400.

34. J.R.R. Tolkien, *Tree and Leaf* (London: Allen & Unwin, 1964), p. 50.

35. Tolkien, *Tree and Leaf*, pp. 40-41.

36. Tolkien, letter to Waldman (see note 16), in Carpenter, *The Letters*, p. 147.

37. Carpenter, *Authorized Biography*, p. 151.

38. C.S. Lewis, as quoted in Smith, p. 13.

39. Tolkien, *Tree and Leaf*, pp. 62-63.

40. C.N. Manlove, *Modern Fantasy: Five Studies* (London: Cambridge University Press, 1975), p. 163.

41. Tolkien, *The Fellowship*, p. 321; Colin Gunton, *King's Theological Review* (1989), vol. 12, no. 1, p. 8. Cited in Pearce, p. 117.

42. Tolkien, *The Fellowship*, pp. 320-321.
43. John Emerich Edward Dalberg Acton, letter to Bishop Mandell Creighton, Apr. 3, 1887, see *Life and Letters of Mandell Creighton* (1904), vol. 1, ch. 13.
44. Graves, www.gospelcom.net/chi/morestories/tolkien.shtml; Paul H. Kocher, *Master of Middle-earth* (Boston: Houghton Mifflin, 1972), p. 76.
45. Tolkien, letter to Waldman (see note 26), in Carpenter, *The Letters*, p. 146; Purtill, p. 110.
46. J.R.R. Tolkien, "On Fairie Stories," in Christopher Tolkien, ed., *J.R.R. Tolkien: The Monsters, and the Critics, and Other Essays* (New York: Houghton Mifflin Company, 1984), pp. 142-143.
47. Tolkien, *The Hobbit*, p. 11. The other kind of magic that exists in Middle-earth is magic within various objects (e.g., weapons, rings, helmets, mirrors). These objects receive special qualities through science or technology. They are created in accordance with the laws of nature as found in Middle-earth.
48. Tolkien, letter to Mitchison, September 25, 1954, in Carpenter, *The Letters*, p. 200.
49. J.R.R. Tolkien, *The Return of the King* (New York: Ballantine Books, 1965; 1983 ed.), p. 299.
50. Tolkien, *The Fellowship*, p. 317.
51. Joseph Pearce, in "J.R.R. Tolkien's Take on the Truth," interview with Pearce by Zenit, www.leaderu.com/humanities/zenit-tolkien.html.

Chapter Six: A Land Called Narnia

1. C.S. Lewis, letter to an American girl, undated. Quoted in Kathryn Lindskoog, *The Lion of Judah in Never-Never Land: God, Man, and Nature in C.S. Lewis's Narnia Tales* (Grand Rapids, MI: Eerdmans Publishing Co., 1973; 1979 ed.), p. 16.
2. Michael Coren, *J.R.R. Tolkien: The Man Who Created The Lord of the Rings* (Toronto: Stiddart, 2001), p. 56. This group included Nevill Coghill (Exeter scholar of medieval literature); Richard Dawkins (professor of Byzantine and modern Greek); George Gordon (president of Magdalen College); and C.T. Onions (editor of the *Oxford English Dictionary*).
3. C.S. Lewis, under May 11, 1926, *The Lewis Papers*, Wade Collection, Wheaton College (Wheaton, IL), as quoted in Michael White, *The Life and Work of J.R.R. Tolkien* (Indianapolis: Alpha, 2002), p. 127; Humphrey Carpenter, *The Inklings* (London: Allen & Unwin, Ltd., 1978), p. 52.
4. A theist is someone who believes there exists a god, usually a personal God.
5. Some of the Inklings also met informally on Tuesday mornings at The Eagle and the Child, an Oxford pub known to regulars as "The Bird and Baby."
6. David Barratt, *C.S. Lewis and His World* (London: Marshall Pickering, 1987), p. 28.
7. *The Lion, the Witch, and the Wardrobe* is the original first book in the Chronicles. But its plot is predated by *The Magician's Nephew* (initially Book VI), which is now being published as Book I. *The Horse and His Boy* (formerly Book V) has been moved into the Book III slot. These alterations to the original order allow the entire saga to flow in chronological order.
8. C.S. Lewis, as quoted in Barratt, p. 31.
9. C.S. Lewis, letter to Maryland fifth-graders, 1954. Quoted in Laurel L. Cornell, "They Don't Know Jack—C.S. Lewis, Political Correctness," *American Enterprise*, Sept. 2001, www.findarticles.com/p/articles/mi_m2185/is_6_12/ai_77607914.
10. Barratt, p. 31.

11. "The Chronicles of Narnia," *Wikipedia*, http://en.wikipedia.org/wiki/The_Chronicles_of_Narnia.
12. See C.S. Lewis, *The Magician's Nephew* (London: The Bodley Head, 1955; in single-volume edition of *The Chronicles of Narnia* [New York: HarperCollins, 2004]), pp. 96-101); C.S. Lewis, *The Lion, the Witch, and the Wardrobe* (London: Geoffrey Bles, 1950; in single-volume edition of *The Chronicles of Narnia* [New York: HarperCollins, 2004]), pp. 185, 191; C.S. Lewis, *The Horse and His Boy* (London: Geoffrey Bles, 1954; in single-volume edition of *The Chronicles of Narnia* [New York: HarperCollins, 2004]), p. 282.
13. Lewis, *The Lion*, p. 185; C.S. Lewis, *The Silver Chair* (London: Geoffrey Bles, 1953; in single-volume edition of *The Chronicles of Narnia* [New York: HarperCollins, 2004]), pp. 557-558, and Lewis, *The Horse*, p. 283.
14. Lewis, *The Horse*, p. 281.
15. C.S. Lewis, *The Voyage of the Dawn Treader* (London: Geoffrey Bles, 1952; in single-volume edition of *The Chronicles of Narnia* [New York: HarperCollins, 2004]), p. 541.
16. C.S. Lewis, *The Last Battle* (London: The Bodley Head, 1956; in single-volume edition of *The Chronicles of Narnia* [New York: HarperCollins, 2004]), p. 744.
17. Paul F. Ford, *Companion to Narnia* (San Francisco: HarperSanFrancisco, 1980), p. 305.
18. Ford, p. 404; Lewis, *The Magician's Nephew*, p. 71.
19. Ford, p. 304.
20. C.S. Lewis, "Membership," first published in *Sobornost*, June 1945. This lecture—originally given by Lewis to the Society of St. Alban and St. Sergius, Oxford—was reprinted in *Transposition and Other Addresses* (1949) and elsewhere (e.g., *The Weight of Glory* [San Francisco: HarperSanFrancisco 2001 ed.]) and quoted in Kathryn Lindskoog, "Sex, Love and Marriage," *The Lewis Legacy*, Summer 2000, issue #85, available at www.discovery.org.

    And again, along similar lines, we have Lewis declaring, "When human souls have become as perfect in voluntary obedience as the inanimate creation is in its lifeless obedience, then they will put on its glory, or rather that greater glory of which Nature is only the first sketch" (C.S. Lewis, as quoted in Cindy Crosby, "For Everything There Is a Season," *Christianity Today*, Nov./Dec. 2004, www.christianitytoday.com/bc/2004/006/19.34.html).
21. Lewis, *The Silver Chair*, pp. 624-625.
22. Lewis, *The Silver Chair*, p. 559.
23. Lewis, *The Silver Chair*, p. 626.
24. Lucy, for example, in *The Lion, the Witch, and the Wardrobe*, fails to obey Aslan's command to come back to him at a certain time. She does not return to him because none of her siblings believe what she has told them about Narnia and Aslan.
25. Ford, pp. 78-82. Ford lists the following—*The Lion, the Witch and the Wardrobe* (Rom. 5:12; Lk. 2:30; Matt. 12:18-20; 26:38; 27:28,29,46; Hos. 11:10-11; Is. 65:16,19; Gen. 2:23; Eph. 6:11-17; 1 Cor. 2:5-8; Heb. 12:2; John 20:22; 6:1-14; 10:16); *Prince Caspian* (Is. 9:1; Mk. 13:29; Jn. 2:9; 6:66); *The Voyage of the Dawn Treader* (Ja. 5:16; 1 Cor. 13:12; Eph. 5:21; Is. 6:6; Jn. 21:12); *The Silver Chair* (Ps. 21:9; 31:5, 103:9; Jn. 7:37-38, 8:11; Deut. 6:4-9; Rom. 14:8; 1 Jn. 1:7; Ex. 4:4, 33:23); *The Horse and His Boy* (Jn. 20:19,27; Lk. 24:39; Matt. 25:21; 1 Peter 5:7; Dan. 4:24-33); *The Magician's Nephew* (Genesis 1:24; 2:19; 3:19; Job 38:7; Ps.19:5; 2 Sam.

18:33; 1 Cor. 15:21; Lk. 19:42); *The Last Battle* (Deut. 33:27; Ps. 77:10; Mk. 13:8,25; Eph. 1:7; Jn. 20:25-29; Rev. 22:2; Lk. 2:7; Matt. 25:21). Consider the following examples:

- *Lewis*: "[Aslan] made no noise, even when the enemies, straining and tugging, pulled the cords so tight that they cut into his flesh" (*The Lion*, p. 180).
  Bible: "He was oppressed and He was afflicted, yet He did not open His mouth; like a lamb that is led to the slaughter, and like a sheep that is silent before its shearers, so He did not open his mouth" (Isaiah 53:7 NASB).
- *Lewis*: "[He was] surrounded by the whole crowd of creatures kicking him, hitting him, spitting on him, jeering at him" (Lewis, (*The Lion*, p. 189).
  Bible: "The men who were guarding Jesus began mocking and beating him. They blindfolded him and demanded, 'Prophesy! Who hit you?' And they said many other insulting things to him" (Lk. 22:63-65).
- *Lewis*: "You would not have called to me unless I had been calling to you" (*The Silver Chair*, p. 558).
  Bible: "No one can come to me unless the Father who sent me draws him" (John 6:44).
- *Lewis*: "'Come and have breakfast,' said the Lamb in its sweet milky voice. "Then they noticed for the first time that there was a fire lit on the grass and fish roasting on it" (*The Voyage*, p. 540).
  Bible: "Jesus said to them, 'Come and have breakfast'" (John 21:12).

26. Lindskoog, *The Lion of Judah*, p. 121.
27. Lewis, *The Lion*, p. 146.
28. Peter Hitchens, "A Labour of Loathing," *The Spectator*, Jan. 18, 2003, www.lewrock well.com/spectator/spec11.html; "Philip Pullman: His Dark Materials—A Not-So Subtle Knife," *Facing the Challenge*, www.facingthechallenge.org/pullman.htm.
29. Philip Pullman, as quoted in John Ezard, "Narnia Books Attacked as Racist and Sexist," *The Guardian*, June 3, 2002, http://books.guardian.co.uk/guardianhayfestival 2002/story/0,11873,726818,00.html; Philip Pullman, interview with David Weich, "Philip Pullman Reaches the Garden," Aug. 31, 2000, www.powells.com/ authors/pullman.html.
30. Philip Pullman, interview during the Readers and Writers Roadshow, July 11, 2002, www.bbc.co.uk/bbcfour/books/readers/clips/preview.shtml?2002/0710/clips/pull man_philip; "Rational Magic," *The Guardian*, Jan. 28, 2000, http://books.guardian. co.uk/reviews/childrenandteens/0,6121,388823,00.html.
31. Philip Pullman, as quoted in Peter Hitchens, "This Is the Most Dangerous Author in Britain," *The Mail on Sunday*, Jan. 27, 2002, p. 63, http://pers-www.wlv.ac.uk/~bu1895 /hitchens.htm.
32. Ed Vulliamy, "Author Angers the Bible Belt, *The Guardian*, Aug. 26, 2001, http://books.guardian.co.uk/bookerprize2001/story/0,1090,543410,00.html; Andrew Carey, writing in *Church of England Newspaper*, June 13, 2002. Quoted in *The Weekly Standard*, as cited in "Pullman Criticizes Lewis for Celebrating Death," *Facing the Challenge*, www.facingthechallenge.org/pplewis4.htm.
33. Amy Welborn, "His Dark Materials," online article, www.amywelborn.com/reviews/ pullman.html.
34. Ford, p. 275.
35. See Don W. King, "The Childlike in George MacDonald and C.S. Lewis," *Mythlore*, Summer 1986, pp. 17-22, 26, http://cslewis.drzeus.net/papers/childlike.html. King is a professor of English at Montreat College.

36. Ford, p. 275. For example, Lucy is the one who makes an allusion to Christ in our world (see *The Last Battle*, p. 744).

37. Ford, pp. 326-329.

38. Lewis, *The Last Battle*, p. 732.

39. Gregg Easterbrook, "In Defense of C.S. Lewis," *The Atlantic Monthly*, Oct. 2001, www.theatlantic.com/doc/prem/200110/easterbrook. For example, Darwin said that the "negro" was an intermediate state between apes and Caucasians (see Charles Darwin, *Descent of Man*, 1871, p. 201). He went so far as to predict that at some point in the relatively near future, all of the "inferior" races would be exterminated in favor of the more civilized White/European race (see Charles Darwin, *Life and Letters*, p. 318)..

40. As a personal example, I mention my wife, who is Asian. She has faced both racism and prejudice, but knows the difference between them. Racists want to harm her; they express hatred toward her, belittle and mock her, and would, if they had the chance, deny her various rights simply because she is not like them.

    But those who have shown prejudice toward her are simply uninformed. Some of them instantly think that just because she is Asian, she eats rice all of the time (in reality, she does not eat rice at all). Others immediately talk more slowly to her because they think she does not understand English (in reality, she is a California "Valley girl" through and through). And when she sings, a few people have actually said, "Wow, you sound great—you don't sound Asian at all." These people are prejudiced. Neither I, nor my wife, would ever say, as Pullman has said of Lewis, that they are "profoundly racist" or "blatantly racist." Most people who hold such stereotypes, do so without malice, and once they receive more information, they often abandon their preconceived ideas. This no doubt would have held true for Lewis had he lived into the 1970s and 1980s.

41. "Pullman Criticizes Lewis for Being Racist and Sexist," www.facingthechallenge.org/pplewis5.htm.

42. Philip Pullman, as quoted in Helena de Bertodano, "I Am the Devil's Party," *The Sunday Telegraph*, Jan. 29, 2002, available at www.telegraph.co.uk; Philip Pullman, as quoted in Susan Roberts, "A Dark Agenda?" Nov. 2002, www.surefish.co.uk/culture/features/pullman_interview.htm; Pullman, as quoted in Eccleshare, http://books.guardian.co.uk/reviews/childrenandteens/0,6121,388823,00.html.

43. Pullman, as quoted in Bertodano, www.telegraph.co.uk.

44. On a personal note, Reepicheep—a talking mouse about one or two feet tall who wears a rapier at his side and a gold headband on his head—is my favorite character. He is the bravest of the brave—always courageous, willing to do battle, calm and cool under pressure, and loyal to the end. He is the only one who actually sails to the land of Aslan, across the Last Sea in the Utter East. In *The Last Battle*, he is the one to welcome the children into heaven, saying, "Welcome in the Lion's name"; and then he gives the invitation for all to "come farther up and further in."

45. Lewis, *The Last Battle*, p. 767.

46. Lewis, *The Last Battle*, p. 767.

47. Pullman, as quoted in Ezard, http://books.guardian.co.uk/guardianhayfestival2002/story/0,11873,726818,00.html.

48. Lewis, *The Last Battle*, p. 135.

49. Pullman, as quoted in Easterbrook, www.theatlantic.com/doc/prem/200110/easterbrook.

50. Pullman, as quoted in Roberts, www.surefish.co.uk/culture/features/pullman_inter view.htm.

51. Mark Ryan and Carole Hausmann Ryan, "Killing God: The Propaganda of His Dark Materials," *Christian Research Journal*, vol. 26, no. 3, 2003, p. 38.

52. Pullman, as quoted in Vulliamy, http://books.guardian.co.uk/bookerprize2001/story/ 0,1090,543410,00.html; Pullman, as quoted in Eccleshare, http://books.guardian. co.uk/reviews/childrenandteens/0,6121,388823,00.html.

53. Mary R. Bowman, "A Darker Ignorance: C.S. Lewis and the Nature of the Fall— Critical Essay," *Mythlore*, Summer 2003, available at www.findarticles.com.

54. Lewis, *The Last Battle*, p. 741; Robert Houston, *Patches of Godlight: The Pattern of Thought of C.S. Lewis* (Athens, GA: University of Georgia, 1981), p. 176. Quoted in Bowman, www.findarticles.com.

55. Lewis, *The Voyage*, p. 541.

56. Philip Pullman, interview with the Readers and Writers Roadshow, July 11, 2002, www.bbc.co.uk/bbcfour/books/readers/clips/preview.shtml?2002/0710/clips/pull man_philip.

57. Peter J. Shakel, *Imagination and the Arts in C.S. Lewis* (Columbia, MO: University of Missouri, 2002), p. ix; C.S. Lewis, *Miracles* (New York: Macmillan, 1972), footnotes, p. 139; Christopher C. McClinch, "Reason, Imagination, and Universalism in C.S. Lewis," thesis submitted to the Faculty of the Virginia Polytechnic Institute and State University, Apr. 17, 2002.

58. C.S. Lewis, "On Three Ways of Writing for Children," in Lewis, *The Chronicles of Narnia* (one-volume edition), p. 777.

Chapter Seven: Welcome to Hogwarts

1. J.K. Rowling, as quoted in Chuck Colson, "Witches and Wizards: The Harry Potter Phenomenon," *Breakpoint Commentary* #91102, Nov. 2, 1999, available at www.pfmonline.net.

2. J.K. Rowling, *Harry Potter and the Sorcerer's Stone* (New York: Scholastic Press, 1997), p. 58.

3. To list all of the occult elements in Harry Potter would be impossible in a note. A few notable instances, however, should be documented: divination (astrology—Book II, pp. 254, 257), clairvoyance (Book IV, pp. 17, 576-577), magick (throughout Books I-VI), herbology (Book I, p. 133), potions (Book I, p. 137), spirit-channeling (Book III, p. 324), necromancy (Book III, p. 162). Regarding the last element, Rowling's characters constantly speak with the spirit realm via ghosts. They commune with spirits such as Professor Binns (one of the Hogwarts teachers), Peeves (a malevolent spirit), Moaning Myrtle (a murdered Hogwarts student), and Nearly Headless Nick (Gryffindor's resident apparition).

4. Raven Grimassi, *Encyclopedia of Wicca & Witchcraft* (St. Paul: Llewellyn Publications, 2000), p. 405.

5. Dawn Marie Nikithser (Hightstown, New Jersey), post #1375, Nov. 19, 2001, Pagan Perspectives, www.witchvox.com/qotw/qwp_detail.html?id=68.

6. "Potter: Modern Fairy-Tale Hero," July-Aug. 2003, *Duke Magazine*, vol. 89, no. 5, www.dukemagazine.duke.edu/dukemag/issues/070803/depgaz8.html.

7. Allan Zola Kronzek and Elizabeth Kronzek, *The Sorcerer's Companion* (New York: Broadway Books, 2001), pp. 32-34, 149-153; Kronzek and Kronzek, pp.28-31.

8. See list of initiation degrees at Ordo Anno Mundi at www.coven-of-cythrawl.com/oam_initiation.htm.

Ordo Anno Mundi	Hogwarts School
"Evocation, spellcasting, ritual, and divination" (1st Degree)	"We will be covering the basic methods of Divination this year" (*Prisoner of Azkaban*, p. 103). "All students should have a copy of each of the following: *The Standard Book of Spells* (Grade 1)" (*Sorcerer's Stone*, p. 66).
"Werewolf" "Animal Transformation" [Transfiguration] (4th Degree)	"Transfiguration is some of the most complex and dangerous magic you will learn at Hogwarts" (*Sorcerer's Stone*, p. 134). "My transformations in those days—were terrible. It is very painful to turn into a werewolf….[My friends] became Animagi….They could each turn into a different animal at will" (*Prisoner of Azkaban*, pp. 353-354).
"magical lore and techniques" [History of Magic] (5th Degree)	"Their very last exam was History of Magic" (*Sorcerer's Stone*, p. 263).

9. The following book titles from Harry Potter are found in Rowling, *Sorcerer's Stone*, p. 66:

Harry Potter	Real-World Occultism
The Standard Book of Spells	Book of Spells (1997) by Arthur Edward Waite
A History of Magic	The History of Magic (1997) by Eliphas Levi
One Thousand Magical Herbs and Fungi	Encyclopedia of Magical Herbs (1985) by Scott Cunningham
Magical Drafts and Potions	Magick Potions: How to Prepare and Use Homemade Oils, Aphrodisiacs, Brews and Much More (1998) by Gurina Dunwich

10. J.K. Rowling, Barnes & Noble Chat, Sept. 8, 1999, www.hogwarts-library.net/reference/interviews/19990908_BarnesNoble.html; J.K. Rowling, Barnes & Noble Chat, Mar. 19, 1999, www.hogwarts-library.net/reference/interviews/19990319_Barnes Noble.html; J.K. Rowling, as quoted in Stephanie Loer. "All About Harry Potter from Quidditch to the Future of the Sorting Hat," *The Boston Globe*, Oct. 18, 1999, available at www.quick-quote-quill.org/index2.html.

More recently Rowling has said, "Ninety–let's say ninety-five percent at least, of the magic in the books is entirely invented by me" (J.K. Rowling, "Harry and Me," interview with the BBC, 2002, available at www.quick-quote-quill.org/index2.html). In another interview she claimed, "The material is almost all from my imagination" (J.K. Rowling, Barnes and Noble & Yahoo Chat, Oct. 20, 2000, available at www.quick-quote-quill.org/index2.html). I could find no information given by Rowling that explained when, why, or how her estimation of the amount of invented "magic" in the books jumped from two-thirds (about 67 percent) to "ninety-five percent" and "almost all."

11. See the "Mythbuster," www.darkforce.com/wicca/myths.htm.

12. Rowling, *Sorcerer's Stone*, p. 291. Satanist Anton LaVey labeled as nonsense any differentiations between white (good) and black (evil) magick: "White magic is supposedly utilized only for good or unselfish purposes, and black magic, we are told, is used only for selfish or 'evil' reasons. Satanism draws no such dividing line. Magic is magic, be it used to help or hinder" (Anton LaVey, *The Satanic Bible* [New York: Avon Books, 1969], p. 51).

13. Starling (Montreal, Quebec), post 1420, Nov. 22, 2001, Pagan Perspectives, www.witchvox.com/qotw/qwp_detail.html?offset=48&id=68.

14. Kronzek and Kronzek, pp. 1, 4, 10, 36, 41, 56, 120, 159, 182, 191, 221, 249.

15. Vablatsky/Blavatsky is mentioned in J.K. Rowling, *Harry Potter and the Prisoner of Azkaban* (New York: Scholastic Books, 1999), p. 53.

16. Leslie A. Shepard, ed., *Encyclopedia of Occultism & Parapsychology* vol. 2, (Detroit: Gale Research, 1991), p. 1250.

17. Rosemary Ellen Guiley, *The Encyclopedia of Witches & Witchcraft* (New York: Checkmark Books, 1999), pp. 5-6.

18. Colin Covert, "A Genuine Touch of Magic," *Star Tribune* (Minneapolis-St. Paul), Nov. 16, 2001, p. 22E, available at startribune.com.

19. Moon Pixie (Elyria, Ohio), post 1435, Nov. 24, 2001, Pagan Perspectives, www.witchvox.com/qotw/qwp_detail.html?offset=60&id=68.

20. Starling, www.witchvox.com/qotw/qwp_detail.html?offset=48&id=68.

21. IO, "The Harry Potter Witchcraft Spellbook," www6.aeonflux.net/~io/index.html.

22. Phyllis Curott, as quoted in Buck Wolf, "Maybe They Can't Fly, but They Love Their Magical Portrayal in the Kid's Book," ABC News Online, http://abcnews.go.com/US/story?id=96531&page=1.

23. Deepti Hajela, "Potter Charms Modern-Day Witches" (Associated Press), May 30, 2000, www.cesnur.org/recens/potter_024.htm.

24. Sarah the Swamp Witch, in "Our Question of the Month: Is Witchcraft a Religion?" posted comment, www.dutchie.org/Tracy/advice.html. In this same Internet thread, another witch explained, "For those who believe that the practice of magic does not involve deity, then witchcraft (with a small 'w') might be the more appropriate term" (Dana). A third witch agreed: "As far as I am concerned, a 'witch' (please note small caps) does not have any pre-defined deity(s) they 'must' worship" (Cserrilyn Sadair).

25. Wren Walker, as quoted in David Yonke, "Some Fear Road to Hell Paved with 'Harry Potter,'" *Bradenton* (Florida) *Herald*, Nov. 24, 2001, www.cesnur.org/2001/potter/nov_16.htm. A reference to this "w" issue also can be found in Isaac Bonewits, *Witchcraft: A Concise History* (Edina, MN: PocketPCpress, 1971, 2001 ed.), excerpt at www.neopagan.net/Witchcraft-Classifying.html, which reads, "witchcraft-with-a-small-w: The beliefs and practices of those modern persons following one or more varieties of Neopagan Witchcraft who refuse to admit it."

26. J.K. Rowling, as quoted in Kathleen Koch, "Success of Harry Potter Bowls Author Over," CNN Online, October 21, 1999, www.cnn.com/books/news/9910/21/rowling.intvu/.

27. "Potter Prompts Course in Witchcraft," Feb. 18, 2002, BBC News, http://news.bbc.co.uk/1/hi/education/1827166.stm.

28. Rowling has stated that younger kids have actually written her after having convinced themselves that the story is true (J.K. Rowling, as quoted in Malcolm Jones, "The Return of Harry Potter!" *Newsweek*, July 1, 2000, p. 4, available at www.quick-quote-quill.org/index2.html.

29. J.K. Rowling, interview with Scholastic Books, Chat #2, Oct. 16, 2000, www.scholastic.com/harrypotter/author/transcript2.htm.

30. Dozens of articles and studies can be accessed from the Parents Television Council Web site at www.parentstv.org/ptc/outsidestudies/main.asp.

31. "An ardent reader of the Harry Potter books becomes familiar with terms such as divination, casting spells, omens, portents, and the weirdness of the occult is softened....[A] child seeing a fortuneteller or palm reader sign will have a sense of recognition rather than suspicion" (Elizabeth A. Wittman, "Occult Trends in Children's Literature," *Homiletic & Pastoral Review*, www.catholic.net/rcc/Periodicals/Homiletic/2000-10/wittman.html).

"The taste for such things, once awakened, may find titillation in play with Ouija boards, Tarot cards, or similar paraphernalia....Some may wish to go further, turning to the Internet or their local library for readily available information on Wiccan rituals or other forms of contemporary magical practice" (Steven D. Greydanus, "Harry Potter vs. Gandalf: An In-Depth Analysis of the Literary use of Magic in the Works of J.K. Rowling, J.R.R. Tolkien, and C.S. Lewis," 2001, Decent Films Online, http://decentfilms.com/commentary/magic.html).

"The most obvious problem, of course, is the author's use of the symbol-world of the occult as her primary metaphor, and occult activities as the dramatic engine of the plots. It presents these to the child reader through attractive role models....Rationally, children know that the fantasy element in the books is not 'real.' But emotionally and subconsciously the young reader absorbs it as real. This is further complicated by the fact that in the world around us there are many opportunities for young people to enter the occult subcultures, where some of Harry's powers are indeed offered as real" (Michael O'Brien, "Why Harry Potter Goes Awry," *Zenit News*, Dec. 6, 2001, www.catholiceducation.org/articles/arts/al0120.html).

32. Heather (Charlotte, North Carolina), message 1432, Nov. 24, 2001, Pagan Perspectives, www.witchvox.com/qotw/qwp_detail.html?offset=60&id=68.

33. Jason (Minneapolis, Minnesota), message #1372, Nov. 19, 2001, Pagan Perspectives, www.witchvox.com/qotw/qwp_detail.html?id=68.

34. DaraLuz (Maiden, North Carolina), message #1367, Nov. 19, 2001, Pagan Perspectives, www.witchvox.com/qotw/qwp_detail.html?id=68.

35. Linda (Milwaukee, Wisconsin), message #1390, Nov. 20, 2001, Pagan Perspectives, www.witchvox.com/qotw/qwp_detail.html?offset=12&id=68.

36. Riannon Silvermoon (New Westminster, British Columbia), message #1378, Nov. 19, 2001, Pagan Perspectives, www.witchvox.com/qotw/qwp_detail.html?id=68.

37. Henbane, "A Dream for Teen Witches," Nov. 2000, Pagan Perspectives, www.witchvox.com/words/words_2000/e_teencraft04.html.

Chapter Eight: Harry Hype

1. "Harry Potter Makes Boarding Fashionable," BBC News, Dec. 13, 1999, http://news.bbc.co.uk/hi/english/education/newsid_563000/563232.stm; Ann Williamson, as quoted in "Harry Potter Makes," http://news.bbc.co.uk/hi/english/education/newsid_563000/563232.stm.

2. John Roach, "Harry Potter Owl Scenes Alarm Animal Advocates," *National Geographic News*, Nov. 16, 2001, http://news.nationalgeographic.com.

3. "The cost of creature comfort," *The Times*, Apr. 13, 2002, www.timesonline.co.uk/printFriendly/0,,1-127-264112,00.html; Lisette Johnston, "Harry Potter Craze 'Putting Owls at Risk,'" Scottish Press Association, Jan. 3, 2005, http://news.scotsman.com/latest.cfm?id=3954085.

4. A reporter from Moscow's *Komsomolskaya Pravda* newspaper who went to the school said children told him they had been inventing potions and ceremonies ("Siberian Potter Fans Drink Poisonous Potion," Apr. 20, 2002, BBC News, http://news.bbc.co.uk/1/hi/world/monitoring/media_reports/1941152.stm.

5. "Stories from the Magic—Newswire: The Magic of Potter," June 29, 2001, www.linkingpage.com/062001.html; cf. Paul Gray, "The Magic of Potter," *Time*, Dec. 25, 2000, www.time.com/time/pacific/magazine/20001225/poy_rowling.html.

6. James Woudhuysen, "The Magic of Mobile, *Spiked-Online*, May 9, 2001, www.spiked-online.com/articles/00000002D0A7.htm.

7. "Buffy draws children to witchcraft," Aug. 4, 2000, http://news.bbc.co.uk/1/hi/entertainment/864984.stm.

8. "The Review," interview with Nigel Bourne, *Good Morning Television*, Aug. 2000, transcript by Lee Borrell, www.fortunecity.com/emachines/e11/86/pagan.html.

9. Sterling Gallagher, as quoted in " 'Harry Potter' Good for New Age Business," *Laurel Leader*, reprinted in *Hpana*, Oct. 2, 2003, www.hpana.com/news.17528.html. Gallagher also noted, "More adults than children come in under the Harry Potter influence."

10. Kronzek and Kronzek, p. xiv.

11 Silver Fire, "Cutting Open the Zip-Locked Mind," Mar. 2002, www.witchvox.com/teen/teen_2002/teen_parents04.html.

12. Knight has written more than a dozen books on witchcraft and neopaganism. She has also been a contributing editor to *Magical Blend* magazine for the past three years and a featured writer for *New Age Retailer* and *Aquarius* magazines.

13. "Sirona's Books," advertisement online at www.dcsi.net/~bluesky/bs3.htm.

14.
   - "The book will delight Wiccans, aspiring dabblers, and Harry Potter fans alike!" ("The Best Book of Modern Wizardry Developments," Aug. 2, 2002, amazon.com).
   - "I liked the 'Harry Potter' theme to the book while explaining what real magic truly is. However, in some instances I thought the Harry Potter theme went a bit far. For example, male Wiccans call themselves Witches, not 'wizards' " ("The Real Life Harry Potter?" May 24, 2002, amazon.com).
   - "I would recommend it to anyone who wants to be a Witch or Wizard. I really liked the fact that Sirona Knight told it like it is and gave a lot of thorough information on many magical topics such as Spellcasting, Potions, Divination, Animal Magic, and Defense Against the Dark Arts. There is a numerous amount of potion recipes in this book and that is something you don't see much in other books. Also there are many spells to start you off. I

was very impressed with how you are taught how to make many of your own magical tools. The divination part is great and gives a description of all of the runes and how to cast your fate using them" (A Great Introduction Into the Magical World," Jan. 22, 2002, amazon.com).

- "When I first picked up this book, I thought it too good to be true. But after reading it, I am astounded by all the information that's in it. It is the closest thing to Harry Potter that I have read" ("Harry Potter Comes to Life," Oct. 24, 2001, amazon.com).
- "The Harry Potter references were obvious in the title and in many of the chapter headings such as Divination and Defense Against the Dark Arts, but upon closer inspection I found this book to be a fairly accurate book about witchcraft and magic and not nearly as gimmicky as the title might suggest....Written in a very kid-accessible style, I was impressed with the solid beginner knowledge of the kind found in most adult books on witchcraft and paganism. I would highly recommend this book for any young adult looking to explore the real world of magick and witchcraft" ("Good Starter Book for Kids," Oct. 11, 2001, amazon.com).

15. "The Real Witch's Handbook," advertisement at http://witchcraft.org/books/KateWest.htm.
16. J.K. Rowling, interview on *Dateline NBC*, June 20, 2003, www.quick-quote-quill.org/articles/2003/0620-dateline-couric.htm.
17. Robert Knight, "A Few Thoughts About Harry," *Culture and Family*, Nov. 21, 2001, www.cultureandfamily.org/articledisplay.asp?id=312&department=CFI&categoryid=cfreport.
18. "Harry Potter's Horoscope," under "Web Sites About Harry Potter," www.sirlinksalot.net/potter.html; cf. "Bless You, Harry Potter. Thanks," Mar. 31, 2002, www.the-leaky-cauldron.org/MTarchives/week_2002_03_31.html.
19. Barbara Schermer, "Harry Potter: Is He Real?—Astrology Has An Answer," www.astrologyalive.com/Harry_Potter.html (see the horoscope at www.astrologyalive.com/HPCompleteChart.html).
20. www.astrologyalive.com/AA-Departments.html#Books. This Web page is accessed from Schermer's page on which she lists all of the Harry Potter books. The link "For Astrology Books Click Here" immediately follows all of Rowling's books (see www.astrologyalive.com/HPBooks.html).
21. See "Real Magick: The Science of Wizardry," advertised by the Discovery Channel, at http://dsc.discovery.com/convergence/realmagick/realmagick.html.
22. The document "Exclusive Download: Harry Potter" that is posted at this Internet resource Web site includes the following exercises (available at www.beachampublishing.com):
    - "Look up the names mentioned on the wizard cards [in *Sorcerer's Stone*]...and list whether they are real or fictional. If they are historical figures, write a paragraph about each magician, witch, or wizard."
    - "Learn about the role of witchcraft in different cultures. Either make a costume for yourself...or use construction paper to design the attire of witches in a specific geographic location."
    - "Write a poem, short play, literary non-fiction, or other form of expression about magic or witchcraft."
23. "Exclusive Download: Harry Potter," www.beachampublishing.com.

24. See "Harry Potter: Love vs. Hate," June 17, 2003, www.the-leaky-cauldron.org/MTarchives/003082.html.
25. See http://cybersleuth-kids.com/sleuth/Language_Arts/Childrens_Literature/Harry_Potter/index1.htm.
26. This site is billed as "The Largest Archive of J.K. Rowling Interviews on the Web." Entering terms such as witchcraft in its search engine brings up neopagan, occult, witchcraft, and Wiccan links.
27. Rowling explains the difference between her world and Narnia thus: "Narnia is literally a different world, whereas in the Harry books you go into a world within a world that you can see if you happen to belong" (J.K. Rowling, as quoted in Jennie Renton, "The Story Behind the Potter Legend: JK Rowling Talks About How She Created the Harry Potter Books and the Magic of Harry Potter's World," Sydney Morning Herald, Oct. 28, 2001, www.quick-quote-quill.org/articles/2001/1001-sydney-renton.htm.
28. Associated Press, "Harry Potter Author Defends Her Work," Oct. 14, 1999, www.quick-quote-quill.org/articles/1999/1099-ap.html; Alan Jacobs, "Harry Potter's Magic," First Things, Jan. 2000, 35-38, www.firstthings.com/ftissues/ft0001/reviews/jacobs.html).
29. Quoted in Robert Knight, The Age of Consent (Dallas: Spence Publishing, 1998), p. 10; Bill Watkins, in The New Absolutes (Minneapolis: Bethany House, 1996) explains, "As truth goes, morality goes....[People] say they believe that what is right for me may be wrong for you, and that no individual, group, or governing body has the right to set the ethical standard for anyone else" (p. 28).
30. Knight, p. 11; J.K. Rowling, "Q & A Session, Vancouver Writers' Festival," Oct. 25, 2000, available at www.quick-quote-quill.org/index2.html; Charles Taylor, "The Plot Deepens" Salon.com, July 10, 2000, available at www.salon.com.
31. In Sorcerer's Stone he begins breaking Hogwarts rules almost immediately after arriving.
32. On page 34 of The Prisoner of Azkaban, Harry lies to a bus driver. On page 155, he lies to Lupin, who is supposed to be his friend. On page 246, he again lies to Lupin, this time doing it "quickly." Harry then lies to Snape on pages 283–285. In Goblet of Fire (New York: Scholastic Books, 2000), Harry lies to Hagrid, a house-elf, Hermione, Professor Snape, Professor Trelawney, and Cornelius Fudge (Rowling, pp. 256, 408, 443, 456, 516, 577, 581)—all without negative consequences.
33. Rowling, Goblet of Fire, p. 722, emphasis added.
34. Rowling, Prisoner, pp. 355-356.
35. Rowling, Prisoner, pp. 28, 204.
36. Rowling, Prisoner, pp. 351-352.
37. Rowling, Prisoner, pp. 192,193.
38. Rowling, Goblet of Fire, pp. 55, 88, 367; pp. 88-89; p. 117.
39. Rowling, Harry Potter and the Chamber of Secrets (New York: Scholastic, 1999), pp. 33, 49, 66.
40. In Goblet of Fire (p. 45), Mr. Weasley illegally connects the Dursley's fireplace to the wizard's network of fireplaces (a magical conduit of travel). "Muggle fireplaces aren't supposed to be connected, strictly speaking," he confesses. "But I've got a useful contact at the Floo Regulation Panel and he fixed it for me." Weasley even breaks rules for others. When the son of a friend landed in trouble for illegally bewitching a Muggle object, he "smoothed the whole thing over," effectively freeing the boy from

punishment (p. 61). Weasley, far from being a model father or wizard, is a liar, hypocrite, and lawbreaker. And as a parent he shows an appalling lack of control over his children.

41. Hagrid performs spells even though he is not supposed to do magic. (He was expelled from Hogwarts during his third year, which means he never graduated to the level of full wizard—*Sorcerer's Stone*, pp. 59, 64.) He repeatedly ignores legal statutes applicable to the entire wizard world. For instance, he raises an "illegal" dragon, violating the "1709 Warlock's Convention" law prohibiting dragon-breeding in Britain (*Sorcerer's Stone*, pp. 230-233). He even asks Harry and his friends to not tell anyone about his criminal activities and disobedience. In *Sorcerer's Stone*, for example, he makes the following request: "If I was ter—er—speed things up a bit, would yeh mind not mentionin' it at Hogwarts?" Harry replies, "Of course not" because he is eager to "see more magic." Later in the book, Hagrid actually allows Harry, Ron, and Hermione to smuggle his illegal dragon out of Hogwarts, with the help of Ron's brother (a Hogwarts graduate) and some of Ron's older postgraduate friends (pp. 64, 237).

42. This aspect of Hagrid's character has been deleted from the movie version of Harry Potter.

43. J.K. Rowling, interview on WBUR, *The Connection*, Oct. 12, 1999, www.hogwartslibrary.net/reference/interviews/19991012_TheConnection.html. In *Sorcerer's Stone*, Rowling even makes reference to this play on words: "Harry watched Hagrid getting redder and redder in the face as he called for more wine" (*Sorcerer's Stone*, pp. 203-204).

44. As Rowling writes, "Filch burst suddenly through a tapestry to Harry's right, wheezing and looking wildly about for the rule-breaker" (*Chamber of Secrets*, p. 125).

45. The following list presents only a small sampling of the many moral and ethical lapses in Harry Potter that occur without any negative results. (*Note:* These instances occurred in the story when no such behavior was necessary in order to combat evil, save a life, or avert disaster.)

- **Harry** disobeys teachers (Book I, pp. 148-150); lies (Book II, pp. 128, 164, 209; Book III, pp. 155, 246, 283-285); disobeys school rules (Book I, pp. 153-158, 209-213; Book II, pp. 164-165); steals (Book II, 186-188), breaks wizard laws (Book I, pp. 237-241; Book II, p. 69), cheats (Book IV, pp. 329, 341).
- **Ron** disobeys school rules (Book I, pp. 153-158, pp. 209-213; Book II, pp. 164-165); lies (Book III, p. 289); steals (Book II, pp. 186-188); breaks wizard laws (Book I, pp. 237-241; Book II, p. 69), uses profanity, swear words, and off-color slang (Book II, p. 259).
- **Hermione** disobeys school rules (Book II, pp. 164-165); steals (Book II, pp. 186-188); cheats (Book IV, pp. 338-339).
- **Hagrid** disobeys conditions of his employment (Book I, pp. 59, 64); breaks wizard laws (Book I, pp. 230-233, 237-241; Book IV, p. 438); encourages children to break rules (Book I, pp. 64, 237); becomes drunk (Book I, pp. 203-204; Book II, 212; Book III, pp. 121, 405); cheats (Book IV, p. 329).
- **Mr. Weasley** breaks wizard laws (Book II, p. 31; Book IV, pp. 45, 61); lies to his wife (Book II, p. 66); uses profanity, swear words, and off-color slang (Book IV, p. 43).

- **Fred and George** disobey school rules (Book III, p. 192), disobey parents (Book II, p. 30; Book IV, pp. 88-89, 117, 367); break wizard laws (Book II, p. 30); lie to parents (Book II, p. 32).
- **Leprechauns** use profanity, swear words, and off-color slang (Book IV, p. 135—give an opposing sports team "the finger").
- **Dumbledore** breaks Hogwarts rules (Book I, pp. 152, 165); lies (Book III, p. 353).

46. J.K. Rowling, as quoted in Deirdre Donahue, "Harry Potter's Appeal: Proof Positive," *USA Today*, December 2, 1999.

47. Toward the end of Book IV, for instance, we see Voldemort rewarding Pettigrew for his faithfulness (p. 649). From the Dark Lord's perspective, he is being "good" to Pettigrew, who helped him rise again even though enemies opposed him. Voldemort also bestows honor upon those who remained true to him and speaks of how he will someday greatly reward them for the suffering they have endured as a result of their faithfulness. To Voldemort, his companions are brave.

48. Michael O'Brien, "Author Michael D. O'Brien Critiques a Literary Phenomenon," www.zenit.org/english/visualizza.phtml?sid=13710.

49. Marcia Montenegro, as quoted in Martha Kleder, "Harry Potter: Seduction of the Occult," *Family Voice*, Nov./Dec. 2001, www.cwfa.org/familyvoice/2001-11/06-12.asp

50. Michael O'Brien, *A Landscape with Dragons* (San Francisco: Ignatius Press, 1998), p. 110.

51. Steven D. Greydanus, "Harry Potter vs. Gandalf: An In-Depth Analysis of the Literary Use of Magic in the Works of J.K. Rowling, J.R.R. Tolkien, and C.S. Lewis," 2001, Decent Films Online, http://decentfilms.com/commentary/magic.htm.

Chapter Nine: The Potter Wars

1. Jack Markowitz, "Rowling's Spell Grows on Parents, Wall Street," *The Tribune-Review* (Pittsburgh, PA), Dec. 26, 2004, www.pittsburghlive.com/x/tribune-review/trib/newcommunity/s_286951.html; Jack Markowitz, "Feeling the Hate from the Fans of 'Totter,'" *The Tribune-Review* (Pittsburgh, PA), Jan. 9, 2005, www.pittsburghlive.com/x/tribune-review/business/s_291025.html.

2. A.S. Byatt, "Harry Potter and the Childish Adult," *New York Times*, July 7, 2003; Colleen McCullough, as quoted in Rodney Chester, "Writing Another Thornbirds Would Be Boring," *The Courier Mail* (Brisbane, Australia), Nov. 25, 2004, as quoted in "Colleen McCullough: 'J.K.R. is a 'lousy writer,'" news update, www.the-leaky-cauldron.org/MTarchives/week_2004_11_21.html.

3. Rev. John Killinger, as quoted in "Just Wild About Harry: Potter Called Christ-like—Minister Compares Boy Wizard to Jesus in New Book," *World Net Daily*, www.worldnetdaily.com/news/article.asp?ARTICLE_ID=31341. Killinger is the author of *God, the Devil, and Harry Potter* (New York: Thomas Dunne Books, 2002), which advances a notion similar to John Granger's (see notes 5 and 6). Another book advocating this same theme is Francis Bridger, *A Charmed Life: The Spirituality of Potterworld* (Garden City, NY: Image Books, 2002).

4. John Granger, *The Hidden Key to Harry Potter* (Port Hadlock, WA: Zossima Press, 2002), p. xi.

5. See Granger, *The Hidden Key*; John Granger, *Looking for God in Harry Potter* (Carol Stream, IL: Salt River, 2004). Granger and I debated each other on Nov. 19, 2004, at California Baptist University.

6. Granger, *Looking for God*, p. xxi; Granger, *The Hidden Key*, p. xv, 140.
7. This perspective also is shared, but to a lesser degree, by youth worker Connie Neal (see *The Gospel According to Harry Potter* and *What's a Christian to Do with Harry Potter?*).
8. Granger, *The Hidden Key*, p. 98; Granger, *Looking for God*, p. 108.
9. J.K. Rowling, interview with Barnes and Noble, Mar. 18, 1999, www.hogwartslibrary.net/reference/interviews/19990319_BarnesNoble.html.
10. Granger, *The Hidden Key*, pp. 99, 183, 198.
11. This was revealed during a World Book Day chat with Rowling in 2004 (see information at www.jkrowling.com). Ginny was once thought to be short for Virginia because the name was erroneously placed in credits for the film *Harry Potter and the Chamber of Secrets* at the Internet Movie Database.
12. Granger, *The Hidden Key*, pp. 252-256.
13. J.K. Rowling, interview with Scholastic.com, Oct. 16, 2000, www.scholastic.com/harrypotter/author/transcript2.htm.
14. Granger, *Looking for God*, p. 105. *Christianity Today* magazine, in reference to *Looking for God in Harry Potter*, repeated Granger's error, noting, "Drawing on his Latin, Granger is keen on discerning the meaning behind Rowling's use of names. The name of Severus Snape suggests a 'severe rebuke,' but it could also predict that character's eventual beheading" (*Christianity Today*, Oct. 2004).
15. J.K. Rowling, AOL online chat, Oct. 2000, http://mugglenet.com/aolchat1.shtml.
16. Granger, *Looking for God*, p. 157.
17. J.K. Rowling, interview with Jeff Jensen, *Entertainment Weekly*, Aug. 4, 2000, available at www.quick-quote-quill.org/index2.html.
18. Granger, *The Hidden Key*, p. 241.
19. J.K. Rowling, interview with Judy O'Malley, "Talking with J.K. Rowling," *Book Links*, July 1999, available at www.quick-quote-quill.org/index2.html.
20. Michelle Arnold, "Harry Potter, Christian Evangelist?" *This Rock*, Sept. 2003, www.catholic.com/thisrock/2003/0309revw.asp.
21. Some feminists interpret the symbolism not only in an alternate way, but also in a negative way, saying that Harry Potter is built on an "underlying symbol system, which betrays a deep reliance on old representations of women as connected to evil, dark magic, and traditional roles of passivity and naiveté....This symbol system is so deeply embedded in the cultural and mythological history of our Westernized and Christian heritage that we embrace it without question or thought as to its deeper meaning....The feminine in *Harry Potter and The Chamber of Secrets* is signified as flesh or blood fed on by masculine forces. This film can also be understood as a metaphor for current societal feminist consciousness: there is a superficial nod to gender equality that only masks a deeply entrenched patriarchal structure in the collective unconscious" (Michelle Yeo, "Harry Potter and the Chamber of Secrets: Feminist Interpretations/Jungian Dreams," University of Victoria, *Studies in Media & Information Literacy Education*, Feb. 2004. vol. 4, issue 1, www.utpjournals.com/jour.ihtml?lp=simile/issue13/yeoX1.html).
22. Prash and Vela, "J.K. Rowling—Rags to Riches—The Harry Potter Way," www.osfa.org.uk/jkrowling.htm.
23. Ken Jacobsen, "Harry Potter and the Secular City: The Dialectical Religious Vision of J.K. Rowling," *Animus: A Philosophical Journal of Our Time*, 2004, vol. 9, www.swgc.mun.ca/animus/current/jacobsen.htm.

24. Kabbalah Made Easy, "Harry Potter and the Kabbalists' Eyes," online article, www.kabbalahmadeeasy.com/prevarticles/harrypotter.html.
25. Carissa Conti, "Harry Potter: Introduction to 4th Density?" July 7, 2003, www.montalk.net/conspiracy/79/harry-potter-introduction-to-4th-density.
26. Michael Bronsk, "Queering Harry Potter," Z *Magazine Online*, Sept. 2003, vol. 16, no. 9, http://zmagsite.zmag.org/Sept2003/bronski0903.html.
27.

Symbol	Christian Uses	Non-Christian Meanings
Griffin	Christ's human/divine nature	Strength, retribution, vigilance (origin: India)
Unicorn	Christ	strength, power, purity (origin: Mesopotamia, China, India)
Phoenix	Christ's death and resurrection	cycles of the sun (origin: Greek, Egyptian)
Centaur	Christ	unpredictability of nature (origin: Greek)

28. Jacobsen, www.swgc.mun.ca/animus/current/jacobsen.htm.
29. Rowling, *Sorcerer's Stone*, p. 215; Rowling, *Chamber of Secrets*, p. 236; Rowling, *Prisoner of Azkaban*, p. 312; Rowling, *Goblet of Fire*, pp. 578-579; Rowling, *Order of the Phoenix*, p. 761.
30. Rowling, *Order of the Phoenix*, pp. 736-737; for example, annual feasts, the sorting hat ceremony, the final awarding of year-end points to various houses at Hogwarts.
31. Gisèle Baxter, "Notes on Bram Stoker's *Dracula*," www.english.ubc.ca/~gmbaxter/dracnote.htm. Baxter is an English professor at the University of British Columbia.
32. Jacobsen, www.swgc.mun.ca/animus/current/jacobsen.htm. For example, Harry Potter includes "Circe" (Homer's *Odyssey*); "Draco" (astrology); "Morgana" (Arthurian legend); Cliodna (Celtic/Druid paganism).
33. John Granger, "So Who is 'The Half Blood Prince' in Harry Potter?" www.hogwarts professor.com/home.php?page=docs/half_blood_prince&PHPSESSID=a6d64789b0 6fc23033adfd2a2c43aa54; Granger, *The Hidden Key*, p. x.
34. Rowling, *Chamber of Secrets*, p. 132; Rowling, *Sorcerer's Stone*, p. 134; Rowling, *Chamber of Secrets*, p. 150, and *Prisoner of Azkaban*, pp. 1-2.
35. Rowling, *Sorcerer's Stone*, p. 220.
36. J.K. Rowling, "Transcript of World Book Day Festival Chat," World Book Day, Mar. 4, 2004, www.hogwarts-library.net/reference/interviews/20040304_WorldBookDay. html.
37. "For a while I thought I was going to vomit if I saw another picture of me captioned with single mother, penniless and divorcee....Seeing it all down there in black and white you think, Jesus Christ, I'm so sad, amn't I? I don't feel that sad" (J.K. Rowling, as quoted in Rosemary Goring, "Harry's Fame," *Scotland on Sunday*, Jan. 17, 1999, available at www.quick-quote-quill.org/index2.html). The word "amn't" is used in Scotland/Ireland as a contraction of "am not."

38. J.K. Rowling, AOL Chat, May 4, 2000, www.aol.co.uk/aollive/transcripts/jkrowling. html; J.K. Rowling, interview on *Dateline NBC*, June 20, 2003, available at www.quick-quote-quill.org/index2.html.

39. Penny Linsenmayer, "Religion and the Harry Potter Series," Harry Potter for Grown-Ups Fan Site, www.hpfgu.org.uk/faq/religion.html. This observation was based on British fan postings at Yahoo message boards (see the article for references).

40. J.K. Rowling, interview with Evan Solomon (Canadian Broadcasting Co.), July 2000, available at www.quick-quote-quill.org/index2.html.

41. J.K. Rowling, interview with Jennie Renton, "The Story Behind the Potter Legend: J.K. Rowling Talks About How She Created the Harry Potter Books and the Magic of Harry Potter's World," *Sydney Morning Herald*, Oct. 28, 2001, available at www.quick-quote-quill.org/index2.html.

42. J.K. Rowling, National Press Club talk, Oct. 20, 1999, transcript, available at www.quick-quote-quill.org/index2.html; J.K. Rowling, interview with Lizo Mzimba, "JK Rowling Talks About Book Four," *BBC Newsround*, July 2000, available at www.quick-quote-quill.org/index2.html; J.K. Rowling, interview with Scholastic. com, "About the Books," transcript, Oct. 16, 2000, available at www.quick-quote-quill.org/index2.html.

43. J.K. Rowling, interview with Jeff Baker, "Harry Potter: Need She Say More?" *The Oregonian*, Oct. 22, 2000, available at www.quick-quote-quill.org/index2.html; J.K. Rowling, interview with Stephen Fry, "J.K. Rowling at the Royal Albert Hall," transcript, June 26, 2003, available at www.quick-quote-quill.org/index2.html.

44. Mark McGarrity, "Harry Potter's Creator Meets Her Public: Author J.K. Rowling Answers Questions from Students at a School in Montclair," *The Star-Ledger* (Newark, NJ), Oct. 16, 1999, available at www.quick-quote-quill.org/index2.html; Rowling, as quoted in Renton, available at www.quick-quote-quill.org/index2.html.

45. See dialogue with a male-witch caller during the interview with J.K. Rowling on WBUR (see note 46).

46. J.K. Rowling, interview on WBUR, *The Connection*, Oct. 12, 1999, www.hogwarts-library.net/reference/interviews/19991012_TheConnection.html. "*Damon:* I want to say blessed be! Are you craft or are you Muggles? *J.K. Rowling:* I am—sorry, say that again, sorry? *Damon:* Are you craft or are you Muggles? *J.K. Rowling:* Am I a Muggle? Yes, I am definitely a Muggle. *Damon:* OK. *J.K. Rowling:* A Muggle with an abnormal amount—er—of knowledge about the wizarding world. *Damon:* Because you do—I'm a—er—magus of about four different magical organizations. You do your homework quite well. *J.K. Rowling:* Yeah—...I know a lot about it, but no, I'm not in any kind of—er—I don't head up my own coven, at all, no!"

47. J.K. Rowling, interview with Evan Solomon, "J.K. Rowling Interview," CBC *NewsWorld: Hot Type*, July 13, 2000, available at www.quick-quote-quill.org/index2.html; Rowling, interview with Jensen, available at www.quick-quote-quill.org/index2.html.

48. Rowling, Barnes & Noble Chat, www.hogwarts-library.net/reference/interviews/19990319_BarnesNoble.html. Even childhood friends, Ian and Vikki Potter, recall how Rowling as a little girl loved dressing up like a witch and making potions. (Danielle Demetiou, "Harry Potter and the source of inspiration," *The Daily Telegraph* [London], July 1, 2000, available at www.quick-quote-quill.org/index2.html).

49. J.K. Rowling, as quoted in Elizabeth Nehren, "Upward and Onward Toward Book Seven," *Los Angeles Times*, Oct. 25, 2000. Elsewhere Rowling has said, "7 is also a magical number" (see interview with WBUR, note 46).

50. Rowling, interview with Judy O'Malley, available at www.quick-quote-quill.org/index2.html.
51. Ralph C. Wood, *The Gospel According to Tolkien* (Louisville, KY: Westminster John Knox Press, 2003), pp. 5, 11.
52. See chapters 3 and 4.
53. Wood, p. 75; Colin Duriez, *A Field Guide to Narnia* (Downers Grove, IL: InterVarsity Press, 2004), p. 65.
54. Joseph Pearce, in "J.R.R. Tolkien's Take on the Truth," interview with Pearce by Zenit, www.leaderu.com/humanities/zenit-tolkien.html.
55. Brian M. Carney, "The Battle of the Books—No Contest. Tolkien Runs Rings Around Potter," *Wall Street Journal*, Nov. 30, 2001, www.cesnur.org/tolkien/010.htm. Carney also provides a pointed comparison between Tolkien's use of a magical Ring in his story and Rowling's use of the Philosopher's Stone: "Contrast Tolkien's careful use of the ring with Ms. Rowling's rather flip use of another great artifact of legend, the philosopher's stone. Alchemists believed the stone would turn lead into gold. As a bonus, it was also thought to confer eternal life. The conceit of 'Harry Potter' is that such a stone has been made and the bad guy wants it. This is a setup worthy of Tolkien; indeed, it mimics his tale in vital respects. But Ms. Rowling's story manages to bring to light none of the moral dilemmas—of mortality, wealth, power—that the existence of the stone naturally suggests. The reader simply accepts as given that both sides want it, no particular importance is assigned to its powers and Harry never shows any interest in using it. He merely wants to keep it away from the bad guy. Once that's accomplished, the stone drops out of the story, like a token at the end of some video game."
56. Steven D. Greydanus—in "Harry Potter vs. Gandalf: An In-Depth Analysis of the Literary Use of Magic in the Works of J.K. Rowling, J.R.R. Tolkien, and C.S. Lewis" (http://decentfilms.com/commentary/magic.html)—lists "Seven Hedges" of protection present in The Lord of the Rings. These "hedges" prove that it is not inconsistent to accept Tolkien while at the same time rejecting Harry Potter. The remainder of this note is a direct quote from Greydanus.

    "There is no slippery slope here, but a substantial differentiation. One may still choose to accept *Harry Potter* as well as Tolkien and Lewis—or one may choose to reject them all—but at any rate there's no arguing that acceptance of Tolkien and Lewis is inconsistent with rejection of *Harry Potter*. Here are the seven hedges in Tolkien and Lewis.

    • Tolkien and Lewis confine the pursuit of magic as a safe and lawful occupation to wholly imaginary realms, with place-names like Middle-earth and Narnia—worlds that cannot be located either in time or in space with reference to our own world, and which stand outside Judeo–Christian salvation history and divine revelation. By contrast, Harry Potter lives in a fictionalized version of our own world that is recognizable in time and space, in a country called England (which is at least nominally a Christian nation), in a time frame of our own era.

    • Reinforcing the above point, in Tolkien's and Lewis's fictional worlds where magic is practiced, the existence of magic is an openly known reality of which the inhabitants of those worlds are as aware as we are of rocket science—even if most of them might have as little chance of actually encountering magic as most of us would of riding in the space shuttle. By contrast, Harry Potter

lives in a world in which magic is a secret, hidden reality acknowledged openly only among a magical elite, a world in which (as in our world) most people apparently believe there is no such thing as magic.

- Tolkien and Lewis confine the pursuit of magic as a safe and lawful occupation to characters who are numbered among the supporting cast, not the protagonists with whom the reader is primarily to identify. By contrast, Harry Potter, a student of wizardry, is the title character and hero of his novels.

- Reinforcing the above point, Tolkien and Lewis include cautionary threads in which exposure to magical forces proves to be a corrupting influence on their protagonists: Frodo is almost consumed by the great Ring; Lucy and Digory succumb to temptation and use magic in ways they shouldn't. By contrast, the practice of magic is Harry Potter's salvation from his horrible relatives and from virtually every adversity he must overcome.

- Tolkien and Lewis confine the pursuit of magic as a safe and lawful occupation to characters who are not in fact human beings (for although Gandalf and Coriakin are human in appearance, we are in fact told that they are, respectively, a semi-incarnate angelic being and an earthbound star). In Harry Potter's world, by contrast, while some human beings (called "Muggles") lack the capacity for magic, others (including Harry's true parents and of course Harry himself) do not.

- Reinforcing the above point, Tolkien and Lewis emphasize the pursuit of magic as the safe and lawful occupation of characters who, in appearance, stature, behavior, and role, embody a certain wizard archetype—white-haired old men with beards and robes and staffs, mysterious, remote, unapproachable, who serve to guide and mentor the heroes. Harry Potter, by contrast, is a wizard-in-training who is in many crucial respects the peer of many of his avid young readers, a boy with the same problems and interests that they have.

- Finally, Tolkien and Lewis devote no narrative space to the process by which their magical specialists acquire their magical prowess. Although study may be assumed as part of the back story, the wizard appears as a finished product with powers in place, and the reader is not in the least encouraged to think about or dwell on the process of acquiring prowess in magic. In the Harry Potter books, by contrast, Harry's acquisition of mastery over magical forces at the Hogwarts School of Wizardry and Witchcraft is a central organizing principle in the story-arc of the series as a whole."

57. See *The Magician's Nephew*.
58. Alan Cochrum, "Harry Potter and the Magic Brew-haha," *Fort-Worth Star Telegram*, Dec. 18, 1999.
59. Cochrum.
60. Edmund Kern, "Harry Potter, Stoic Boy Wonder," *The Chronicle of Higher Education*, Nov. 16, 2001, http://chronicle.com/free/v48/i12/12b01801.htm.
61. Michael O'Brien, "Harry Potter and the Paganization of Children's Culture," *Catholic Culture*, www.catholicculture.org/docs/doc_view.cfm?recnum=3816.
62. See Rowling, *Chamber of Secrets* (pp. 253, 259, 310) and *Goblet of Fire* (pp. 43, 62, 127, 232, 344, 470, 561, 626).
63. Rowling, *Goblet of Fire*, p. 111; Rowling, *Chamber of Secrets*, pp. 130-131.

64. See Rowling, *Sorcerer's Stone*, p. 177, and *Chamber of Secrets*, p. 216; Rowling, *Chamber of Secrets*, pp. 136-137; Rowling, *Goblet of Fire* pp. 195, 541, 201.

65. Rowling, interview with O'Malley, available at www.quick-quote-quill.org/index2.html; Leslie Brody, "Students Meet the Real Wizard Behind the Harry Potter Craze," *The Record* (Bergen-Hackensack, NJ), Oct. 14, 1999, available at www.quick-quote-quill.org/index2.html. Another journalist recorded this comment in different words: "The great thing about being a writer is that you have a chance to get back at those people who wronged you" (McGarrity, available at www.quick-quote-quill.org/index2.html).

66. Rowling, *Sorcerer's Stone*, pp. 59, 90.

67. Rowling, *Sorcerer's Stone*, p. 80.

68. Rowling, *Sorcerer's Stone*, p. 182; Rowling, *Prisoner of Azkaban*, pp. 280-281.

69. J.K. Rowling, "Comic Relief Live Chat," transcript, Mar. 2001, available at www.quick-quote-quill.org/index2.html.

70. Curt Brannan, "What About Harry Potter?" online article, www.tbcs.org/papers/article04.htm. Brannan is associated with The Bear Creek School, a Christian liberal arts educational institution.

71. Rowling, interview with Judy O'Malley, available at www.quick-quote-quill.org/index2.html.

72. "My greatest [childhood] fantasy would have been to find out that I had powers that I'd never dreamt of, that I was special, that 'these people couldn't be my parents, I'm far more interesting than that.' ...So I just took that one stage further, and I thought, 'What's the best way of breaking free of that? Okay, you're magic!'" (J.K. Rowling, interview with Margot Adler, *All Things Considered* [NPR Radio], Oct. 13, 1999, available at www.quick-quote-quill.org/index2.html).

  Journalist: "I suggest that this essentially is a book about power and this delights her." *Rowling:* "Yes. Absolutely. Kids are so powerless, however happy they are. The idea that we could have a child who escapes from the confines of the adult world and goes somewhere where he has power, both literally and metaphorically, really appealed to me" (J.K. Rowling, as quoted in Anne Johnstone, "Happy Ending, and that's for Beginners," *The Herald*, June 24, 1997, available at www.quick-quote-quill.org/index2.html).

  "Kids are incredibly powerless because everything is determined for them, so a rich fantasy life in which they do have power is almost inevitable. And a middle-class boarding school is a world where they are free of their parents. Being an orphan is very liberating in a book. I think it's a common fantasy of children that somehow these parents aren't their parents" (J.K. Rowling, as quoted in Eddie Gibb, "Tales from a Single Mother," *The Sunday Times*, June 29, 1997, available at www.quick-quote-quill.org/index2.html).

73. Edmund Kern, "Wild About Harry (Potter)," *Lawrence Today*, Summer 2001, www.lawrence.edu/news/pubs/lt/spring04/kern2.shtml.

74. James Morone, "Cultural Phenomena: Dumbledore's Message," *The American Prospect*, Dec. 17, 2001, www.prospect.org/print/V12/22/morone-j.html.

75. Morone, www.prospect.org/print/V12/22/morone-j.html.

76. Rowling, interview with WBUR, www.hogwarts-library.net/reference/interviews/19991012_TheConnection.html.

77. Rowling, interview with Scholastic.com, available at www.quick-quote-quill.org/index2.html; Rowling, as quoted in Renton, available at www.quick-quote-quill.org/index2.html.

78. Deirdre Donahue, "Harry Potter 'Fire' Sale Casts Spell Tonight," *USA Today*, July 7, 2000; Al Lautenslager, "Mega Potter Means Mega Marketing, or Is That: Mega Marketing Means Mega Potter," Market for Profits, 2003, www.market-for-profits.com/set_media_reprint5.html.

79. AP, "Book Sales Plunge," May 13, 2004, available at cbsnews.com.

80. Diane Penrod, "The Trouble with Harry: A Reason for Teaching Media Literacy to Young Adults," *The Writing Instructor*, Dec. 2001, available at writinginstructor.com.

Chapter Ten: Marketers and Moneymakers

1. Team Media Literacy, "An Introduction to Media Literacy," available at http://medialiteracy.net.

2. Teenage Research Unlimited, "TRU Projects Teens Will Spend $169 Billion in 2004," available at www.teenresearch.com.

3. Elaine Ashcroft, "Children as Consumers—News/Reference," *PENPages*, Department of Family & Human Development (Utah State University), available at www.penpages.psu.edu.

4. This term "refers to the children's ability to nag their parents into purchasing items they may not otherwise buy" (Media Awareness Network, "How Marketers Target Kids," online article, www.media-awareness.ca/english/parents/marketing/marketers_target_kids.cfm.

5. Media Awareness Network, www.media-awareness.ca/english/parents/marketing/marketers_target_kids.cfm.

6. T.R. Reid, "All Aboard the Publicity Train," July 9, 2000, *Washington Post* (foreign service), p. C9.

7. Anne Johnstone, "We Are Wild About Harry," Jan. 26, 1999, *The Herald*, www.the-leaky-cauldron.org/quickquotes/articles/1999/0199-herald-johnstone.html.

8. Anne Johnstone, "Happy Ending, and That's for Beginners," *The Glasgow Herald*, June 24, 1997, available at www.quick-quote-quill.org/index2.html.

9. Eddie Gibb, "Tales from a Single Mother," *Sunday Times*, 29 June 1997, available at www.quick-quote-quill.org/index2.html.

10. Richard Savill, "Harry Potter and the Mystery of J.K.'s Lost Initial," *The Daily Telegraph*, July 19, 2000, available at www.quick-quote-quill.org/index2.html. Rowling has explained, "My real name is Joanne Rowling. My publishers wanted another initial, so I gave myself my favourite grandmother's name as a middle name, which was Kathleen" ("Exclusive: Writer J.K. Rowling Answers Her Readers' Questions," *Toronto Star*, Nov. 3, 2001, available at www.quick-quote-quill.org/index2.html).

11. "J.K. Rowling's Diary," *Sunday Times*, July 26, 1998, available at www.quick-quote-quill.org/index2.html.

12. Carmel Brown, "Harry Potter Cashing in on Pester Power," *Socialist Review*, Sept. 2000, issue 244, http://pubs.socialistreviewindex.org.uk/sr244/brown.htm.

13. "J.K. Rowling's Diary," available at www.quick-quote-quill.org/index2.html; see article listed under "What Happened in 1997" at www.quick-quote-quill.org/qq1997.html.

14. Brown, http://pubs.socialistreviewindex.org.uk/sr244/brown.htm; commentator, *60 Minutes* (New York: CBS), voice-over, transcript at www.harrypotterspage.com/60minutes.htm.

15. Scholastic is listed as a "media" company by *Crain's New York Business*, "the only publication dedicated to exclusive coverage of business in New York City" (see Subscription Center, https://sec.crain.com/cnw/cgi-bin/circulation.pl?USER-ID=).

16. See Martin Arnold, "Making Books; Sign of Success: 'Read It Again!'" Dec. 17, 1998, *New York Times.*

17. "Name Selling to Kids, Harry Potter Makes Marketing Magic for Scholastic Selling to Kids," June 28, 2000, *Selling to Kids,* www.findarticles.com/p/articles/mi_m0FVE/is_12_5/ai_63061455.

18. "Name Selling to Kids," www.findarticles.com/p/articles/mi_m0FVE/is_12_5/ai_63061455.

19. Lisa Biank Fasig, "Harry Carries: The Magic of Marketing," *Providence Journal,* June 21, 2003, p. A1, available at www.northernlight.com.

20. Britt Beemer, as quoted in Fasig, available at www.northernlight.com; Stephen Brown., as quoted in Fasig, available at www.northernlight.com.

21. "Harry Potter Special: The Book Comes to Life," *Hello!* available at www.hello magazine.com.

22. Jyotsna Kapur, *Jump Cut: A Review of Contemporary Media,* 2003, no. 46, available at www.ejumpcut.org.

23. Martin Lindstrom, "Is Harry Committing Suicide?" *ClickZ Network: Solutions for Marketers,* Dec. 4, 2001, www.clickz.com/experts/brand/brand/article.php/932631.

24. Kapur, available at www.ejumpcut.org; James Oakley, as quoted in Al Lautenslager, "Mega Potter Means Mega Marketing; or Is That: Mega Marketing Means Mega Potter?" *Market for Profits,* 2003, www.market-for-profits.com/set_media_reprint5.html.

25. The Chartered Institute of Marketing, "Harry Potter Works Marketing Magic, *News,* Oct. 9, 2001, www.cim.co.uk/cim/new/html/preRel.cfm?year=2001.

26. Scholastic Corporation, "Form 10-K" for the fiscal year ended May 31, 2004, Securities and Exchange Commission File No. 000-19860.

27. ICFAI Center for Management Research, "ICMR Case Catalogue," Nov. 2004, Case #MKTG079, http://icmr.icfai.org/PDF/Marketing.PDF. The ICFAI Center for Management Research (ICMR), a constituent of ICFAI University, an international company in India, develops quality courseware and management case studies.

28. Victor C. Strasburger, "Children and the Media: What Parents Need to Know," online article, available at keepkidshealthy.com.

29. Strasburger, available at keepkidshealthy.com; Kaiser Family Foundation, "Parents, Media and Public Policy: A Kaiser Family Foundation Survey," Fall 2004, p. 13.

30. See *Kids & Media @ the New Millennium* (1999) and *Zero to Six: Electronic Media in the Lives of Infants, Toddlers and Preschoolers* (2003) by the Kaiser Family Foundation, available at www.kff.org.

31. Gary Ruskin, "Will Ashcroft Stand Up for Children or Corporations?" *Commercial Alert,* Jan. 16, 2001, available at www.commercialalert.org.

32. Media Awareness Network, "Special Issues for Young Children," online article, www.media-awareness.ca/english/parents/marketing/issues_kids_marketing.cfm.

33. Diane Penrod, "The Trouble with Harry: A Reason for Teaching Media Literacy to Young Adults," *The Writing Instructor,* Dec. 2001, available at writinginstructor.com. Penrod teaches at Rowan University, Glassboro, NJ.

34. American Psychological Association, "Television Advertising Leads To Unhealthy Habits in Children; Says APA Task Force," www.apa.org/releases/childrenads.html.

35. Gary Ruskin, "Why They Whine: How Corporations Prey on Our Children," *Mothering* magazine, Nov./Dec., 1999, reprinted in *Commercial Alert,* available at www.commercialalert.org.

36. Todd Zwillich, "Adults Get Low Grades on Drinking, Drugs; Adolescents Say Parents Do Poorly in Preventing Smoking, Alcohol Use," *WebMD Medical News*, June 22, 2004, www.nccf-cares.org/media10.htm.

37. Cristine Russell, "'The Talk' with Kids Should Occur Early, Often," Apr. 6, 1999, *The Washington Post*, p. Z10.

38. Strasburger, available at keepkidshealthy.com.

39. Canadian Paediatric Society (CPS), "Impact of Media Use on Children and Youth," Psychosocial Paediatrics Committee, www.cps.ca/english/statements/PP/pp03-01.htm.

40. "'Desperate Housewives' Appeals to Young Viewers, Too," *Broadcasting & Cable*, Dec. 28, 2004.

41. Parents Television Council, "Desperate Housewives," available at www.parentstv.org.

42. Cartoon Network, "Adult Swim: Frequently Asked Questions," www.cartoonnetwork.com/gen/asfaq/index.html.

43. Aubree Bowling, "Worst TV Show of the Week: *Without a Trace*," Parents Television Council, www.parentstv.org/PTC/publications/bw/2005/0102worst.asp.

44. AP, "Those Who Watch Shows with Sexual Content More Likely to Have Sex," Sept. 6, 2004, available at www.msnbc.msn.com.

45. Survey conducted by the Rand Corporation and published in the Sept. 2004 issue of *Pediatrics*.

46. Parents Television Council, "It's Just Harmless Entertainment: Oh Really?" online article, www.parentstv.org/ptc/facts/mediafacts.asp.

47. AP, "Those Who Watch Shows," available at www.msnbc.msn.com.

48. AP, "Those Who Watch Shows," available at www.msnbc.msn.com.

49. Strasburger, available at www.healthology.com.

50. American Psychiatric Association, "Psychiatric Effects of Media Violence," position statement, available at www.psych.org.

51. Lt. Col. David Grossman, as quoted in "Psychologist: TV, Games Teach Killing," May 11, 1999, Sentinel Wire Services, available at www.hollandsentinel.com; cf. Tim Madigan, *The Arizona Republic*, May 27, 1999.

52. Terry Price, "Helping Kids Make Sense of the Media," Nov. 19, 2003, *Toronto Star*, available at www.thestar.com.

53. Dale Frost Stillman, "Will the Real Jack#@% Please Stand Up?" New Jersey State Bar Foundation, www.njsbf.com/njsbf/student/eagle/fall02-1.cfm; cf. Lee Margulies, "Child's Death Prompts MTV to Retool 'Beavis,'" *Los Angeles Times*, Oct. 14, 1993, p. F1.

54. John Murray, "Children and Television Violence," *Kansas Journal of Law and Public Policy*, 4(30), 1993, p. 7.

55. John Charles Kunich, "Natural Born Copycat Killers and the Law of Shock Torts," *Washington University Law Quarterly*, Winter 2000, p. 1197.

56. American Academy of Pediatrics, Commission on Communications, "Media Violence," policy statement, *Pediatrics*, issue 949, 1995, available at www.aap.org. Quoted in Canadian Council on Social Development (CCSD), *Children's Exposure to Violence in Canada: What It Means for Parents Research Report and Forum Proceedings*, Sept. 2003, www.ccsd.ca/pubs/2003/violence/ccsd_violence.pdf.

57. Dan Weiss, "Wrestling with Perversity," *Real and Unreal*, Winter 2000, p. 15, available at www.americasfuture.org/doublethink/winter2000/dtWinter2000.pdf; Louise I. Gerdes, ed., *Professional Wrestling* (Farmington Hills, MI: Greenhaven Press, 2003), "Introduction," www.enotes.com/professional-wrestling/.

58. For example, on April 25, 2001, three teens raced their car toward a friend standing in the road. The boy was supposed to jump out of the way at the last second, but he failed to do so in time and bounced off the car hood. Fortunately, he walked away with only a broken leg and some internal injuries. The teenagers admitted to copying a *Jackass* stunt (see "Teen Injures Friend in Alleged 'Jackass Stunt,'" *News Net 5*, Apr. 25, 2000, available at www.newsnet5.com).

59. In 2004, 16-year-old Bobbi MacKinnon died after being thrown 75 feet from a merry-go-round spinning at approximately 60 mph. It was a Jackass stunt she was trying to duplicate (see "Girl Killed After Copying TV Stunt," available at http://cbs5.com/news). MacKinnon's mother said: "I had no idea that she watched the show" (Quoted in M.S. Enkoji, "Stunt Inspired by TV Show Turns Tragic," *Modesto Bee*, Jan. 21, 2004, available at http://modbee.com).

   In 2003, 15-year-old Paul Rouen died in what police said was an attempt to imitate the Jackass stunt known as "Car Surfing," which involves riding the hood of a fast-moving car (AP, Dec. 17, 2002).

   In 2002, 18-year-old Adam Ports died after he and his three friends tried to duplicate a stunt while in the back of a fast-moving truck. Ports fell from the truck and died of head injuries (AP, "Police: 18-Year-Old Dies from 'Jackass' Stunt," Nov. 26, 2002, www.newsnet5.com/news/1801136/detail.html).

60. "MTV Defends Itself After Youth Burned in 'Copycat' Incident," CNN.com, Jan. 29, 2001. MTV disavowed all responsibility, pointing to the warning aired with the program: "The following show features stunts performed by professionals and/or total idiots under very strict control and supervision. MTV and the producers insist that neither you or anyone else attempt to re-create or perform anything you have seen on this show" (CNN, http://archives.cnn.com/2001/SHOWBIZ/TV/01/29/mtv.fire.02/).

   Journalist John Kiesewetter highlighted what the program has shown: "They put on a show making cult heroes out of global village idiots being pushed down a flight of stairs in a laundry basket…being hurled from a shopping cart into bushes…getting zapped by an electronic dog collar…leaping into a plastic pool full of elephant dung…or complaining to a waitress after slipping dog poop onto their restaurant plate. They show a kid running into an intersection and knocking a skateboarder off his wheels, onto his butt, in the middle of the street. They show some guy riding a child's plastic big wheel bike into the street in front of a car—and let you hear the camera operators laugh at the prank" (John Kiesewetter, "Real Jackasses Are MTV Programmers," *The Cincinnati Enquirer*, available online at www.enquirer.com).

61. See www.theamericanjackass.com/.

62. See www.freewebs.com/ckms/thebigvid1.htm.

63. See www.LNDL.net/.

64. See http://originallife.8m.com/custom2.html.

65. Testimony of Leonard D. Eron, Professor of Psychology and Senior Research Scientist at the University of Michigan, before the Senate Committee on Commerce, Science and Transportation, May 18, 1999, as quoted in "Children, Violence, and the Media: A Report for Parents and Policy Makers," prepared by Majority Staff Senate Committee on the Judiciary, Sept. 14, 1999, http://judiciary.senate.gov/oldsite/mediavio.htm.

66. Do It Now Foundation, "Ceasefire: What We Can Do to Stop Violence in Our Schools," Nov. 2001, p. 2; Greg Toppo, "48 School Deaths Highest in Years," *USA Today*, June 27, 2004.

67. There are many examples of this kind of behavior. In 2003, for example, "four teens in Cleveland, Ohio, were arrested for allegedly videotaping themselves randomly urinating in public and using stun guns on homeless people" (Rasheed Oluwa, "'Jackass' Imitators Are New Menace," *Poughkeepsie Journal*, available at www.poughkeepsiejournal.com).

In addition to the cases cited in this chapter, also see: "Police: Three Teens Taped Themselves Beating Homeless Men," *Northwest Indiana Times*, Aug, 20, 2003, available at http://nwitimes.com; "Teen Sentenced in Jogger Attack," Apr. 4, 2003, *The Wenatchee World*, available at www.wenworld.com; Linda Spice and Mike Johnson, "Seventh-, Eighth-Graders Taped Themselves Drinking, Police Say," *Milwaukee Journal Sentinel*, Dec. 22, 1999, available at www.jsonline.com/news.

68. A series of important articles on this case, including online video clips of the horrific brutality, can be found at www.reviewjournal.com/news/311boyz/.

69. "Violent Amateur Videos on Rise," Nov. 19, 2002, *CBS News*, www.cbsnews.com.

70. Ken Druck, "Violent Amateur Videos, www.cbsnews.com; Ron Kaufman, "How Television Images Affect Children," online article, www.turnoffyourtv.com/health education/children.html.

71. American Psychiatric Association, "Psychiatric Effects," available at www.psych.org.

72. Price, available at www.thestar.com.

73. Quoted in Dean Schabner, "The Makings of a *Jackass* Kid: Children Can't Filter Media, Psychologists Say," May 8, 2001, ABC News, available in Google Cache.

74. Quoted in Schabner.

75. Jim Rutenberg, "Violence Finds a Niche in Children's Cartoons," Jan. 28, 2001, *New York Times*, found at nytimes.com

76. Rutenberg, available at nytimes.com; Strasburger, available at keepkidshealthy.com.

77. Consider the following, all from Suzanne M. Chamberlin, "Toxic Television," *The Australian Family*, Nov. 2002, p. 3, www.family.org.au/journal/2002/j20021103.html.

    • *Violence:* "Leading child psychologist Dr. George Gerbner notes that children who watch violent shows are more likely to strike at a playmate, bicker, or disobey authority, and are less willing to share than those children who watched non-violent programs. A study in Canada showed that two years after television was introduced to a remote city called Notel, reports of physical aggression by children increased 160 percent."

    • *Desensitization:* "According to author H. Featherstone in the *Harvard Education Letter*, children who watch a lot of television are less bothered by violence and less likely to see anything wrong with it. In several studies, children who watched a violent program were less quick to call for assistance or intervene when, afterwards, they saw younger children fighting."

    • *Aggressiveness:* "Researchers Liebert and Sprafkin found that steady consumption of violence on television creates anti-social attitudes in all individuals and a perception that violence is the first-resort in problem solving."

    • *The future:* "Another study by psychologist L.R. Huesmann revisited adults who watched an above-average amount of violence on television as youths. What he found was that 59 percent of those who were interviewed as children had been involved in more than the typical number of aggressive acts later in life—including domestic violence and traffic violations."

78. Chamberlin, www.family.org.au/journal/2002/j20021103.html.

79. Mile Falcon, "David Proval: 'Reality TV' Means Honest Depictions of Sexuality," *USA Today*, Oct. 24, 2002; Jim Henson, as quoted in National Teacher Training

Institute, "Instructional Television Programming, 2001-2002," p. 1, available at www.wbra.org/html/edserv/ntti/nttipdf/03itv.pdf.

Chapter Eleven: Time for a Reality Check

1. National Institute of Mental Health, "Teenage Brain: A Work in Progress," *NIH Publication No. 01-4929*, 2001, www.nimh.nih.gov/publicat/teenbrain.cfm.

2. Johanna Seltz, "Teen Brains Are Different," *The Boston Globe*, May 28, 2000, www.loni.ucla.edu/media/News/BG_05282000.html.

3. Renate Caine and Geoffrey Caine, *Making Connections: Teaching and the Human Brain* (White Plains, NY: Pearson Learning, 1994), p. 18. Quoted in David M. Considine, "Media and Youth: The Wonder Years or Risky Business?" *Telemedium: The Journal of Media Literacy*, Fall 2002, p. 13, available at www.ci.appstate.edu.

4. However, from the 1960s to the early 1970s there was a spate of Dracula films released by Britain's Hammer Studios. The movies were rather gory compared to other films of that era.

5. Lynn Schofield Clark, *From Angels to Aliens: Teenagers, the Media, and the Supernatural* (New York: Oxford University Press, 2003), p. 66.

6. B.A. Robinson, "Teenagers and Wicca," www.religioustolerance.org/wic_teen1.htm.

7. *New Worlds of Mind and Spirit* (St. Paul: Llewellyn Publications), Sept/Oct. 1996, p. 6.

8. Phyllis Curott, as quoted in "Blair Witch Offends Witches: A Practicing Witch on the Summer's Hottest Flick," Aug. 18, 1999, online chat, ABC News. A transcript of this interview is now available only at the Google cache of pages. It can be accessed by entering "Blair Witch Offends Witches" in the search engine and clicking the "cached" link under the return "ABCNEWS.com: Chat Transcript: Phyllis Curott, a Practicing Witch."

9. Ruth La Ferla, "Like Magic, Witchcraft Charms Teenagers," *New York Times*, Feb. 13, 2000.

10. Pat Devin, interview with Douglas Eby, "About Consulting on the Movie: 'The Craft,'" *Cinefantastique*, 1996, http://talentdevelop.com/pdevin.html.

11. Devin, http://talentdevelop.com/pdevin.html.

12. Patrick Goodenough, "Paganism Finds Growing Interest Among UK Children," CNS News Service, Aug. 25, 2000, available at www.cnsnews.com.

13. Andy Norfolk, as quoted in Goodenough, available at www.cnsnews.com.

14. Cynthia A. Freeland, as quoted in Thomas Hargrove and Guido H. Stempel III, "Survey: Some People Believe in Ghosties, Ghoulies, and Bumps," Oct. 30, 1999, http://web.gosanangelo.com/archive/99/october/30/3.htm.

15. Clark, p. 68.

16. See http://yahooligans.yahoo.com/; John Carvel, "Fear over Web Access to Occult," *The Guardian*, Apr. 22, 2000, available at www.guardian.co.uk.

17. Daniel McGrory, "Children Seduced by Forces of Satanism on the Internet," *The Times*, Aug, 28, 2001, www.zenit.org/german/visualizza.phtml?sid=9195; Ben Russell, "Buffy 'Prompting Pupils to Access the Occult,'" *The Independent*, Apr. 22, 2000, www.cesnur.org/testi/buffy_001.htm.

18. Steven D. Greydanus, "Harry Potter vs. Gandalf: An In-Depth Analysis of the Literary Use of Magic in the Works of J.K. Rowling, J.R.R. Tolkien, and C.S. Lewis," 2001, Decent Films Online, http://decentfilms.com/commentary/magic.html.

19. Quoted in Media Awareness Network, "How Marketers Target Kids," online article, www.media-awareness.ca/english/parents/marketing/marketers_target_kids.cfm; Media

Awareness Network, "Marketing: Special Issues for Tweens and Teens," online article, www.media-awareness.ca/english/parents/marketing/issues_teens_marketing.cfm.

20. Media Awareness Network, "Movies: Special Issues for Tweens and Teens," online article, www.media-awareness.ca/english/parents/movies/teens_movies.cfm.

21. The NC-17 rating is not listed because it is so rarely used. (Only three such films were released in 2004.) No one under 17 is admitted—period. The movies contain very explicit violence, intense sexuality (including protracted full nudity), or both. Several *hard* R-rated movies, however, come close to NC-17, which means all movies must be judged carefully.

22. This particular vulgarity has appeared in a variety of PG-13 films, such as *All the President's Men* (1976), *The Kids Are Alright* (1979), and *The Right Stuff* (1983). The MPAA has arbitrarily allowed it to be used once in any PG-13 film.

23. • **1992**: Four teens rob a bank in emulation of a robbery in the movie *Point Break*. From prison, one of the teens (a former contender for the U.S. Olympic team) tells reporters, "I never would have done it if I hadn't seen [the movie]. It looked pretty d*** easy, [I thought] we could do that" (D.A. Winston, "The Bad News Bank Robbers," *Cleveland Plain Dealer,* July 26, 1992).

• **1993**: Three teenagers try to copy a stunt from *The Program*, which showed a college football hero proving his bravery by lying down in the middle of a road at night. In the movie, the hero is fine. But in real life, one teen is killed and another critically injured. About two dozen kids apparently were playing the same "game" that night at another location (M. Hines, "Not Like the Movie: A Dare to Test Nerves Turns Deadly," *New York Times,* Oct. 19, 1993).

• **1994**: *The Crow* incites Canadian teens to dress like characters from the movie and torch several cars. "We see a link with *The Crow*," said Det. Sgt. Yvon Lacasse. "Since it came out, there seem to have been fires everywhere" ("Movie Blamed in Arson Spree," *Toronto Sun,* Nov. 17, 1994, available at www.torontosun.com).

• **1997**: An eight-year-old girl is killed after being shot in the head by another child. The children, according to police, were acting out a scene from *Set It Off,* a movie they had watched on videotape" (Brigitte Greenberg, "Police Say Movie Linked to Fatal Shooting of Young Girl," read into Senate Congressional Report, Feb. 13, 1997, http://thomas.loc.gov/cgi-bin/query/z?r1 05:S13FE7-617:).

• **1999**: An 11-year-old boy accidentally hangs himself, but before doing so he tells his friends about a movie that "included a hanging" ("Boy Hanged in 'Movie' Tragedy," *Toronto Sun,* Oct. 15, 1999, as quoted in "Canadian Incidents," *The Free Radical,* www.fradical.com/canadian_incidents.htm);

• **2001**: Another Canadian teen, 18 years old, dies in an automobile crash while street racing like the actors in *The Fast and the Furious* ("Vancouver Drag Race Claims Teenage Driver's Life," *Globe and Mail,* June 18, 2001, as cited in "Media Related Injuries, Deaths, Crimes: Canada," *The Free Radical,* www.fradical.com/Canadian_copycat_incidents.htm).

24. Jyotsna Kapur, "Free Market, Branded Imagination—Harry Potter and the Commercialization of Children's Culture," *Jump Cut: A Review of Contemporary Media,* Summer 2003, no. 46, www.ejumpcut.org/currentissue/kapur.potter/index.html.

25. Online Advancement of Student Information Skills, "Media Literacy Defined," http://oasis.fiu.edu/Ch8/ch8page2.htm.
26. David M. Considine, "Putting the ME in MEdia Literacy," *The Middle Ground*, Oct. 2002, p. 2, available at www.ci.appstate.edu/programs/edmedia/medialit/.
27. Quoted in Considine, p. 1.
28. Kaiser Family Foundation, "Teens Say Sex on TV Influences Behavior of Peers," 2002, press release, available at www.kff.org.
29. Strasburger, available at keepkidshealthy.com.

Chapter Twelve: Does Anyone Have a Question?

1. American Academy of Pediatrics, "Television and the Family," www.aap.org/family/tv1.htm; and "The Ratings Game: Choosing Your Child's Entertainment," www.aap.org/family/ratingsgame.htm.
2. Dana Corby, "Harry Potter and the Cuckoo's Egg," www.witchvox.com/words/words_2003/e_harry01.html.
3. "J.K. Rowling's Success Story," *Mega East*, www.megaeast.com/default.asp?section=main&page=rowling.com.
4. For example, a seven-year-old wrote to a newspaper in Britain, saying, "I like Harry Potter because he is rather cheeky—he isn't always good" (Jasmine War, letter to the editor, *London Times*, June 29, 2000, available at www.londontimes.co.uk). And an 11-year-old in America told the *New York Times* that she likes reading the books because it's "like we're reading about ourselves. . . . They like to do stuff like we like to do. They like to get in trouble" (Megan Campenelle. Quoted in Jodi Wilgoren, "Don't Give Us Little Wizards, the Anti-Potter Parents Cry," *New York Times*, Nov. 1, 1999).
5. In *Prisoner of Azkaban* he did request that the traitorous Peter Pettigrew be allowed to live. But this is not sacrificial love, it is simply deciding to not murder, which is exactly what Professor Lupine and Sirius Black (good characters) were willing to do.
6. The character of Madame Trelawney, according to J.K. Rowling herself, has made two accurate predictions. As of Book V, the first prediction had not yet been revealed. However, the second prediction occurred in *Prisoner of Azkaban*. The scene depicts a classic episode of spirit-channeling, also known as mediumship. Like Trelawney, spiritists claim to speak forth prophecies or words of knowledge using voices not like their own, and then afterward, do not remember what has transpired. This is precisely what Rowling describes (see *Prisoner of Azkaban*, p. 324).
7. Here is where people who do not have Rowling's level of knowledge about the occult can fall woefully shy of understanding how deeply she is depicting the occult. If *Goblet of Fire* is read carefully, it will be seen that Harry is indeed clairvoyant to a certain degree, especially with things having to do with Voldemort. He can actually see things and hear things—accurately. What is interesting about Harry's crystal-ball scene is how he really "sees" nothing in the crystal ball. Nevertheless, what he says actually does come to pass. This is because within the occult tradition most seers, or clairvoyants, almost always (especially when young) do not know they have such powers and can accurately make predictions. It is something they must grow into, usually after many years of simply knowing things. We see this same level of imma-ture powers depicted when Harry releases the snake in *Sorcerer's Stone*. He has no idea he made this happen. The fact that Harry is "making up" what he says in his scene with Trelawney and then that what he says just "coincidentally" comes true, is not an accident.

8. Josh London, "Harry Potter Is Great," Dec. 7, 2001, *Spintech*, available at www.spin techmag.com.
9. James Morone, "What the Muggles Don't Get: Why Harry Potter Succeeds While the Morality Police Fail," *Brown Alumni* magazine, July/Aug. 2001, available at www.brownalumnimagazine.com/storydetail.cfm?ID=210.
10. Judith Krug, as quoted in "The 'Harry Potter' Books: Craze and Controversy," available online at www.familyhaven.com/books/harrypotter.html.
11. Michael O'Brien, interview with Zenit News Agency, "Why Harry Potter Goes Awry," Dec. 6, 2001, www.zenit.org/english/visualizza.phtml?sid=13710.
12. From conversations with Marcia Montenegro (former astrologer and occultist), Douglas Groothuis (professor of philosophy, Denver Seminary), Steve Russo (occult expert), Dr. Ron Rhodes (former senior researcher at the Christian Research Institute), to name but a few.
13. Gene Edward Veith, "Censoring 'Kum Ba Ya,'" Sept. 2, 2000, *World* magazine, available at www.worldmag.com.
14. See American Academy of Pediatrics, Commission on Communications, "Media Violence," policy statement, *Pediatrics*, issue 949, 1995, available at www.aap.org. Quoted in Canadian Council on Social Development (CCSD), *Children's Exposure to Violence in Canada: What It Means for Parents Research Report and Forum Proceedings*, Sept. 2003, www.ccsd.ca/pubs/2003/violence/ccsd_violence.pdf.
15. Bernice Cullinan, *Literature and the Child* (New York: Harcourt Brace Jovanovich, 1989), p. 280.
16. O'Brien, www.zenit.org/english/visualizza.phtml?sid=13710.
17. Doreen Valiente, *An ABC of Witchcraft* (New York: St. Martins Press, 1973), p. 60.
18. J.D. Douglas and Merrill C. Tenney, eds., *The New International Dictionary of the Bible* (Grand Rapids, MI: Zondervan, 1987 edition), p. 1067; Francis Brown et al., eds., *The New Brown-Driver-Briggs-Gesenius Hebrew and English Lexicon* (Peabody, MA: Hendrickson, 1979), s.v. 3784; and Geoffrey W. Bromiley, *The International Standard Bible Encyclopedia* (Grand Rapids: Eerdman's, 1979; rev. ed.), vol. 2, s.v. "magic, magician," pp. 213-219.
19. Cited in John Ankerberg, "Questions About Harry Potter," www.johnankerberg.org/hp-articles/hp-questions.htm.
20. O'Brien, www.zenit.org/english/visualizza.phtml?sid=13710.

Appendix A: What's So Bad About Occultism?

1. Gordon Michael Scallion, interview with Art Bell, *Coast to Coast*, Dec. 8, 1995, Internet transcript available at www.nhne.com/interviews/intbellinterview.html.
2. For an in-depth explanation of all of Scallion's predictions, see Richard Abanes, *End-Time Visions: The Road to Armageddon?* (New York: Four Walls, Eight Windows, 1998), pp. 53-55.
3. See Abanes, pp. 56-58.
4. Roland Seidel, "Astrology Overview," *The Skeptic*, available at www.skeptics.com. au/journal/astrol.htm.
5. Elliot Miller, *A Crash Course on the New Age Movement* (Grand Rapids, MI: Baker Books, 1989), p. 36.
6. See Jason Barker, "Youth and the Occult," *The Watchman Expositor*, vol. 15, no. 6, 1998, www.watchman.org/occult/teenwitch.htm.
7. Randall Tedford, "An Answer to the Call: Something Has to Be Done," May 14, 1999, available at www.oakridger.com.

8. Lori Gray, "Preventing Violence," *Education Report*, January 6, 1998; cf. Reid Kimbrough and John Evans, *Pathological Maturity* (Cincinnati: Custom Publishing, 1999).
9. Norvin Richards, as quoted in "Satanic Crimes on the Rise in Alabama," available at the Alabama Center for Justice, www.alabamacenterforjustice.com/devilwor.htm.

Index

Rick Warren and the Purpose That Drives Him

An Insider Looks at the Phenomenal Bestseller

Richard Abanes

Rick Warren's *The Purpose-Driven Life* has sold more than 20 million copies and has spent months on the *New York Times* bestseller list. Whether you're of the Christian faith or not, you've probably been intrigued by Warren's teachings, in addition to his way of "doing church."

Bestselling author Richard Abanes—a former staff member at Warren's church—takes a balanced and positive look at issues that have been raised about the "purpose-driven" concepts. In a compact format that will inform you and increase your understanding, he offers...

- a concise history of how Warren's work has grown into what it is today, and an inside view of Warren as a man who loves God and wants to serve Him

- a user-friendly point/counterpoint section dealing with criticisms, concerns, and worries that have recently been expressed—with an aim to correcting misperceptions

- an exclusive interview with Warren in which Abanes candidly asks the questions that you want and need to have answered

You'll come away informed about—even inspired by—the story of a man and what his God is doing through him.

What Is Fact? What Is Fiction?

The Truth Behind the Da Vinci Code
A Challenging Response to the Bestselling Novel
Richard Abanes

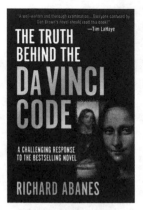

"All descriptions of artwork, architecture, documents, and secret rituals in this novel are accurate."

With these startling words, The Da Vinci Code—author Dan Brown's megaselling thriller—kicks you into high gear. After 454 nonstop pages, you've discovered a lot of shocking facts about history and Christianity...or have you?

Award-winning investigative journalist Richard Abanes takes you down to the murky underpinnings of this multi- million-copy blockbuster that has confused so many readers. What do you really learn when the novel's assumptions are unearthed and scrutinized?

- **The Code:** *Jesus was married to Mary Magdalene, whom he named leader of the church before his death.*
- **The Truth:** *This fantasy has no support even from the "Gnostic gospels" mentioned in the book, let alone from the historical data.*

- **The Code:** *Since the year 1099, a supersecret society called "The Priory of Sion" has preserved knowledge of Jesus and Mary's descendants.*
- **The Truth:** *Today's "Priory of Sion" was founded in the early 1960s by a French con man who falsified documents to support the story of Jesus' "bloodline."*

- **The Code:** *As a "Priory" leader and pagan goddess-worshipper, Leonardo da Vinci coded secret knowledge about Jesus and Mary into his paintings.*
- **The Truth:** *Da Vinci had no known ties to any secret societies. Any obscure images in his paintings likely reflect his personal creativity.*

Probing, factual, and revealing, The Truth Behind the Da Vinci Code gives you the straightforward information you need to separate the facts from the fiction.

Other Books by Richard Abanes

Becoming Gods
A Closer Look at 21st-Century Mormonism

Did You Know Mormons Hope to Eventually Become Gods?

This and other Latter-day Saint doctrines can lead to misunderstanding when you interact with Mormon friends, neighbors, and co-workers. Richard Abanes' thorough yet accessible approach helps you understand not only what today's Mormons believe, but also how they think about and defend their faith. The award-winning journalist offers the results of his research into many key teachings and beliefs, such as—

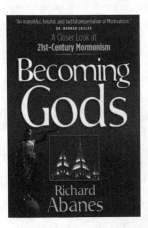

- who God is, who Jesus is, and what it means for us to participate in their divine nature
- why Joseph Smith and his visions have such a central place in the hearts of Mormons
- what role the Book of Mormon and other authoritative writings play in LDS beliefs
- how Mormons are now dealing with evangelicals' criticisms of their faith
- how you can effectively talk to 21st-century Mormons about their religion

"An insightful, helpful, and tactful presentation of Mormonism."
—Dr. Norman Geisler

ALSO BY RICHARD ABANES

One Nation Under Gods:
A History of the Mormon Church

Witchcraft Goes Mainstream
Uncovering Its Alarming Impact on You and Your Family
Brooks Alexander

The Halloween witch is dead.

The old crone on a broomstick is gone. In her place is a young, hip, sexually magnetic woman who worships a goddess and practices socially acceptable magic

As witchcraft goes mainstream, this new image, or some other aspect of the rapidly growing pagan religious movement, shapes the identity of more and more of your coworkers and neighbors...or maybe even your friends and family members. What do you do or say when you and your children meet someone like this?

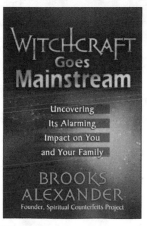

Brooks Alexander, founder of the Spiritual Counterfeits Project, pointedly answers the tough questions:

- What do modern witches believe? Are they really following ancient pagan traditions or worshiping the devil?

- What does the widespread acceptance of witchcraft today mean for you?

- How can you respond to protect your loved ones and reach out with the love of Jesus?

Weighing our ever-changing spiritual surroundings within a biblical framework, *Witchcraft Goes Mainstream* will help you chart a course for yourself and your family and see the light of God more clearly in a darkening culture.

A CHAMPION'S
PRAYER
Journey